A
DIARY WITHOUT
DATES

and

THE
HAPPY
FOREIGNER

by

Enid Bagnold

Printed on acid free ANSI archival quality paper.

ISBN: 978-1-78139-440-3

Contents

A DIARY WITHOUT DATES

I.
OUTSIDE THE GLASS DOORS

I like discipline. I like to be part of an institution. It gives one more liberty than is possible among three or four observant friends.

It is always cool and wonderful after the monotone of the dim hospital, its half-lit corridors stretching as far as one can see, to come out into the dazzling starlight and climb the hill, up into the trees and shrubberies here.

The wind was terrible to-night. I had to battle up, and the leaves were driven down the hill so fast that once I thought it was a motor-bicycle.

Madeleine's garden next door is all deserted now: they have gone up to London. The green asphalt tennis-court is shining with rain, the blue pond brown with slime; the little statues and bowls are lying on their sides to keep the wind from putting them forcibly there; and all over the house are white draperies and ghost chairs.

When I walk in the garden I feel like a ghost left over from the summer too.

I became aware to-night of one face detaching itself from the rest. It is not a more pleasing face than the others, but it is becoming conspicuous to me.

Twice a week, when there is a concert in the big hall, the officers and the V.A.D.'s are divided, by some unspoken rule—the officers sitting at one side of the room, the V.A.D.'s in a white row on the other.

When my eyes rest for a moment on the motley of dressing-gowns, mackintoshes, uniforms, I inevitably see in the line one face set on a slant, one pair of eyes forsaking the stage and fixed on me in a steady, inoffensive beam.

This irritates me. The very lack of offence irritates me. But one grows to look for everything.

Afterwards in the dining-room during Mess he will ask politely: "What did you think of the concert, Sister? Good show...."

How wonderful to be called Sister! Every time the uncommon name is used towards me I feel the glow of an implied relationship, something which links me to the speaker.

My Sister remarked: "If it's only a matter of that, we can provide thrills for you here very easily."

The name of my ... admirer ... is, after all, Pettitt. The other nurse in the Mess, who is very grand and insists on pronouncing his name in the French way, says he is "of humble origin."

He seems to have no relations and no visitors.

Out in the corridor I meditate on love.

Laying trays soothes the activity of the body, and the mind works softly.

I meditate on love. I say to myself that Mr. Pettitt is to be envied. I am still the wonder of the unknown to him: I exist, walk, talk, every day beneath the beam of his eye, impenetrable.

He fell down again yesterday, and his foot won't heal. He has time before him.

But in a hospital one has never time, one is never sure. He has perhaps been here long enough to learn that—to feel the insecurity, the impermanency.

At any moment he may be forced to disappear into the secondary stage of convalescent homes.

Yes, the impermanency of life in a hospital! An everlasting dislocation of combinations.

Like nuns, one must learn to do with no nearer friend than God.

2

Bolts, in the shape of sudden, whimsical orders, are flung by an Almighty whom one does not see.

The Sister who is over me, the only Sister who can laugh at things other than jokes, is going in the first week of next month. Why? Where? She doesn't know, but only smiles at my impatience. She knows life—hospital life.

It unsettles me as I lay my spoons and forks. Sixty-five trays. It takes an hour to do. Thirteen pieces on each tray. Thirteen times sixty-five ... eight hundred and forty-five things to collect, lay, square up symmetrically. I make little absurd reflections and arrangements—taking a dislike to the knives because they will not lie still on the polished metal of the tray, but pivot on their shafts, and swing out at angles after my fingers have left them.

I love the long, the dim and lonely, corridor; the light centred in the gleam of the trays, salt-cellars, yellow butters, cylinders of glass....

Impermanency.... I don't wonder the Sisters grow so secret, so uneager. How often stifled! How often torn apart!

It's heaven to me to be one of such a number of faces.

To see them pass into Mess like ghosts—gentleman, tinker, and tailor; each having shuffled home from death; each having known his life rock on its base ... not talking much—for what is there to say?—not laughing much for they have been here too long—is a nightly pleasure to me.

Creatures of habit! All the coloured dressing-gowns range themselves round the two long tables—this man in this seat, that man by the gas-fire; this man with his wheel-chair drawn up at the end, that man at the corner where no one will jostle his arm.

Curious how these officers leave the hospital, so silently. Disappearances.... One face after another slips out of the picture, the unknown heart behind the face fixed intently on some other centre of life.

I went into a soldiers' ward to-night to inquire about a man who has pneumonia.

Round his bed there stood three red screens, and the busy, white-capped heads of two Sisters bobbed above the rampart.

It suddenly shocked me. What were they doing there? Why the screens? Why the look of strain in the eyes of the man in the next bed who could see behind the screens?

I went cold and stood rooted, waiting till one of them could come out and speak to me.

3

Soon they took away the screen nearest to me; they had done with it.

The man I was to inquire for has no nostrils; they were blown away, and he breathes through two pieces of red rubber tubing: it gave a more horrible look to his face than I have ever seen.

The Sister came out and told me she thought he was "not up to much." I think she means he is dying.

I wonder if he thinks it better to die.... But he was nearly well before he got pneumonia, had begun to take up the little habits of living. He had been out to tea.

Inexplicable, what he thinks of, lying behind the screen.

To-night I was laying my trays in the corridor, the dim corridor that I am likely often to mention—the occasional blue gas-lamps hanging at intervals down the roof in a dwindling perspective.

The only unshaded light in the corridor hangs above my head, making the cutlery gleam in my hands.

The swish-swish of a lame foot approached down the stone tiling with the tapping, soft and dull, of a rubber-tipped walking-stick.

He paused by the pillar, as I knew he would, and I busied myself with an added rush and hurry, an added irritating noise of spoons flung down.

He waited patiently, shyly. I didn't look up, but I knew his face was half smiling and suppliant.

"We shall miss you," he said.

"But I shall be back in a week!"

"We shall miss you ... laying the trays out here."

"Everything passes," I said gaily.

He whistled a little and balanced himself against his stick.

"You are like me, Sister," he said earnestly; and I saw that he took me for a philosopher.

He shuffled on almost beyond the circle of light, paused while my lips moved in a vague smile of response, then moved on into the shadow. The low, deep quiet of the corridor resumed its hold on me. The patter of reflection in my brain proceeded undisturbed.

"You are like me!" The deepest flattery one creature pays its fellow ... the cry which is uttered when another enters "our country."

4

Far down the corridor a slim figure in white approaches, dwarfed by the smoky distance; her nun-like cap floating, her scarlet cape, the "cape of pride," slipped round her narrow shoulders.

How intent and silent They are!

I watched this one pass with a look half-reverence, half-envy. One should never aspire to know a Sister intimately. They are disappointing people; without candour, without imagination. Yet what a look of personality hangs about them....

To-night ... Mr. Pettitt: "Sister!"

"Yes, Mr. Pettitt."

"Do you ever go to theatres? Do you like them?"

At the risk of appearing unnatural, I said, "Not much."

"Oh ... I thought.... H'm, that's a pity. Don't you like revues?"

"Oh, yes...."

"I thought you'd take me to a *matinée* one afternoon."

"Oh, charming! I can't get leave in the afternoons, though."

"You often have a day off."

"Yes, but it's too soon to ask for another."

"Well, how about Wednesday, then?"

"Too soon. Think of the new Sister, and her opinion of me! That has yet to be won."

"Well, let me know, anyway...."

(Staved off!)

The new Sister is coming quite soon: she has a medal.

Now that I know *my* Sister must go I don't talk to her much; I almost avoid her. That's true hospital philosophy.

I must put down the beauty of the night and the woman's laugh in the shadowy hedge....

I walked up from the hospital late to-night, half-past eight, and hungry ... in the cold, brilliant moonlight; a fine moon, very low, throwing long, pointed shadows across the road from the trees and hedges.

5

As one climbs up there is a wood on the right, the remains of the old wooded hill; sparse trees, very tall; and to-night a star between every branch, and a fierce moon beating down on the mud and grass.

I had on my white cap and long blue coat, very visible. The moon swept the road from side to side: lovers, acting as though it were night, were lit as though it was day.

I turned into the wood to take a message to a house set back from the road, and the moonlight and the night vapour rising from the marshy ground were all tangled together so that I could hardly see hedge from field or path.

I saw a lit cigarette-end, and a woman's laugh came across the field as naturally as if a sheep had bleated in the swampy grass. It struck me that the dark countryside was built to surround and hide a laugh like hers—the laugh of a lover, animal and protesting.

I saw the glowing end of the cigarette dance in a curve and fall to the ground, and she laughed again more faintly.

Walking on in the middle of the moonlight, I reached the gate I was looking for, ran up the pebbly drive to the dining-room window, gave my message, and returned.

I slipped my cap off my hair and pushed it into my pocket, keeping under the shadow of the hedge and into the quiet field.

They were whispering: "Do you?" "I do...." "Are you?" "I am...." crushed into the set branches of the hedge.

The Mess went vilely to-night. Sister adds up on her fingers, and that's fatal, so all the numbers were out, and the *chef* sent in forty-five meats instead of fifty-one. I blushed with horror and responsibility, standing there watching six hungry men pretending to be philosophers.

The sergeant wolfed the cheese too. He got it out from under my very eyes while I was clearing the tables and ate it, standing up to it in the pantry with his back to me when I went in to fetch a tray.

Whenever I see that broad khaki back, the knickered legs astride, the flexed elbow-tips, I know that his digestion is laying up more trouble for him.

Benks, the Mess orderly, overeats himself too. He comes to the bunk and thrusts his little smile round the door: "Sister, I got another of them sick 'eadaches," very cheerfully, as though he had got something worth having. She actually retorted, "Benks, you eat too much!" one day, but he only swung on one leg and smiled more cheerfully than ever.

The new Sister has come. That should mean a lot. What about one's habits of life...?

The new Sister has come, and at present she is absolutely without personality, beyond her medal. She appears to be deaf.

I went along to-night to see and ask after the man who has his nose blown off.

After the long walk down the corridor in almost total darkness, the vapour of the rain floating through every open door and window, the sudden brilliancy of the ward was like a haven.

The man lay on my right on entering—the screen removed from him.

Far up the ward the Sister was working by a bed. Ryan, the man with his nose gone, was lying high on five or six pillows, slung in his position by tapes and webbing passed under his arms and attached to the bedposts. He lay with his profile to me—only he has no profile, as we know a man's. Like an ape, he has only his bumpy forehead and his protruding lips—the nose, the left eye, gone.

He was breathing heavily. They don't know yet whether he will live.

When a man dies they fetch him with a stretcher, just as he came in; only he enters with a blanket over him, and a flag covers him as he goes out. When he came in he was one of a convoy, but every man who can stand rises to his feet as he goes out. Then they play him to his funeral, to a grass mound at the back of the hospital.

It takes all sorts to make a hospital.

For instance, the Visitors....

There is the lady who comes in to tea and wants to be introduced to every one as though it was a school-treat.

She jokes about the cake, its scarcity or its quantity, and makes a lot of "fun" about two lumps of sugar.

When she is at her best the table assumes a perfect and listening silence—not the silence of the critic, but the silence of the absorbed child treasuring every item of talk for future use. After she goes the joy of her will last them all the evening.

There is the lady who comes in to tea and, sitting down at the only unlaid table, cries, "Nurse! I have no knife or plate or cup; and I prefer a glass of boiling water to tea. And would you mind sewing this button on my glove?"

There is the lady who comes in and asks the table at large: "I wonder if any one knows General Biggens? I once met him...."

Or: "You've been in Gallipoli? Did you run across my young cousin, a lieutenant in the...? Well, he was only there two days or so, I suppose...." exactly as though she was talking about Cairo in the season.

To-day there was the Limit.

She sat two paces away from where I sit to pour out tea. Her face was kind, but inquisitive, with that brown liver-look round the eyes and a large rakish hat. She comes often, having heard of him through the *padre*, to see a Canadian whom she doesn't know and who doesn't want to see her.

From two places away I heard her voice piping up: "Nurse, excuse my asking, but is your cap a regulation one, like all the others?"

I looked up, and all the tea I was pouring poured over the edge. Mr. Pettitt and Captain Matthew, between us, looked down at their plates.

I put my hand to my cap. "Is anything wrong? It ought to be like the others."

She leant towards me, nodding and smiling with bonhomie, and said flatteringly, "It's so prettily put on, I thought it was different."

And then (horror): "Don't you think nurse puts her cap on well?" she asked Captain Matthew, who, looking harder than ever at his plate and reddening to the ears, mumbled something which did not particularly commit him since it couldn't be heard.

The usual delighted silence began to creep round the table, and I tried wildly to divert her attention before our end became a stage and the rest of the table an audience.

"I think it's so nice to see you sitting down with them all," she cooed; "it's so cosy for them."

"Is your cup empty?" I said furiously, and held out my hand for it. But it wasn't, of course; she couldn't even do that for me.

She shook hands with me when she went away and said she hoped to come again. And she will.

There was once a lady who asked me very loudly whether I "saw many horrible sights," and "did the V.A.D.'s have to go to the funerals?"

8

And another who cried out with emotion when she saw the first officer limp in to Mess, "And can some of them *walk*, then!" Perhaps she thought they came in to tea on stretchers, with field-bandages on. She quivered all over, too, as she looked from one to the other, and I feel sure she went home and broke down, crying, "What an experience ... the actual wounds!"

Shuffle, shuffle, up the corridor to-night, as I was laying my trays. Captain Matthew appeared in the circle of light, his arm and hand bound up and his pipe in his mouth.

He paused by me. "Well...." he said companionably, and lolled against a pillar.

"You've done well at tea in the way of visitors," I remarked. "Six, wasn't it?"

"Yes," he said, "and now I've got rid of 'em all, except one."

"Where's the one?"

"In there." He pointed with his pipe to the empty Mess-Room. "He's the father of a subaltern of mine who was killed."

"He's come to talk to you about it?"

"Yes."

But he seemed in no hurry to go in, waiting against the pillar and staring at the moving cutlery.

He waited almost three minutes, then he sighed and went in.

Biscuits to put out, cheese to put out. How wet this new cheese is, and fresh and good the little bits that fall off the edge! I never eat cheese at home, but here the breakings are like manna.

And pears, with the old shopman's trick, little, bitten ones at the bottom, fine ones at the top. Soft sugar, lump sugar, coffee. As one stirs the coffee round in the tin the whole room smells of it, that brown, burnt smell.

And then to click the light on, let down the blind, stir the fire, close the door of the little bunk, and, looking round it, think what exhilaration of liberty I have here.

Let them pile on the rules, invent and insist; yet behind them, beneath them, I have that strong, secret liberty of an institution that runs like a wind in me and lifts my mind like a leaf.

So long as I conform absolutely, not a soul will glance at my thoughts—few at my face. I have only to be silent and conform, and I might be in so far a land that even the eye of God had lost me.

I took the plate of biscuits, the two plates of cheese, one in each hand and one balanced with a new skill on my arm, and carried them into the dining-room, where the tables were already laid and only one light kept on as yet for economy's sake.

Low voices.... There in the dimmest corner sat Captain Matthew, his chin dug deep in his grey dressing-gown, and beside him a little elderly man, his hat on his knees, his anxious, ordinary face turned towards the light.

A citizen ... a baker or a brewer, tinker, tailor, or candlestick-maker...?

There had been the buying of the uniform, the visits to the camp in England, the parcels to send out—always the parcels—week by week. And now nothing; no more parcels, no more letters, silence.

Only the last hungry pickings from Captain Matthew's tired memory and nervous speech.

I turned away with a great shrinking.

In a very few minutes the citizen went past my bunk door, his hat in his hand, his black coat buttoned; taking back to his home and his family the last facts that he might ever learn.

At the end of the passage he almost collided with that stretcher which bears a flag.

Of the two, the stretcher moved me least.

My Sister is afraid of death. She told me so. And not the less afraid, she said, after all she has seen of it. That is terrible.

But the new Sister is afraid of life. She is shorter-sighted.

The rain has been pouring all day.

To-night it has stopped, and all the hill is steam and drizzle and black with the blackness that war has thrust upon the countryside.

My Sister has gone.

Two nights ago I went up to a dinner at Madeleine's and to stay the night. My Sister said, "Go and enjoy yourself!" And I did. It is very amusing, the change into rooms full of talk and light; I feel a glow of pleasure as I climb to the room Madeleine calls mine and find the reflection of the fire on the blue wall-paper.

10

The evening wasn't remarkable, but I came back full of descriptions to the bunk and Sister next day.

I was running on, inventing this and that, making her laugh, when suddenly I looked up, and she had tears in her eyes.

I wavered and came to a stop. She got up suddenly and moved about the room, and then with a muttered "Wash my hands," disappeared into the corridor.

I sat and thought: "Is it that she has her life settled, quietly continuous, and one breaks in...? Does the wind from outside hurt?"

I regretted it all the evening.

Yesterday I arrived at the hospital and couldn't find the store-cupboard keys, then ran across to her room and tapped at the door. Her voice called "Come in!" and I found her huddled in an arm-chair, unnerved and white. I asked her for the keys, and when she gave them to me she held out her hand and said: "I'm going away to-morrow. They are sending me home; they say I'm ill."

I muttered something with a feeling of shock, and going back to my bunk I brooded.

The new Sister came in, and a new V.A.D. too, explaining that my former companion was now going into a ward.

A sense of desolation was in the air, a ruthlessness on the part of some one unknown. "Shuffle, shuffle ... they shuffle us like cards!"

I rose and began to teach the new V.A.D. the subtle art of laying trays. She seemed stupid.

I didn't want to share my trays with her. I love them; they are my recreation. I hung over them idly, hardly laying down the spoons I held in my hand, but, standing with them, chivied the new V.A.D. until her movements became flustered and her eye distraught.

She was very ugly. I thought: "In a day or two I shall get to like her, and then I shan't be able to chivy her."

Out in the corridor came a tremendous tramping, boots and jingling metal. Two armed men with fixed bayonets arrived, headed by a sergeant. The sergeant paused and looked uncertainly this way and that, and then at me.

I guessed their destination. "In there," I nodded, pointing through a closed glass door, and the sergeant marched his men in and beyond the door.

11

An officer had been brought back under arrest; I had seen him pass with his escort. The rumour at tea had been that he had extended his two days' leave into three weeks.

The V.A.D. looked at me questioningly but she didn't dare, and I couldn't bear, to start any elucidations on the subject.

I couldn't think; she worried me. Her odds and ends of conversation pecked at me like a small bird. She told me a riddle which filled me with nausea, and finally a limerick which I had heard three times in the Mess.

I left her and went into the bunk.

Here the new Sister had installed herself, gentle and pink and full of quiet murmurs.

The rain, half snow, half sleet, dabbled against the window-pane, and I lifted the blind to watch the flakes stick and melt on the glass.

The V.A.D., her trays finished, appeared in the doorway. The little room seemed full of people.

"There's a concert," I said, looking at the V.A.D. with distaste.

She looked at me uncertainly: "Aren't you coming?"

"No," I said, "I've a note to write," forgetting that the new Sister might not allow such infringements. She gave no sign.

The V.A.D. gave in and disappeared concertwards.

The Sister rose too and went out into the kitchen to consult with the *chef*.

I slipped out behind her and down the steps into the garden—into the wet, dark garden, down the channels that were garden-paths, and felt my way over to the Sisters' quarters.

My Sister hadn't moved. There by the gas-fire, her thin hand to her face, she sat as she had two hours before.

"Come in," she offered, "and talk to me."

Her collar, which was open, she tried to do up. It made a painful impression on me of weakness and the effort to be normal.

I remembered that she had once told me she was so afraid of death, and I guessed that she was suffering now from that terror.

But when the specialist is afraid, what can ignorance say...?

Life in the bunk is wretched (except that the new V.A.D. tells fortunes by hands).

The new Sister is at the same time timid and dogged. She looks at me with a sidelong look and gives me little flips with her hand, as though (*a*) she thought I might break something and (*b*) that she might stave it off by playfulness.

Pain....

To stand up straight on one's feet, strong, easy, without the surging of any physical sensation, by a bedside whose coverings are flung here and there by the quivering nerves beneath it ... there is a sort of shame in such strength.

"What can I do for you?" my eyes cry dumbly into his clouded brown pupils.

I was told to carry trays from a ward where I had never been before—just to carry trays, orderly's work, no more.

No. 22 was lying flat on his back, his knees drawn up under him, the sheets up to his chin; his flat, chalk-white face tilted at the ceiling. As I bent over to get his untouched tray his tortured brown eyes fell on me.

"I'm in pain, Sister," he said.

No one has ever said that to me before in that tone.

He gave me the look that a dog gives, and his words had the character of an unformed cry.

He was quite alone at the end of the ward. The Sister was in her bunk. My white cap attracted his desperate senses.

As he spoke his knees shot out from under him with his restless pain. His right arm was stretched from the bed in a narrow iron frame, reminding me of a hand laid along a harp to play the chords, the fingers with their swollen green flesh extended across the strings; but of this harp his fingers were the slave, not the master.

"Shall I call your Sister?" I whispered to him.

He shook his head. "She can't do anything. I must just stick it out. They're going to operate on the elbow, but they must wait three days first."

His head turned from side to side, but his eyes never left my face. I stood by him, helpless, overwhelmed by his horrible loneliness.

Then I carried his tray down the long ward and past the Sister's bunk. Within, by the fire, she was laughing with the M.O. and drinking a cup of tea—a harmless amusement.

13

"The officer in No. 22 says he's in great pain," I said doubtfully. (It wasn't my ward, and Sisters are funny.)

"I know," she said quite decently, "but I can't do anything. He must stick it out."

I looked through the ward door once or twice during the evening, and still his knees, at the far end of the room, were moving up and down.

It must happen to the men in France that, living so near the edge of death, they are more aware of life than we are.

When they come back, when the postwar days set in, will they keep that vision, letting it play on life ... or must it fade?

And some become so careless of life, so careless of all the whims and personalities and desires that go to make up existence, that one wrote to me:

"The only real waste is the waste of metal. The earth will be covered again and again with Us. The corn will grow again; the bread and meat can be repeated. But this metal that has lain in the earth for centuries, the formation of the beginning, that men have sweated and grubbed for ... that is the waste."

What carelessness of worldly success they should bring back with them!

Orderlies come and go up and down the corridor. Often they carry stretchers—now and then a stretcher with the empty folds of a flag flung across it.

Then I pause from laying my trays, and with a bunch of forks in my hand I stand still.

They take the stretcher into a ward, and while I wait I know what they are doing behind the screens which stand around a bed against the wall. I hear the shuffle of feet as the men stand to attention, and the orderlies come out again, and the folds of the flag have ballooned up to receive and embrace a man's body.

Where is he going?

To the mortuary.

Yes ... but where else...?

Perhaps there is nothing better than the ecstasy and unappeasement of life?

14

II.
INSIDE THE GLASS DOORS

My feet ache, ache, ache...!
End of the first day.

Life in a ward is all scurry and rush. I don't reflect; I'm putting on my cap anyhow, and my hands are going to the dogs.

I shall never get to understand Sisters; they are so strange, so tricky, uncertain as collies. Deep down they have an ineradicable axiom: that any visitor, any one in an old musquash coat, in a high-boned collar, in a spotted veil tied up at the sides, any one with whom one shakes hands or takes tea, is more important than the most charming patient (except, of course, a warded M.O.).

For this reason the "mouths" of the pillow-cases are all turned to face up the ward, away from the door.

I think plants in a ward are a barbarism, for as they are always arranged on the table by the door, it is again obvious that they are intended only to minister to the eye of the visitor, that race of gods.

In our ward there are eighteen fern-pots, some in copper, some in pink china, three in mauve paper, and one hanging basket of ferns. All of these have to be taken out on the landing at night and in again in the morning, and they have to be soaked under the tap.

The Sisters' minds are as yet too difficult for me, but in the minds of the V.A.D.'s I see certain salient features. I see already manifested in them the ardent longing to be alike. I know and remember this longing; it was present through all my early years in a large boarding-school; but there it was naturally corrected by the changes of growth and the inexpertness of youth. Here I see for the first time grown women trying with all the concentration of their fuller years to be as like one another as it is possible to be.

There is a certain dreadful innocence about them too, as though each would protest, "In spite of our tasks, our often immodest tasks, our minds are white as snow."

And, as far as I can see, their conception of a white female mind is the silliest, most mulish, incurious, unresponsive, condemning kind of an ideal that a human creature could set before it.

At present I am so humble that I am content to do all the labour and take none of the temperatures, but I can see very well that it is when I reach a higher plane that all the trouble will begin.

The ranklings, the heart-burnings, the gross injustices.... Who is to make the only poultice? Who is to paint the very septic throat of Mr. Mullins, Army Service Corps? Who is to—dizzy splendour—go round with the M.O. should the Sister be off for a half-day?

These and other questions will form the pride and anguish of my inner life.

It is wonderful to go up to London and dine and stay the night with Madeleine after the hospital.

The hospital—a sort of monotone, a place of whispers and wheels moving on rubber tyres, long corridors, and strangely unsexed women moving in them. Unsexed not in any real sense, but the white clothes, the hidden hair, the stern white collar just below the chin, give them an air of school-girlishness, an air and a look women don't wear in the world. They seem unexpectant.

Then at Madeleine's ... the light, the talk, the deep bath got ready for me by a maid, instead of my getting it ready for a patient....

Not that I mind getting it ready; I like it. Only the change! It's like being turn and turn about maid and mistress.

There is the first snow here, scanty and frozen on the doorstep.

I came home last night in the dark to dinner and found its faint traces on the road and in the gutter as I climbed the hill. I couldn't see well; there were stars, but no moon. Higher up it was unmistakable; long white tracks frozen in the dried mud of the road, and a branch under a lamp thickened with frozen snow.

Shall I ever grow out of that excitement over the first bit of snow...?

I felt a glow of pride in the hill, thinking:

"In London it's all slush and mud. They don't suspect what we've got here. A suburb is a wonderful place!"

After a wet and muddy day in London I've seen the trains pull into Charing Cross with snow piled on the roofs of the carriages, and felt a foot taller for joy that I was one of those fortunates who might step into a train and go down into a white countryside.

It is the same excitement to wake up early to an overnight fall and see down the Dover Road for miles no foot of man printed, but only the birds' feet. Considering the Dover Road has been a highway since the Romans, it really is a fine moment when you realize its surface has suddenly become untrodden and unexplored as any jungle.

Alas, the amount of snow that has set me writing!... two bucketfuls in the whole garden!

When a Medical Officer goes sick, or, in other words, when an M.O. is warded, a very special and almost cynical expression settles on his face. Also the bedside manner of the Visiting Officer is discarded as he reaches the bed of the sick M.O.

"My knees are very painful," says the sick M.O., but it is a despondent statement, not a plea for aid.

The Visiting Officer nods, but he does not suggest that they will soon be better.

They look at each other as weak human beings look, and:

"We might try...?" says the Visiting Officer questioningly.

The M.O. agrees without conviction, and settles back on his pillows. Not for him the comfortable trust in the divine knowledge of specialists. He can endure like a dog, but without its faith in its master.

The particular M.O. whose knees are painful is, as a matter of fact, better now. He got up yesterday.

Mooning about the ward in a dressing-gown, he stared first out of one window into the fog and then out of another.

Finally, just before he got back into bed, he made an epigram.

"Nurse," he said, "the difference between being in bed and getting up is that in bed you do nothing, but when you get up there's nothing to do...."

I tucked him up and put the cradle over his knees, and he added, "One gets accustomed to everything," and settled back happily with his reading-lamp, his French novel, and his dictionary.

The fog developed all day yesterday, piling up white and motionless against the window-panes. As night fell a little air of excitement ran here and there amongst the V.A.D.'s.

"How shall we get home...?" "Are the buses running?" "Oh no, the last one is stuck against the railings outside!" "My torch has run out...."

By seven o'clock even the long corridor was as dim as the alley outside. No one thought of shutting the windows—I doubt whether they will shut ... and the fog rolled over the sill in banks and round the open glass doors, till even the white cap of a Sister could hardly be seen as she passed.

I am pleased with any atmospheric exaggeration; the adventure of going home was before me....

At eight I felt my way down over the steps into the alley; the torch, held low on the ground, lighted but a small, pale circle round my shoes. Outside it was black and solid and strangely quiet.

In the yard a man here and there raised his voice in a shout; feet strayed near mine and edged away.

At the cross-roads I came on a lantern standing upon the ground, and by it drooped the nose of a benighted horse; the spurt of a match lit the face of its owner.

Up the hill, the torch held low against the kerbstone, the sudden looming of a black giant made me start back as I nearly ran my head into a telegraph-post....

I was at the bottom of the sea; fathoms and fathoms of fog must stand above my head.

Suddenly a dozen lights showed about me, then the whole sky alight with stars, and naked trees with the rime on them, bristling; the long road ran up the hill its accustomed steel colour, the post office was there with its red window, the lean old lamp-post with its broken arm....

I had walked out of the fog as one walks out of the sea on to a beach!

Looking back, I could see the pit behind me; the fog standing on the road like a solid wall, straight up and down. Again I felt a pride in the hill. "Down there," I thought, "those groping feet and shouting voices; that man and that horse ... they don't guess!"

18

I walked briskly up the hill, and presently stepped on to the pavement; but at the edge of the asphalt, where tufted grass should grow, something crackled and hissed under my feet. Under the torchlight the unnatural grass was white and brittle with rime, fanciful as a stage fairy scene, and the railings beyond it glittered too.

I slid in the road as I turned down the drive; a sheet of ice was spread where the leaky pipe is, and the steps up to the house door were slippery.

But oh, the honeysuckle and the rose-trees...! Bush, plant, leaf, stem, rimed from end to end. The garden was a Bond Street jeweller's!

Perhaps the final chapter on Mr. Pettitt....

In the excitement of the ward I had almost forgotten him; he is buried in the Mess, in the days when I lived on the floor below.

To-night, as I was waiting by the open hatch of the kitchen for my tray to be filled with little castles of lemon jelly, the hot blast from the kitchen drawing stray wisps of hair from beneath my cap, I saw the familiar limping figure—a figure bound up with my first days at the hospital, evoking a hundred evenings at the concerts, in the dining-room. I felt he had been away, but I didn't dare risk a "So you're back!"

He smiled, blushed, and limped past me.

Upstairs in the ward, as I was serving out my jellies, he arrived in the doorway, but, avoiding me, hobbled round the ward, visiting every bed but the one I was at at the moment. Then he went downstairs again.

I passed him on the stairs. He can't say he didn't have his opportunity, for I even stopped with my heavy tray and spoke to him.

Half an hour later he was back in the ward again (not his ward), and this time he found the courage of hysteria. There in the middle of the ward, under the glaring Christmas lights, with the eyes of every interested man in every bed glued upon us, he presented me with a fan wrapped in white paper: "A little present I bought you, nurse." I took it, eyes sizzling and burning holes in my shoulders, and stammered my frantic thanks.

"You do like it, nurse?" he said rapidly, three times in succession.

And I: "I do, I do, I do...."

"I thought you would. You do like it?"

"Oh, just what I wanted!"

"That's all right, then. Just a little Christmas present."

19

We couldn't stop. It was like taking too much butter for the marmalade and too much marmalade for the butter.

He leaves the hospital in a day or two.

The fog is still thick. To-night at the station after a day off I found it white and silent. Touching the arm of a man, I asked him the all-important question: "Are the buses running?"

"Oh no...."

And the cabs all gone home to bed, and I was hungry!

What ghosts pass ... and voices, bodyless, talking intimately while their feet fall without a stir on the grass of the open Heath.

I was excited by the strange silent fog.

But my left shoe began to hurt me, and stopping at the house of a girl I knew, I borrowed a country pair of hers: no taller than I, she takes two sizes larger; they were like boats.

I started to trudge the three miles home in the boats: the slightest flick of the foot would have sent one of them flying beyond the eye of God or man. After a couple of miles the shoes began to tell, and I stood still and lifted up one foot behind me, craning over my shoulder to see if I could catch sight of the glimmer of skin through the heel of the stocking. The fog was too thick for that.

Another half-mile and I put my finger down to my heel and felt the wet blood through a large hole in my stocking, so I took off the shoes and tied them together ... and, more silent than ever in the tomb of fog, padded along as God had first supposed that woman would walk, on the wet surface of the road.

A warded M.O. is pathetic. He knows he can't get well quicker than time will let him. He has no faith.

To-morrow I have to take down all the decorations that I put up for Christmas. When I put them up I never thought I should be the one to take them down. When I was born no one thought I should be old.

While I was untying a piece of holly from the electric-light cords on the ceiling and a patient was holding the ladder for me, a young *padre* came and pretended to help us, but while he stood with us he whispered to the patient, "Are you a communicant?" I felt a wave of heat and anger; I could have dropped the holly on him.

They hung up their stockings on Christmas night on walking-sticks hitched over the ends of the beds and under the mattresses. Such big stockings! Many of them must have played Father Christmas in their own homes, to their own children, on other Christmases.

On Christmas Eve I didn't leave the hospital till long after the Day-Sisters had gone and the Night-Sisters came on. The wards were all quiet as I walked down the corridor, and to left and right through the glass doors hung the rows of expectant stockings.

Final and despairing postscript on Mr. Pettitt.

When a woman says she cannot come to lunch it is because she doesn't want to.

Let this serve as an axiom to every lover: A woman who refuses lunch refuses everything.

The hospital is alive; I feel it like a living being.

The hospital is like a dream. I am afraid of waking up and finding it commonplace.

The white Sisters, the ceaselessly-changing patients, the long passages, the sudden plunges into the brilliant wards ... their scenery hypnotizes me.

Sometimes in the late evening one walks busily up and down the ward doing this and that, forgetting that there is anything beyond the drawn blinds, engrossed in the patients, one's tasks—bed-making, washing, one errand and another—and then suddenly a blind will blow out and almost up to the ceiling, and through it you will catch a glimpse that makes you gasp, of a black night crossed with bladed searchlights, of a moon behind a crooked tree.

The lifting of the blind is a miracle; I do not believe in the wind.

A new Sister on to-night ... very severe. We had to make the beds like white cardboard. I wonder what she thinks of me.

Mr. Pettitt (who really is going to-morrow) wandered up into the ward and limped near me. "Sister...." he began. He *will* call me "Sister." I frowned at him. The new Sister glanced at him and blinked.

He was very persistent. "Sister," he said again, "do you think I can have a word with you?"

"Not now," I whispered as I hurried past him.

21

"Oh, is that so?" he said, as though I had made an interesting statement, and limped away, looking backwards at me. I suppose he wants to say good-bye.

He sat beside Mr. Wicks's bed (Mr. Wicks who is paralysed) and looked at me from time to time with that stare of his which contains so little offence.

It is curious to think that I once saw Mr. Wicks on a tennis-lawn, walking across the grass.... Mr. Wicks, who will never put his foot on grass again, but, lying in his bed, continues to say, as all Tommies say, "I feel well in meself."

So he does; he feels well in himself. But he isn't going to live, all the same.

Still his routine goes on: he plays his game of cards, he has his joke: "Lemonade, please, nurse; but it's not from choice!"

When I go to clear his ash-tray at night I always say, "Well, now I've got something worth clearing at last!"

And he chuckles and answers, "Thought you'd be pleased. It's the others gets round my bed and leaves their bits."

He was once a sergeant: he got his commission a year ago.

My ruined charms cry aloud for help.

The cap wears away my front hair; my feet are widening from the everlasting boards; my hands won't take my rings.

I was advised last night on the telephone to marry immediately before it was too late.

A desperate remedy. I will try cold cream and hair tonics first.

There is a tuberculosis ward across the landing. They call it the T.B. ward.

It is a den of coughs and harrowing noises.

One night I saw a negro standing in the doorway with his long hair done up in hairpins. He is the pet of the T.B. ward; they call him Henry.

Henry came in to help us with our Christmas decorations on Christmas Eve, and as he cleverly made wreaths my Sister whispered to me, "He's never spitting ... in the ward!"

But he wasn't, it was part of his language—little clicks and ticks. He comes from somewhere in Central Africa, and one of the T.B.'s told me, "He's only got one wife, nurse."

He is very proud of his austerity, for he has somehow discovered that he has hit on a country where it is the nutty thing only to have one wife.

No one can speak a word of his language, no one knows exactly where he comes from; but he can say in English, "Good morning, Sister!" and "Christmas Box!" and "One!"

Directly one takes any notice of him he laughs and clicks, holding up one finger, crying, "One!"

Then a proud T.B. (they regard him as the Creator might regard a humming-bird) explains: "He means he's only got one wife, nurse."

Then he did his second trick. He came to me with outstretched black hand and took my apron, fingering it. Its whiteness slipped between his fingers. He dropped it and, holding up the hand with its fellow, ducked his head to watch me with his glinting eyes.

"He means," explained the versatile T.B., "that he has ten piccaninnies in his village and they're all dressed in white."

It took my breath away; I looked at Henry for corroboration. He nodded earnestly, coughed and whispered, "Ten!"

"How do you know he means that?" I asked. "How can you possibly have found out?"

"We got pictures, nurse. We showed 'im kids, and 'e said 'e got ten—six girls and four boys. We showed 'im pictures of kids."

I had never seen Henry before, never knew he existed. But in the ward opposite the poor T.B.'s had been holding conversations with him in window-seats, showing him pictures, painfully establishing a communion with him ... Henry, with his hair done up in hairpins!

Although they showed him off with conscious pride, I don't think he really appeared strange to them, beyond his colour. I believe they imagine his wife as appearing much as their own wives, his children as the little children who run about their own doorsteps. They do not stretch their imaginations to conceive any strangeness about his home surroundings to correspond with his own strangeness.

To them Henry has the dignity of a man and a householder, possibly a rate-payer.

He seems quite happy and amused. I see him carrying a bucket sometimes, sharing its handle with a flushed T.B. They carry on animated conversations as they go downstairs, the T.B. talking the most. It reminds me of a child and a dog.

What strange machinery is there for getting him back? Part of the cargo of a ship ... one day ... "a nigger for Central Africa...."

"Where's his unit?"

"Who knows! One nigger and his bundle ... for Central Africa!"

The ward has put Mr. Wicks to Coventry because he has been abusive and violent-tempered for three days.

He lies flat in his bed and frowns; no more jokes over the lemonade, no wilfulness over the thermometer.

It is in these days that Mr. Wicks faces the truth.

I lingered by his bed last night, after I had put his tea-tray on his table, and looked down at him; he pretended to be inanimate, his open eyes fixed upon the white rail of the bed. His bedclothes were stretched about him as though he had not moved since his bed was made, hours before.

His worldly pleasures were beside him—his reading-lamp, his Christmas box of cigars, his *Star*—but his eyes, disregarding them, were upon that sober vision that hung around the bedrail.

He began a bitter conversation:

"Nurse, I'm only a ranker, but I had a bit saved. I went to a private doctor and paid for myself. And I went to a specialist, and he told me I should never get this. I paid for it myself out of what I had saved."

We might have been alone in the world, he and I. Far down at the other end of the room the men sat crouched about the fire, their trays before them on chairs. The sheet of window behind Mr. Wicks's head was flecked with the morsels of snow which, hunted by the gale, obtained a second's refuge before oblivion.

"I'd sooner be dead than lying here; I would, reely." You hear that often in the world. "I'd sooner be dead than——" But Mr. Wicks meant it; he would sooner be dead than lying there. And death is a horror, an end. Yet he says lying there is worse.

"You see, I paid for a specialist myself, and he told me I should never be like this."

There was nothing to be said.... One must have one's tea. I went down the ward to the bunk, and we cut the pink iced cake left over from Christmas....

I did not mean to forget him, but I forgot him. From birth to death we are alone....

But one of the Sisters remembered him.

"Mr. Wicks is still in the dumps," she remarked.

"What is really the matter with him, Sister?"

"Locomotor ataxy." And she added as she drank her tea, "It's his own fault."

"Oh, hush, hush!" my heart cried soundlessly to her, "You can't judge the bitterness of this, nun, from your convent...!"

Alas, Mr. Wicks!... No wonder you saved your money to spend upon specialists! How many years have you walked in fear of this? He took your money, the gentleman in Harley Street, and told you that you might go in peace. He blessed you and gave you salvation.

And the bitterest thing of all is that you paid for him like an officer and he was wrong.

How the blinds blew and the windows shook to-night...! I walked out of the hospital into a gale, clouds driving to the sea, trees bending back and fore across the moon.

I walked till I was warm, and then I walked for happiness.

The maddening shine of the moon held my eyes, and I walked in the road like a fool, watching her—till at last, bringing my eyes down, the telegraph-posts were small as blades of grass on the hill-side and the shining ribbon tracks in the mud on the road ran up the hill for ever. They go to Dover, and Dover is France—and France leads anywhere.

To what a lost enchantment am I recalled by the sight of a branch across the moon? Something in childhood, something which escapes yet does not wither....

As I passed the public-house on the crest of the hill, all black and white in the cold moonlight, a heavy door swung open and, with a cough and a deep, satisfied snuffle, a man coming out let a stream of gas-light across the road. If I were a man I should certainly go to public-houses. All that polished brass and glass boxed up away from the moon and the shadows would call to me. And to drink must be a happy thing when you have climbed the hill.

25

The T.B. ward is a melancholy place. There is a man in a bed near the door who lies with his mouth open; his head is like a bird-cage beneath a muslin cloth. I saw him behind his screens when I took them over a little lukewarm chicken left from our dinner.

There was a dark red moon to-night, and frost. Our orderly said, "You can tell it's freezing, nurse, by the breath," as he watched mine curl up in smoke in the icy corridor. I like people who notice things....

Out in the road in front of the hospital I couldn't get the motor-bicycle to work, and sat crouched in the dark fiddling with spanners.

The charwomen came out of the big gate in the dark talking and laughing, all in a bunch. One of them stepped off the pavement near me and stopped to put her toe through the ice in the gutter.

"Nah, come on, Mrs. Toms!"

"I always 'ave to break it, it's ser nice an' stiff," she said as she ran after them.

To be a Sister is to have a nationality.

As there are Icelanders urbane, witty, lazy ... and yet they are all Icelanders ... so there are cold, uproarious, observant, subservient, slangy, sympathetic, indifferent, and Scotch Sisters, and yet....

Sister said of a patient to-day, "He was a funny man."

A funny man is a man who is a dark horse: who is neither friendly nor antagonistic; who is witty; who is preoccupied; who is whimsical or erratic—funny qualities, unsafe qualities.

No Sister could like a funny man.

In our ward there are three sorts of men: "Nothing much," "nice boys," and Mr. Wicks.

The last looms even to the mind of the Sister as a Biblical figure, a pillar of salt, a witness to God's wrath.

The Sister is a past-mistress of such phrases as "Indeed!" "That is a matter of opinion," "We shall see..." "It is possible."

I have discovered a new and (for me) charming game which I play with my Sister. It is the game of telling the truth about the contents of my mind when asked.

Yesterday Sister was trying to get some coal out of the coal-bin with a shovel that turned round and round on its handle; she was unsuccessful.

I said, "Let me, Sister!"

She said, "Why?"

And I: "Because I think I can do it better."

"Why should you think that?"

"Because all human beings do," I said, and, luckily, she smiled.

She was washing her caps out in a bowl in the afternoon when I came on.

"Good afternoon, Sister," I said. "Ironing?"

"I am obviously only washing as yet," she said.

"It's because I think so quickly, Sister," I said; "I knew you would iron next."

I dined with Irene last night after the hospital.

I refused to believe what she told me about the last bus passing at half-past nine, and so at a quarter to ten I stood outside "The Green Lamp" and waited.

Ten minutes passed and no bus.

With me were two women waiting too—one holding a baby; the other, younger, smarter, dangling a purse.

At last I communicated my growing fears: "I believe the last has gone...."

We fixed our six eyes on the far corner of the road, waiting for the yellow lights to round it, but only the gas-lamps stood firm in their perspective.

"Oh my, Elsie!" said the woman with the baby, "you can't never walk up to the cross-roads in the dark alone!"

"I wouldn't make the attempt, not for anything!" replied the younger one firmly.

Without waiting for more I stepped into the middle of the road and started on my walk home; the very next sentence would have suggested that Elsie and I should walk together.

She wouldn't "make the attempt...." Her words trailed through my mind, conjuring up some adventure, some act of bravery and daring.

The road was the high road, the channel of tarmac and pavements that she probably walked along every day; and now it was the selfsame high road, the same flagstones, hedges, railings, but with the cloak of night upon them.

It wasn't man she feared; even in the dark I knew she wasn't that kind. She would be awfully capable—with man. No, it was the darkness, the spooky jungle of darkness: she feared the trees would move....

"I wouldn't make the attempt, not for anything"; and the other woman had quite agreed with her.

I knew where I was by the smells and the sounds on the road— the smell of the lines of picketed horses behind the railings, the sharp and sudden stamp of the sick ones in the wooden stables, and, later on, the glitter of water in the horse-troughs.

I thought: "I am not afraid.... Is it because I am more educated, or have less imagination?"

"Halt! Who goes there?"

"Friend," I said, thrilling tremendously.

He approached me and said something which I couldn't make anything of. Presently I disentangled, "You should never dread the baynit, miss."

"But I'm not dreading," I said, annoyed, "I ... I love it."

He said he was cold, and added: "I bin wounded. If you come to that lamp you can see me stripe."

We went to the lamp. "It's them buses," he complained, "they won't stop when I halt 'em."

"But why do you want to stop them? They can't poison the horse-troughs."

"It's me duty," he said. "There's one comin'."

A bus, coming the opposite way, bore down upon us with an unwieldy rush and roar—the last bus, in a hurry to get to bed.

"You'll see," he said pessimistically.

"'Alt! 'Alt, there!" The bus, with three soldiers hanging on the step, rushed past us, and seemed to slow a little. The sentry ran a few paces towards it, crying "'Alt!" But it gathered speed and boomed on again, buzzing away between the gas-lamps. He returned to me sadly.

"I don't believe they can hear," I said, and gave him some chocolates and went on.

As I passed the hospital gates it seemed there was a faint, a very faint, sweet smell of chloroform....

I was down at the hospital to-night when the factory blew up over the river.

The lights went out, and as they sank I reached the kitchen hatchway with my tray. At the bottom of the stairs I could see through the garden door the sky grown sulphur and the bushes glowing, while all the panes of glass turned incandescent.

Then the explosion came; it sounded as though it was just behind the hospital. Two hundred panes of glass fell out, and they made a noise too.

Standing in the dark with a tray in my hand I heard a man's voice saying gleefully, "I haven't been out of bed this two months!"

Some one lit a candle, and by its light I saw all the charwomen from the kitchen bending about like broken weeds, and every officer was saying, "There, there now!"

We watched the fires till midnight from the hill.

I went over this morning early. We were thirty-two in a carriage—Lascars, Chinese, children, Jews, niggers from the docks.

Lascars and children and Jews and I, we fought to get off the station platform; sometimes there wasn't room on the ground for both my feet at once.

The fires were still burning and smouldering there at midday, but a shower of rime fell on it, so that it looked like an old ruin, something done long ago.

At Pompeii, some one told me, one looked into the rooms and they were as they had been left—tables laid.... Here, too, I saw a table laid for the evening meal with a bedstead fallen from the upper floor astraddle across it. The insides of the houses were coughed into their windows, basket-chairs hanging to the sills, and fire-irons.

Outside, the soil of the earth turned up; a workman's tin mug stuck and roasted and hardened into what looks like solid rock—a fossil, as though it had been there for ever.

London is only skin-deep. Beneath lies the body of the world.

The hump under the blankets rolls over and a man's solemn face appears upon the pillow.

"Can you get me a book, nurse?"

"Yes. What kind do you like?"

"Nothing fanciful; something that might be true."

"All right!"

"Oh—and nurse...?"

"Yes?"

"Not sentimental and not funny, I like a practical story."

I got him "Lord Jim."...

Another voice: "Nurse, is there any modern French poetry in that bookcase?"

"Good heavens, no! Who would have brought it here?"

(Who are they all ... these men with their differing tastes?)

Perhaps the angels feel like this as they trail about in heaven with their wings flapping on their thin white legs....

"Who were you, angel?"

"I was a beggar outside San Marco."

"Were you? How odd! I was an Englishman."

The concerts that we give in the ward touch me with some curious emotion. I think it is because I am for once at rest in the ward and have time to think and wonder.

There is Captain Thomson finishing his song. He doesn't know what to do with his hands; they swing. He is tall and dark, with soft eyes—and staff badges.

Could one guess what he is? Never in a dozen years.... But I *know*!

He said to me last night, "Nurse, I'm going out to-morrow."

I leant across the table to listen to him.

"Nurse, if you ever want any *crêpe de Chine* ... for nightgowns ... mind, at wholesale prices...."

"I have bought some at a sale."

"May I ask at what price?"

"Four-and-eleven a yard."

"Pity! You could have had it from me at three!"

He gave me his business card. "That's it, nurse," he said, as he wrote on the back of it. "Drop me a line to that address and you'll get any material for underwear at trade prices."

30

He booked one or two orders the night he went away—not laughingly, not as a joke, but with deep seriousness, and gravely pleased that he was able to do what he could for us. He was a traveller in ladies' underwear. I have seldom met any one so little a snob....

Watch Mr. Gray singing....

One hand on the piano, one on his hip:

"I love every mouse in that old-fashioned house."

"That fellow can sing!" whispers the man beside me.

"Is he a professional?" I asked as, finishing, the singer made the faintest of bows and walked back to his chair.

"I think he must be."

"He is, he is!" whispered Mr. Matthews, "I've heard him before."

They know so little about each other, and they don't ask. It is only I who wonder—I, a woman, and therefore of the old, burnt-out world. These men watch without curiosity, speak no personalities, form no sets, express no likings, analyse nothing. They are new-born; they have as yet no standards and do not look for any.

Ah, to have had that experience too!... I am of the old world.

Again and again I realize, "A nation in arms...."

Watchmakers, jewellers, station-masters, dress-designers, actors, travellers in underwear, bank clerks ... they come here in uniforms and we put them into pyjamas and nurse them; and they lie in bed or hobble about the ward, watching us as we move, accepting each other with the unquestioning faith of children.

The outside world has faded since I have been in the hospital. Their world is often near me—their mud and trenches, things they say when they come in wounded.

The worst of it is it almost bores me to go to London, and London was always my Mecca. It is this garden at home, I think. It is so easy not to leave it.

When you wake up the window is full of branches, and last thing at night the moon is on the snow on the lawn and you can see the pheasants' footmarks.

Then one goes to the hospital....

When Madeleine telephones to me, "I'm living in a whirl...." it disturbs me. Suddenly I want to too, but it dies down again.

Not that it is their world, those trenches. When they come in wounded or sick they say at once, "What shows are on?"

Mr. Wicks has ceased to read those magazines his sister sends him; he now stares all day at his white bedrail.

I only pass him on my way to the towel-cupboard, twice an evening, and then as I glance at him I am set wondering all down the ward of what he thinks, or if he thinks....

I may be quite wrong about him; it is possible he doesn't think at all, but stares himself into some happier dream.

One day when he is dead, when he is as totally dead as he tells me he hopes to be, that bed with its haunted bedrail will bend under another man's weight. Surely it must be haunted? The weight of thought, dream or nightmare, that hangs about it now is almost visible to me.

Mr. Wicks is an uneducated and ordinary man. In what manner does his dream run? Since he has ceased to read he has begun to drop away a little from my living understanding.

He reflects deeply at times.

To-night, as I went quickly past him with my load of bath-towels, his blind flapped a little, and I saw the moon, shaped like a horn, behind it.

Dropping my towels, I pulled his blind back:

"Mr. Wicks, look at the moon."

Obedient as one who receives an order, he reached up to his supporting handle and pulled his shoulders half round in bed to look with me through the pane.

The young moon, freed from the trees, was rising over the hill.

I dropped the blind again and took up my towels and left him.

After that he seemed to fall into one of his trances, and lay immovable an hour or more. When I took his dinner to him he lifted his large, sandy head and said:

"Seems a queer thing that if you hadn't said 'Look at the moon' I might have bin dead without seeing her."

"But don't you ever look out of the window?"

The obstinate man shook his head.

32

There was a long silence in the ward to-night. It was so cold that no one spoke. It is a gloomy ward, I think; the pink silk on the electric lights is so much too thick, and the fire smokes dreadfully. The patients sat round the fire with their "British warms" over their dressing-gowns and the collars turned up.

Through the two glass doors and over the landing you can see the T.B.'s moving like little cinema figures backwards and forwards across the lighted entrance.

Suddenly—a hesitating touch—an ancient polka struck up, a tune remembered at children's parties. Then a waltz, a very old one too. The T.B.'s were playing dance music.

I crept to their door and looked. One man alone was taking any notice, and he was the player; the others sat round coughing or staring at nothing in particular, and those in bed had their heads turned away from the music.

The man whose face is like a bird-cage has now more than ever a look of ... an empty cage. He allows his mouth to hang open: that way the bird will fly.

What is there so rapturous about the moon?

The radiance of a floating moon is unbelievable. It is a figment of dream. The metal-silver ball that hung at the top of the Christmas tree, or, earlier still, the shining thing, necklace or spoon, the thing the baby leans to catch ... the magpie in us....

Mr. Beecher is to be allowed to sleep till eight. He sleeps so badly, he says. He woke up crying this morning, for he has neurasthenia.

That is what Sister says.

He should have been in bed all yesterday, but instead he got up and through the door watched the dead T.B. ride away on his stretcher (for the bird flew in the night).

"How morbid of him!" Sister says.

He has seen many dead in France and snapped his fingers at them, but I agree with him that to die of tuberculosis in the backwaters of the war isn't the same thing.

It's dreary; he thought how dreary it was as he lay awake in the night.

But then he has neurasthenia....

Pity is exhaustible. What a terrible discovery! If one ceases for one instant to pity Mr. Wicks he becomes an awful bore. Some days, when the sun is shining, I hear his grieving tenor voice all over the ward, his legendary tale of a wrong done him in his promotion. The men are kind to him and say "Old man," but Mr. Gray, who lies in the next bed to him, is drained of everything except resignation. I heard him say yesterday, "You told me that before...."

We had a convoy last night.

There was a rumour at tea-time, and suddenly I came round a corner on an orderly full of such definite information as:

"There's thirty officers, nurse; an 'undred an' eighty men."

I flew back to the bunk with the news, and we sat down to our tea wondering and discussing how many each ward would get.

Presently the haughty Sister from downstairs came to the door: she held her thin, white face high, and her rimless glasses gleamed, as she remarked, overcasually, after asking for a hot-water bottle that had been loaned to us:

"Have you many beds?"

"Have they many beds?" The one question that starts up among the competing wards.

And, "I don't want any; I've enough to do as it is!" is the false, cloaking answer that each Sister gives to the other.

But my Sisters are frank women; they laughed at my excitement—themselves not unstirred. It's so long since we've had a convoy.

The gallants of the ward showed annoyance. New men, new interests.... They drew together and played bridge.

A little flying boy with bright eyes said in his high, piping voice to me across the ward:

"So there are soldiers coming into the ward to-night!"

I paused, struck by his accusing eyes.

"What do you mean? Soldiers...?"

"I mean men who have been to the front, nurse."

The gallants raised their eyebrows and grew uproarious.

The gallants have been saying unprofessional things to me, and I haven't minded. The convoy will arm me against them. "Soldiers are coming into the ward."

Eight o'clock, nine o'clock.... If only one could eat something! I took a sponge-finger out of a tin, resolving to pay it back out of my tea next day, and stole round to the dark corner near the German ward to eat it. The Germans were in bed; I could see two of them. At last, freed from their uniform, the dark blue with the scarlet soup-plates, they looked— how strange!—like other men.

One was asleep. The other, I met his eyes so close; but I was in the dark, and he under the light of a lamp.

I knew what was happening down at the station two miles away; I had been on station duty so often. The rickety country station lit by one large lamp; the thirteen waiting V.A.D.'s; the long wooden table loaded with mugs of every size; kettles boiling; the white clock ticking on; that frowsy booking clerk....

Then the sharp bell, the tramp of the stretcher-bearers through the station, and at last the two engines drawing gravely across the lighted doorway, and carriage windows filled with eager faces, other carriage windows with beds slung across them, a vast Red Cross, a chemist's shop, a theatre, more windows, more faces....

The stretcher-men are lined up; the M.O. meets the M.O. with the train; the train Sisters drift in to the coffee-table.

"Here they come! Walkers first...."

The station entrance is full of men crowding in and taking the steaming mugs of tea and coffee; men on pickaback with bandaged feet; men with only a nose and one eye showing, with stumbling legs, bound arms. The station, for five minutes, is full of jokes and witticisms; then they pass out and into the waiting chars-à-bancs.

A long pause.

"Stretchers!"

The first stretchers are laid on the floor.

There I have stood so often, pouring the tea behind the table, watching that littered floor, the single gas-lamp ever revolving on its chain, turning the shadows about the room like a wheel—my mind filled with pictures, emptied of thoughts, hypnotized.

But last night, for the first time, I was in the ward. For the first time I should follow them beyond the glass door, see what became of them, how they changed from soldiers into patients....

The gallants in the ward don't like a convoy; it unsexes us.

Nine o'clock ... ten o'clock.... Another biscuit. Both Germans are asleep now.

At last a noise in the corridor, a tramp on the stairs.... Only walkers? No, there's a stretcher—and another...!

Now reflection ends, my feet begin to move, my hands to undo bootlaces, flick down thermometers, wash and fetch and carry.

The gallants play bridge without looking up. I am tremendously fortified against them: for one moment I fiercely condemn and then forget them. For I am without convictions, antipathies, prejudices, reflections. I only work and watch, watch....

Our ward is divided: half of it is neat and white and orderly; the other half has khaki tumbled all over it—"Sam Brownes," boots, caps, mud, the caked mud from the "other side."

But the neat beds are empty; the occupants out talking to the new-comers, asking questions. Only the gallants play their bridge unmoved. They are on their mettle, showing off. Their turn will come some day.

Now it only remains to walk home, hungry, under a heavy moon.

The snow is running down the gutters. What a strange and penetrating smell of spring! February ... can it be yet?

The running snow is uncovering something that has been delayed. In the garden a blackbird made a sudden cry in the hedge. I did smell spring, and I'm starving....

I thought last night that a hospital ward is, above all, a serene place, in spite of pain and blood and dressings. Gravity rules it and order and a quiet procession of duties.

Last night I made beds with the eldest Sister. The eldest Sister is good company to make beds with; she is quiet unless I rouse her, and when I talk she smiles with her eyes. I like to walk slowly round the ward, stooping and rising over the white beds, flicking the sheets mechanically from the mattress, and finally turning the mattress with an ease which gives me pleasure because I am strong.

In life nothing is too small to please....

Once during the evening the eldest Sister said to me:

"I am worried about your throat. Is it no better?"

And from the pang of pleasure and gratitude that went through me I have learnt the value of such remarks.

In every bed there is some one whose throat is at least more sore than mine....

Though I am not one of those fierce V.A.D.'s who scoff at sore throats and look for wounds, yet I didn't know it was so easy to give pleasure.

The strange, disarming ways of men and women!

I stood in the bunk to-night beside the youngest Sister, and she looked up suddenly with her absent stare and said, "You're not so nice as you used to be!"

I was dumbfounded. Had I been "nice"? And now different....

What a maddening sentence, for I felt she was going to refuse me any spoken explanation.

But one should not listen to what people say, only to what they mean, and she was one of those persons whose minds one must read for oneself, since her words so often deformed her thoughts.

The familiarity and equality of her tone seemed to come from some mood removed from the hospital, where her mistrustful mind was hovering about a trouble personal to herself.

She did not mean "You are not so nice...." but "You don't like me so much...."

She was so young, it was all so new to her, she wanted so to be "liked"! But there was this question of her authority....

How was she to live among her fellows?

Can one afford to disdain them? Can one steer happily with indifference? Must one, to be "liked," bend one's spirit to theirs? And, most disturbing question of all, is to be "liked" the final standard?

Whether to wear, or not to wear, a mask towards one's world? For there is so much that is not ripe to show—change and uncertainty....

As she sat there, unfolding to me the fogs of her situation, her fresh pink face clouded, her grand cap and red cape adding burdens of authority to the toil of growth, I could readily have looked into the glass to see if my hair was grey!

"Then there is nothing you condemn?" said the youngest Sister finally, at the close of a conversation.

I have to-day come up against the bedrock of her integrity; it is terrible. She has eternal youth, eternal fair hair, cold and ignorant judgments. On things relating to the world I can't further soften her; a man must do the rest.

"A gentleman ... a gentleman...." I am so tired of this cry for a "gentleman."

Why can't they do very well with what they've got!

Here in the wards the Sisters have the stuff the world is made of laid out, bedded, before their eyes; the ups and downs of man from the four corners of the Empire and the hundred corners of social life, helpless and in pyjamas—and they're not satisfied, but must cry for a "gentleman"!

"I couldn't make a friend of that man!" the youngest Sister loves to add to her criticism of a patient.

It isn't my part as a V.A.D. to cry, "Who wants you to?"

"I couldn't trust that man!" the youngest Sister will say equally often.

This goes deeper....

But whom need one trust? Brother, lover, friend ... no more. Why wish to trust all the world?...

"They are not real men," she says, "not men through and through."

That's where she goes wrong; they are men through and through—patchy, ordinary, human. She means they are not men after her pattern.

Something will happen in the ward. Once I have touched this bedrock in her I shall be for ever touching it till it gets sore!

One should seek for no response. They are not elastic, these nuns....

In all honesty the hospital is a convent, and the men in it my brothers.

This for months on end....

For all that, now and then some one raises his eyes and looks at me; one day follows another and the glance deepens.

"Charme de l'amour qui pourrait vous peindre!"

Women are left behind when one goes into hospital. Such women as are in a hospital should be cool, gentle; anything else becomes a torment to the "prisoner."

For me, too, it is bad; it brings the world back into my eyes; duties are neglected, discomforts unobserved.

But there are things one doesn't fight.

"Charme de l'amour...." The ward is changed! The eldest Sister and the youngest Sister are my enemies; the patients are my enemies—even Mr. Wicks, who lies on his back with his large head turned fixedly my way to see how often I stop at the bed whose number is 11.

Last night he dared to say, "It's not like you, nurse, staying so much with that rowdy crew...." The gallants ... I know! But one among them has grown quieter, and his bed is No. 11.

Even Mr. Wicks is my enemy.

He watches and guards. Who knows what he might say to the eldest Sister? He has nothing to do all day but watch and guard.

In the bunk at tea I sit among thoughts of my own. The Sisters are my enemies....

I am alive, delirious, but not happy.

I am at any one's mercy; I have lost thirty friends in a day. The thirty-first is in bed No. 11.

This is bad: hospital cannot shelter this life we lead, No. 11 and I. He is a prisoner, and I have my honour, my responsibility towards him; he has come into this room to be cured, not tormented.

Even my hand must not meet his—no, not even in a careless touch, not even in its "duty"; or, if it does, what risk!

I am conspired against: it is not I who make his bed, hand him what he wishes; some accident defeats me every time.

Now that I come to think of it, it seems strange that the Sisters should be my enemies. Don't we deserve sympathy and pity, No. 11 and I? From women, too....

Isn't there a charm hanging about us? Aren't we leading magic days? Do they feel it and dislike it? Why?

I feel that the little love we have created is a hare whose natural fate is to be run by every hound. But I don't see the reason.

We can't speak, No. 11 and I, only a whispered word or two that seems to shout itself into every ear. We don't know each other.

Last night it was stronger than I. I let him stand near me and talk. I saw the youngest Sister at the far end of the ward by the door, but I didn't move; she was watching. The moment I took my eyes from her I forgot her.... That is how one feels when one is desperate; that is how trouble comes.

Later, I stood down by the hatch waiting for the tray of fish, and as I stood there, the youngest Sister beside me, he came down, for he was up and dressed yesterday, and offered to carry the tray. For he is reckless, too....

She told him to go back, and said to me, looking from her young, condemning eyes, "I suppose he thinks he can make up for being the cause of all the lateness to-night."

"Sister...." and then I stopped short. I hated her. Were we late? I looked at the other trays. We were not late; it was untrue. She had said that because she had had to wrap her barb in something and hadn't the courage to reprove me officially. I resented that and her air of equality. Since I am under her authority and agree to it, why dare she not use it?

As for me, I dared not speak to her all the evening. She would have no weapons against me. If I am to remember she is my Sister I must hold my hand over my mouth.

She would not speak to me, either. That was wrong of her: she is in authority, not I.

It is difficult for her because she is so young; but I have no room for sympathy.

At moments I forget her position and, burning with resentment, I reflect, " ... this schoolgirl...."

To-day I walked down to the hospital thinking: "I must be stronger. It is I who, in the inverted position of things, should be the stronger. He is being tortured, and he has no release. He cannot even be alone a moment."

But at the hospital gates I thought of nothing but that I should see him.

In the bunk sat the eldest Sister, writing in a book. It passed through my head that the two Sisters had probably "sat" on my affairs together. I wondered without interest what the other had told her. Putting on my cap, I walked into the ward.

Surely his bed had had a pink eiderdown!

I walked up the ward and looked at it; but I knew without need of a second glance what had happened.

His bed was made in the fashion in which we make an empty bed, a bed that waits for a new patient. His locker was empty and stood open, already scrubbed. I smiled as I noticed they hadn't even left me that to do.

No one volunteered a word of explanation, no one took the trouble to say he had gone.

These women.... I smiled again. Only the comic phrase rang in my head "They've properly done me in! Properly done me in...."

I went downstairs and fetched the trays, and all the time the smile was on my lips. These women.... Somehow I had the better of the Sister. It is better to be in the wrong than in the right.

His friends looked at me a little, but apparently he had left no message for me.

Later I learnt that he had been taken to another hospital at two, while I came on at three.

Once during the evening the eldest Sister mentioned vaguely, "So-and-so has gone."

And I said aloud, after a little reflection, "Yes ... in the nick of time, Sister."

During the evening I realized that I should never see him again. It was here in this ward the thing had grown. The hare we had started wouldn't bear the strain of any other life. He might write, but I shouldn't go and see him.

"He must be wild," I thought with pity.

41

The feeling between us would die anyhow; better throw in my strength with the Sister's and help her hurl it now towards its death. I looked at her bent head with a secret triumph.

Then, slowly: "How ... permanently am I in disgrace?"
And she: "Not at all ... now."

Behind the stone pillar of the gateway is one dirty little patch of snow; I saw it even in the moonless darkness.

The crown of the hill here holds the last snows, but for all that the spring smell is steaming among the trees and up and down the bracken slopes in the garden next door.

There is no moon, there are no stars, no promise to the eye, but in the dense, vapouring darkness the bulbs are moving. I can smell what is not earth or rain or bark.

The curtain has been drawn over No. 11; the Sister holds the corners tightly against the window-frame. He is outside, somewhere in the world, and I am here moving among my thirty friends; and since it isn't spring yet, the lights are lit to hide the twilight. The Sister's eyes talk to me again as we make beds—yes, even bed No. 11 with a little jaundice boy in it. They let me make it now!

Last night we had another concert in the ward.

A concert demoralizes me. By reason of sitting on the beds and talking to whom one wills, I regain my old manners, and forget that a patient may be washed, fed, dressed but not talked to. My old manners were more gracious, but less docile.

Afterwards we wheeled the beds back into their positions. I bumped Mr. Lambert's as I wheeled it, and apologized.

"I'm not grumbling," he smiled from his pillow.

"You never do," I answered.

"You don't know me, nurse!"

And I thought as I looked down at him "I shall never know him better or so well again...."

Indeed a Sister is a curious creature. She is like a fortress, unassailable, and whose sleeping guns may fire at any minute.

42

I was struck with a bit of knowledge last night that will serve me through life, i.e. that to justify oneself is the inexcusable fault. It is better to be in the wrong than in the right.

A Sister has an "intimate life."

It occurs when she goes off duty; that is to say, it lies between 8.45, when she finishes her supper, and 10 o'clock, when she finishes undressing.

That is why one Sister said to me, "If I hadn't taken up nursing I should have gone in for culture."

I don't laugh at that.... To have an intimate life one must have a little time.

Who am I that I can step in from outside to criticize? The hospital is not my life. I am expectant....

But for them here and now is the business of life.

As the weeks go by I recognize the difficulty of keeping the life of the Sisters and the V.A.D.'s out of the circle of my thoughts. Their vigorous and symmetrical vision of the ward attacks me; their attitude towards the patients, which began by offending me, ends by overtaking me.

On the whole the Sisters loathe relations. They look into the ward and see the mothers and sisters and wives camped round the beds, and go back into the bunk feeling that the ward doesn't belong to them.

The eldest Sister said to me yesterday: "Shut the door, nurse; there's Captain Fellows's father. I don't want him fussing round."

On that we discussed relations, and it seemed to me that it was inevitable that a Sister should be the only buffer between them and their pressing anxieties.

"No, a relation is the last straw.... You don't understand!" she said.

I don't understand, but I am not specialized.

Long ago in the Mess I said to *my* Sister, laughing: "I would go through the four years' training just to wear that cap and cape!"

And she: "You couldn't go through it and come out as you are...."

Mr. Wicks has set his heart on crutches.

"If you won't try me on them I'll buy me own and walk out of here!"

Then I realize the vanity of his threat and the completeness of his imprisonment, and hurry to suggest a new idea before he sees it too....

We set him on crutches....

He is brave. He said with anger, "I can't stand on these, they're too long. You go and ask for some shorter ones...."

And thus together we slurred over the fact of that pendulous, nerveless body which had hung from the crutches like an old stocking.

But all the evening he was buried in his own silence, and I suppose he was looking at the vision on the bedrail.

A boy of seventeen was brought in yesterday with pneumonia.

He was so ill that he couldn't speak, and we put screens round his bed. All the other patients in the ward immediately became convalescents.

I helped Sister to wash him, holding him on his side while he groaned with pain; and Sister, no longer cynical, said, "There you are Sonnie, it's almost finished...."

When I rolled back the blanket it gave me a shock to see how young his feet were —clean and thin, with the big toe curling up and the little toes curling back.

"Will you brush my hair?" he managed to say to me, and when I had finished: "This is a pretty ward...."

It isn't, but I am glad it seems so to him.

The boy is at his worst. Whenever we come near him he lifts his eyes and asks, "What are you going to do now?"

But to whatever we do he submits with a terrible docility.

Lying there propped on his pillow, with his small yellow face staring down the ward, he is all the centre of my thoughts; I am preoccupied with the mystery that is in his lungs.

Five days ago he was walking on his legs: five days, and he is on the edge of the world—to-night looking over the edge.

There is no shell, no mark, no tear.... The attack comes from within.

The others in the ward are like phantoms.

When I say to-morrow, "How is the boy?" what will they say?

The sun on the cobwebs lights them as it lights the telephone-wires above. The cocks scream from every garden.

To-day the sky is like a pale egg-shell, and aeroplanes from the two aerodromes are droning round the hill.

I think from time to time, "Is he alive?"

Can one grow used to death? It is unsafe to think of this....

For if death becomes cheap it is the watcher, not the dying, who is poisoned.

His mother buys a cake every day and brings it at tea-time, saying, "For the Sisters' tea...."

It is a bribe, dumbly offered, more to be on the safe side of every bit of chance than because she really believes it can make the slightest difference.

Now that I have time to think of it, her little action hurts me, but yesterday I helped to eat it with pleasure because one is hungry and the margarine not the best.

Aches and pains....
Pains and aches....

I don't know how to get home up the long hill....

Measles....

(Unposted.)

"DEAR SISTER,—Four more days before they will let me out of bed.... Whatever I promise to a patient in future I shall do, if I have to wear a notebook hanging on my belt.

"By which you will see that I am making discoveries!

45

"The quality of *expectation* in a person lying horizontally is wrought up to a high pitch. One is always expecting something. Generally it is food; three times a day it is the post; oftener it is the performance of some promise. The things that one asks from one's bed are so small: 'Can you get me a book?' 'Can you move that vase of flowers?' 'When you come up next time could you bring me an envelope?'

"But if one cannot get them life might as well stop.

"The wonder to me is how they stood me!

"I was always cheerful—I thought it a merit; I find instead it is an exasperation.

"I make a hundred reflections since my eyes are too bad to read. I stare at the ceiling, and if a moth comes on it—and just now that happened, or I would not have thought of mentioning it—I watch the pair of them, the moth and its leaping shadow, as they whirl from square to square of the smoke-ripened ceiling. This keeps my thoughts quiet.

"Then in the daytime there is the garden, the dog that crosses the lawn, the gardener talking to himself, the girl who goes to feed the hens....

"I don't say that in any of these things I find a substitute for reading, but since I can't and mayn't read....

"I am thinking, you know, of the beds down the right-hand side of the ward.

"There's Mr. Wicks, now: he has his back to the road with the trams on it.

"Do you see anything in that?

"I do. But then I have the advantage of you; my position is horizontal.

"Mr. Wicks's position is also ... strictly ... horizontal. It seems to me that if he could see those trams, mark Saturdays and Sundays by the increase of passengers, make little games to himself involving the number of persons to get on and off (for the stopping-place is within view: I know, for I looked) it might be possible to draw him back from that apathy which I too, as well as you, was ceasing to notice.

"Mr. Wicks, Sister, not only has his back to the road with trams on it, but for eleven months he has had his eyes on the yellow stone of the wall of the German ward; that is, when they are not on his own bed-rail....

"But if his bed were turned round to range alongside the window...? For he is a man with two eyes; not one who can write upon a stone wall with his thoughts.

"And yet ... it would be impossible! There's not a ward in the hospital whose symmetry is so spoilt.

"And that, you know, is a difficulty for you to weigh. How far are you a dictator?

"I have been thinking of my rôle and yours.

"In the long run, however 'capable' I become, my soul should be given to the smoothing of pillows.

"You are barred from so many kinds of sympathy: you must not sympathize over the deficiencies of the hospital, over the food, over the M.O.'s lack of imagination, over the intolerable habits of the man in the next bed; you must not sigh 'I know ...' to any of these plaints.

"Yours is the running of the ward. Yours the isolation of a crowned head.

"One day you said a penetrating thing to me:

"'He's not very ill, but he's feeling wretched. Run along and do the sympathetic V.A.D. touch!'

"For a moment I, just able to do a poultice or a fomentation, resented it.

"But you were right.... One has one's *métier.*"

III.
"THE BOYS ..."

So now one steps down from chintz covers and lemonade to the Main Army and lemon-water.

And to show how little one has one's eye upon the larger issues, the thing that upset me most on coming into a "Tommies'" ward was the fact that instead of twenty-six lemons twice a day for the making of lemonade I now squeeze two into an old jug and hope for the best about the sugar.

Smiff said to-day, "Give us a drop of lemon, nurse...." And the Sister: "Go on with you! I won't have the new nurse making a pet of you...."

I suppose I'm new to it, and one can't carry on the work that way, but, God knows, the water one can add to a lemon is cheap enough!

Smiff had a flash of temper to-night. He said: "Keepin' me here starin' at green walls this way! Nothing but green, nine blessed months!"

His foot is off, and to-night for the first time the doctor had promised that he should be wheeled into the corridor. But it was forgotten, and I am too new to jog the memory of the gods.

It's a queer place, a "Tommies'" ward. It makes me nervous. I'm not simple enough; they make me shy. I can't think of them like the others do, as "the boys"; they seem to me full-grown men.

I suffer awfully from my language in this ward. I seem to be the only V.A.D. of whom they continually ask, "What's say, nurse?" It isn't that I use long words, but my sentences seem to be inverted.

An opportunity for learning to speak simple Saxon....

"An antitetanic injection for Corrigan," said Sister. And I went to the dispensary to fetch the syringe and the needles.

"But has he any symptoms?" I asked. (In a Tommies' ward one dare ask anything; there isn't that mystery which used to surround the officers' illnesses.)

"Oh no," she said, "it's just that he hasn't had his full amount in France."

So I hunted up the spirit-lamp and we prepared it, talking of it.

But we forgot to talk of it to Corrigan. The needle was into his shoulder before he knew why his shirt was held up.

His wrath came like an avalanche; the discipline of two years was forgotten, his Irish tongue was loosened. Sister shrugged her shoulders and laughed; I listened to him as I cleaned the syringe.

I gathered that it was the indignity that had shocked his sense of individual pride. "Treating me like a cow...." I heard him say to Smiff— who laughed, since it wasn't his shoulder that carried the serum. Smiff laughed: he has been in hospital nine months, and his theory is that a Sister may do anything at any moment; his theory is that nothing does any good—that if you don't fuss you don't get worse.

Corrigan was angry all day; the idea that "a bloomin' woman should come an' shove something into me systim" was too much for him. But he forgets himself: there are no individualists now; his "system" belongs to us.

Sister said, laughing, to Smiff the other day, "Your leg is mine."

"Wrong again; it's the Governmint's!" said Smiff. But Corrigan is Irish and doesn't like that joke.

There are times when my heart fails me; when my eyes, my ears, my tongue, and my understanding fail me; when pain means nothing to me....

In the bus yesterday I came down from London sitting beside a Sister from another ward, who held her hand to her ear and shifted in her seat.

She told me she had earache, and I felt sorry for her.

As she had earache we didn't talk, and I sat huddled in my corner and watched the names of the shops, thinking, as I was more or less forced to do by her movements, of her earache.

What struck me was her own angry bewilderment before the fact of her pain. "But it hurts.... You've no idea how it hurts!" She was surprised.

Many times a day she hears the words, "Sister, you're hurtin' me.... Couldn't you shift my heel? It's like a toothache," and similar sentences. I hear them in our ward all the time. One can't pass down the ward without some such request falling on one's ears.

She is astonished at her earache; she is astonished at what pain can be; it is unexpected. She is ready to be angry with herself, with her pain, with her ear. It is monstrous, she thinks....

The pain of one creature cannot continue to have a meaning for another. It is almost impossible to nurse a man well whose pain you do not imagine. A deadlock!

One has illuminations all the time!

There is an old lady who visits in our ward, at whom, for one or two unimportant reasons, it is the custom to laugh. The men, who fall in with our moods with a docility which I am beginning to suspect is a mask, admit too that she is comic.

This afternoon, when she was sitting by Corrigan's bed and talking to him I saw where her treatment of him differed from ours. She treats him as though he were an individual; but there is more in it than that.... She treats him as though he had a wife and children, a house and a back garden and responsibilities: in some manner she treats him as though he had dignity.

I thought of yesterday's injection. That is the difference: that is what the Sisters mean when they say "the boys."...

The story of Rees is not yet ended in either of the two ways in which stories end in a hospital. His arm does not get worse, but his courage is ebbing. This morning I wheeled him out to the awful sleep again—for the third time.

They will take nearly anything from each other. The only thing that cheered Rees up as he was wheeled away was the voice of Pinker crying, "Jer want white flowers on yer coffin? We'll see to the brass 'andles!"

From Pinker, a little boy from the Mile End Road, they will stand anything. He is the servant of the ward (he says), partly through his good nature and a little because he has two good arms and legs. "I ain't no skivvy," he protests all the time, but every little odd job gets done.

Rees, when he wakes, wakes sobbing and says, "Don' go away, nurse...." He holds my hand in a fierce clutch, then releases it to point in the air, crying "There's the pain!" as though the pain filled the air and rose to the rafters. As he wakes it centralizes, until at last comes the moment when he says, "Me arm aches cruel," and points to it. Then one can leave him.

It was the first time I had heard a man sing at his dressing. I was standing at the sterilizer when Rees's song began to mount over the screen that hid him from me. ("Whatever is that?" "Rees's tubes going in.")

It was like this: "Ah ... ee ... oo, Sister!" and again: "Sister ... oo ... ee ... ah!" Then a little scream and his song again.

I heard her voice: "Now then, Rees, I don't call that much of a song." She called me to make his bed, and I saw his left ear was full of tears.

O visitors, who come into the ward in the calm of the long afternoon, when the beds are neat and clean and the flowers out on the tables and the V.A.D.'s sit sewing at splints and sandbags, when the men look like men again and smoke and talk and read ... if you could see what lies beneath the dressings!

When one shoots at a wooden figure it makes a hole. When one shoots at a man it makes a hole, and the doctor must make seven others.

I heard a blackbird sing in the middle of the night last night— two bars, and then another. I thought at first it might be a burglar whistling to his mate in the black and rustling garden.

But it was a blackbird in a nightmare.

Those distant guns again to-night....

Now a lull and now a bombardment; again a lull, and then batter, batter, and the windows tremble. Is the lull when *they* go over the top?

I can only think of death to-night. I tried to think just now, "What is it, after all! Death comes anyway; this only hastens it." But that won't do; no philosophy helps the pain of death. It is pity, pity, pity, that I feel, and sometimes a sort of shame that I am here to write at all.

Summer.... Can it be summer through whose hot air the guns shake and tremble? The honeysuckle, whose little stalks twinkled and shone that January night, has broken at each woody end into its crumbled flower.

Where is the frost, the snow?... Where are the dead?

Where is my trouble and my longing, and the other troubles, and the happiness in other summers?

Alas, the long history of life! There is that in death that makes the throat contract and the heart catch: everything is written in water.

We talk of tablets to the dead. There can be none but in the heart, and the heart fades.

There are only ten men left in bed in the ward. Sometimes I think, "Will there never be another convoy?"

And then: "Is not one man alone sufficient matter on which to reflect?" "One can find God in a herring's head...." says a Japanese proverb.

When there is not much to do in the ward and no sound comes from behind the screens, when there has not been a convoy for weeks, when the little rubber tubes lie in the trolley-drawer and the syringe gives place to the dry dressing—then they set one of us aside from the work of the ward to sit at a table and pad splints.

It isn't supposed to be a job we care for, and I am keeping up the delusion, but all the time I run my seams straight, pull the horsehair out to the last fine shred, turn in my corners as the corners of a leather book are turned, so that I may be kept at it, although out of cunning I appear to grumble and long to be released.

One does not wash up when one makes splints, one does not change the pillow-cases—forcing the resentful pillow down, down till the corners of the case are filled—nor walk the ward in search of odd jobs.

But these are not the reasons....

Just as I liked the unending laying of the trays in the corridor, so making splints appears to me a gentle work in which one has time to look at and listen to the ward with more penetrating eyes, with wider ears—a work varied by long conversations with Pinker about his girl and the fountain-pen trade.

But I ought not to have asked if she were pretty.

At first he didn't answer and appeared to be thinking very seri-ously—of a way out, perhaps.

"Does fer me all right," he presently said.

The defence of his girl occupied his attention, for after a few minutes he returned to it: "Sensible sort of girl. She ain't soft. Can cook an' all that."

I went on sewing my splint.

Almost reluctantly he pursued: "Got 'er photograph 'ere." But he did not get up at once, and we turned to the fountain-pens. "Any nib," he said, "crossed ever so, *I* could mend it. Kep' the books too; we was al-ways stocktaking."

Now I think of it, fountain-pen shops always *are* stocktaking. They do it all down the Strand, with big red labels across the front.

He rose suddenly and crossed to his locker to look for her pho-tograph, returning after a few minutes with a bundle of little cardboards. The first I turned over was that of a pretty fair-haired girl. "Is that her?" I asked. "She's pretty!" "That's 'er young sister," he answered. I turned over the rest, and he pointed out his family one by one—last of all his girl.

There are some men who are not taken in by a bit of fair hair.

One knows what these cheap photographs are, how they distort and blacken. The girl who looked at me from this one appeared to be a monster.

She had an enormous face, enormous spectacles, bands of gal-vanized iron drawn across her forehead for hair....

"Ther's just them two, 'er an 'er sister. 'Er sister ain't got a feller yet."

I praised his girl to Pinker, and praised Pinker to myself.

"A girl friend," he said, "keeps yer straighter than a man. Makes yer punctual."

"So she won't wait for you when you are late?"

"Not a minute over time," he said with pride. "I used to be a ter-ror when I first knew 'er; kep' 'er waitin' abaht. She soon cured me, did F. Steel."

"You are a funny little bird, Pinker," said the Sister, passing.

"Lil bird, am I?" He tucked his cardboards carefully into his locker and followed her up the ward firing repartee.

I sewed my splint. In all walks of life men keep one waiting. I should like to ask the huge and terrible girl about her cure.

53

Monk is the ugliest man I have ever seen. He has a squint and a leer, his mouth drops at both sides, he has no forehead, and his straight, combed hair meets his eyebrows—or rather, his left eyebrow, since that one is raised by a cut. He has the expression of a cut-throat, and yet he is quite young, good-tempered, and shy.

When Monk was working at a woollen belt Pinker said: "Workin' that for yer girl?... You got a girl, Monk?"

Monk squinted sidelong at Pinker and rubbed his hands together like a large ape.

"'E ain't got no girl," shrilled Pinker. "Monk ain't got no girl. You don' know what a girl is, do yer, Monk?"

Although they do much more to help each other than I ever saw done in the officers' ward, yet one is always saying things that I find myself praying the other hasn't heard.

In the next bed to Monk lies Gayner, six foot two, of the Expeditionary Force. Wounded at Mons, he was brought home to England, and since then he has made the round of the hospitals. He is a good-looking, sullen man who will not read or write or sew, who will not play draughts or cards or speak to his neighbour. He sits up, attentive, while the ulcers on his leg are being dressed, but if one asks him something of the history of his wound his tone holds such a volume of bitterness and exasperation that one feels that at any moment the locks of his spirit might cease to hold.

" ... ever since Mons, these ulcers, on and off?"

"Yes."

"Oh well, we must cure them now."

Her light tone is what he cannot endure. He does not believe in cure and will not believe in cure. It has become an article of faith: his ulcers will never be cured. He has a silent scorn of hospitals. He can wind a perfect bandage and he knows the rules; beyond that he pays as little attention as possible to what goes on.

When his dressing is over he tilts his thin, intelligent face at the ceiling. "Don't you ever read?" I asked him.

"I haven't the patience," he replied. But he has the patience to lie like that with his thin lips compressed and a frown on his face for hours, for days ... since Mons....

I have come to the conclusion that he has a violent soul, that he dare not talk. It is no life for a man.

I said to Pinker this morning, "I wish you'd hurry up over your bath; I've got to get it scrubbed out by nine."

"Don't you hurry me, nurse," said Pinker, "it's the on'y time I can think, in me bath."

I should like to have parried with Pinker (only my language is so much more complicated than it ought to be) that thinking in one's bath is a self-deception. I lay in my own bath last night and thought very deep thoughts, but often when we think our thoughts are deep they are only vague. Bath thoughts are wonderful, but there's nothing "to" them.

We had a heated discussion to-day as to whether the old lady who leaves a tract beneath a single rose by each bedside could longer be tolerated.

"She is a nuisance," said the Sister; "the men make more noise afterwards because they set her hymns to ragtime."

"What good does it do them?" said the V.A.D., " ... and I have to put the roses in water!"

I rode the highest horse of all: "Her inquiries about their souls are an impertinence. Why should they be bothered?"

These are the sort of things they say in debating societies. But Life talks differently....

Pinker said, "Makes the po'r ole lady 'appy!"

As one bends one's head low over the splint one sits unnoticed, a part of the furniture of the ward. The sounds of the ward rise and fill the ears; it is like listening to a kettle humming, bees round a bush of flowers, the ticking of a clock, the passing of life....

Now and then there are incidents, as just now. Two orderlies came in with a stretcher to fetch Mr. Smith (an older man than Smiff and a more dignified) away to a convalescent home. Mr. Smith has never been to France, but walked into our ward one day with a sore on his foot which had to be cut. He was up and dressed in his bedraggled khaki uniform when the stretcher-bearers came for him.

He looked down his nose at the stretcher. "I don't much like the look of that," he said. The stretcher-bearers waited for him.

He stood irresolute. "I never bin in one of them, and I don't want to make a start."

"Its bad luck to be our name," called out Smiff, waving his amputated ankle. "Better get your hand in!"

Mr. Smith got in slowly and departed from the ward, sitting bolt upright, gripping the sides with his hands.

Some of the wards and the Sisters' bunks are charming at this time of the year, now that larkspur and rambler-roses are cheap in the market.

But the love of decoration is not woman's alone. Through the dispensary hatchway I saw three empty poison-bottles, each with a poppy stuck in its neck.

Everything in the dispensary is beautiful—its glasses, its flames, its brass weights, its jars and globes; but much more beautiful because it is half a floor higher than the corridor in which we stand and look up into it, through a hatchway in the wall. There is something in that: one feels like Gulliver.

No woman has ever been into this bachelors' temple.

On tapping at a small square panel set in the wall of the corridor the panel flies up and a bachelor is seen from the waist to the knees. If he feels well and my smile is humble he will stoop, and I see looking down at me a small worn face and bushy eyebrows, or a long ascetic face and bleached hair, or a beard and a pair of bearded nostrils.

Between them the three old things, priests in their way, measure and weigh and mix and scold and let up the panel and bang it down through the long day, filling the hospital with their coloured bottles, sealed packets of pills, jars and vaccines, and precious syringes in boxes marked "To be returned at once" (I never knew a Sister fail to toss her head when she saw this message).

It is a very social spot outside the panel of the dispensary: each V.A.D. goes there each morning as one might do one's marketing, and, meeting there, puts down her straw basket, taps at the panel, and listens to the scolding of the old men with only half an ear.

For the bachelors amuse themselves when they are not mixing and weighing by inventing odd rules and codes of their own, and, reaching a skinny arm through the hatchway, they pin them on, little scraps of paper which fall down and are swept to heaven in the charwomen's pails.

And the V.A.D.'s, who are not at all afraid, because one cannot be afraid of a man of whom one has never seen more than half, turn a blind eye to the slips and a deaf ear to the voices, bringing their bottles and their jars just in the manner they were taught to do when first they entered the hospital. And they gossip! They have just seen the morning papers on all the beds; they have just heard about the half-days for the week; they have collected little rags and ends of news as they came along the corridor.

They gossip. And once a bearded bachelor thumped the panel down almost on my finger, leaving three startled faces staring at a piece of painted wood. But a little dark girl worked the panel up an inch with her nails and cajoled through the crack.

I have said before that the long corridor is wonderful. In the winter afternoons and evenings, when the mist rolled up and down over the tiles like the smoke in a tunnel, when one walked almost in darkness and peered into the then forbidden wards, when dwarfs coming from the G block grew larger and larger till the A block turned them into beings of one's own size, the corridor always made a special impression on me.

But in the summer mornings it is remarkable too. Then regiments of charwomen occupy it, working in close mass formation. Seven will work abreast upon their knees, flanked by their pails, their hands moving backwards and forwards in so complicated a system that there appears to be no system at all.

Patches of the corridor are thick with soapsuds; patches are dry. The art of walking the corridor in the morning can be learnt, and for a year and five months I have done it with no more than a slip and a slide.

But yesterday I stepped on a charwoman's hand. It was worse than stepping on a puppy: one knows that sickening lift of the heart, as though the will could undo the weight of the foot....

The stagger, the sense of one's unpardonable heaviness.... I slipped on her hand as on a piece of orange-peel, and, jumping like a chamois, sent the next pail all over the heels of the front rank.

It was the sort of situation with which one can do nothing.

I met a friend yesterday, one of the old Chelsea people. He has followed his natural development. Although he talks war, war, war, it is from his old angle, it wears the old hall-mark.

He belongs to a movement which believes it "feels the war." Personal injury or personal loss does not enter the question; the heart of this movement of his bleeds perpetually, but impersonally. He claims for it that this heart is able to bleed more profusely than any other heart, individual or collective, in ... let us limit it to England!

In fact it is the only blood he has noticed.

When the taxes go up he says, "Well, now perhaps it will make people feel the war!" For he longs that every one should lose their money so that at last they may "feel the war," "stop the war" (interchangeable!)

He forgets that even in England a great many quite stupid people would rather lose their money than their sons.

How strange that these people should still picture the minds of soldiers as filled with the glitter of bright bayonets and the glory of war! They think we need a vision of blood and ravage and death to turn us from our bright thoughts, to still the noise of the drum in our ears. The drums don't beat, the flags don't fly....

He should come down the left-hand side of the ward and hear what the dairyman says.

"I 'ates it, nurse; I 'ates it. Them 'orses'll kill me; them drills.... It's no life for a man, nurse."

The dairyman hasn't been to the Front; you needn't go to the Front to hate the war. Sometimes I get a glimpse from him of what it means to the weaklings, the last-joined, feeble creatures.

"Me 'ead's that queer, nurse; it seems to get queerer every day. I can't 'elp worryin'. I keep thinkin' of them 'orses."

Always the horses....

I said to Sister, "Is No. 24 really ill?"

"There's a chance of his being mental," she said. "He is being watched."

Was he mental before the war took him, before the sergeant used to whip the horses as they got to the jumps, before the sergeant cried out "Cross your stirrups!"?

It isn't his fault; there are strong and feeble men.

A dairyman's is a gentle job; he could have scraped through life all right. He sleeps in the afternoon, and stirs and murmurs: "Drop your reins.... Them 'orses, sergeant! I'm comin', sergeant; don't touch 'im this time!" And then in a shriller voice, "Don't touch 'im...." Then he wakes.

Poor mass of nerves.... He nods and smiles every time one looks at him, frantic to please.

There are men and men. Scutts has eleven wounds, but he doesn't "mind" the war. God made many brands of men, that is all; one must accept them.

But war finds few excuses; and there are strange minnows in the fishing-net. Sometimes, looking into the T.B. ward, I think: "It almost comes to this: one must spit blood or fight...."

"Why don't you refuse?" my friend would say to the dairyman. "Why should you fight because another man tells you to?"

It isn't so simple as that, is it, dairyman? It isn't even a question of the immense, vague machinery behind the sergeant, but just the sergeant himself; it isn't a question of generals or politicians of great wrongs or fierce beliefs ... but of the bugle which calls you in the morning and the bugle which puts you to bed at night.

Well, well.... The dairyman is in hospital, and that is the best that he can hope for.

I read a book once about a prison. They too, the prisoners, sought after the prison hospital, as one seeks after one's heaven.

It is so puffed up of my friend to think that his and his "movement's" are the only eyes to see the vision of horror. Why, these others *are* the vision!

This afternoon I was put at splints again.

I only had an inch or two to finish and I spun it out, very happy.

Presently the foot of a bed near me began to catch my attention: the toe beneath the sheets became more and more agitated, then the toes of the other foot joined the first foot, beating a frenzied tattoo beneath the coverings. I looked up.

Facing me a pair of blue eyes were bulging above an open mouth, the nostrils were quivering, the fingers were wrung together. It was Gayner, surely seeing a ghost.

I rose and went to his bed.

"My jaws want to close," he muttered. "I can't keep them open."

I jumped and went for Sister, who took the news in a leisurely fashion, which reproved me for my excitement. Feeling a fool, I went and sat down again, taking up my splint. But there was no forgetting Gayner.

I tried to keep my eyes on my work, but first his toes and then his hands filled all my mind, till at last I had to look up and meet the eyes again.

Still looking as though he had seen a ghost—a beast of a ghost...! In hospital since Mons.... "I wonder how many men he has seen die of tetanus?" I thought.

"He's got the jumps," I thought.

So had I. Suppose Sister was wrong! Suppose the precious minutes were passing! Suppose...! She was only the junior Sister.

"Shall I get you some water?" I said at last. He nodded, and gulped in a horrible fashion. I got him the mug, and while he drank I longed, but did not dare, to say, "Are you afraid of ... that?" I thought if one could say the word it might break down that dumb fright, draw the flesh up again over those bulging eyes, give him a sort of anchor, a confessional, even if it was only me. But I didn't dare. Gayner is one of those men so pent up, so rigid with some inner indignation, one cannot tamper with the locks.

Again I went and sat down.

When next I looked up he was sweating. He beckoned to me: "Ask Sister to send for the doctor. I can't stand this."

I went and asked her.

She sucked her little finger thoughtfully.

"Give him the thermometer," she said. He couldn't take it in his mouth, " ... for if I shut my lips they'll never open." I put it under his arm and waited while his feet kicked and his hands twisted. He was normal. Sister smiled.

But by a coincidence the doctor came, gimlet-eyed.

"Hysteria...." he said to Sister in the bunk.

"Is no one going to reassure Gayner?" I wondered. And no one did.

Isn't the fear of pain next brother to pain itself? Tetanus or the fear of tetanus—a choice between two nightmares. Don't they admit that?

So, forbidden to speak to him, I finished my splint till tea-time. But I couldn't bring myself to sit down to it, for fear that the too placid resumption of my duties should outrage him. I stood up.

Which helped me, not him.

After the dressings are over we scrub the dishes and basins in the annexe.

In the annexe, except that there is nothing to sit on, there is leisure and an invitation to reflection.

Beneath the windows legions of white butterflies attack the cabbage-patch which divides us from the road; beyond the road there is a camp from which the dust flows all day.

When the wind is from the north the dust is worse than ever and breaks like a surf over the cabbages, while the butterflies try to rise above it; but they never succeed, and dimly one can see the white wings beating in the whirlpool.

I shall never look at white butterflies again without hearing the sounds from the camp, without seeing the ring of riders, without thinking, perhaps, of the dairyman and of the other "dairymen."

The butterflies do not care for noise. When, standing beside the cabbage-patch, the bugler blows the dinner-bugle, they race in a cloud to the far corner and hover there until the last note is sounded.

I think it is I who am wrong when I consider the men as citizens, as persons of responsibility, and the Sister right when she says "the boys."

Taken from their women, from their establishments, as monks or boys or even sheep are housed, they do not want, perhaps, to be reminded of an existence to which they cannot return; until a limb is off, or the war ends.

To what a point they leave their private lives behind them! To what a point their lives are suspended....

On the whole, I find that in hospital they do not think of the future or of the past, nor think much at all. As far as life and growth goes it is a hold-up!

There is really not much to hope for; the leave is so short, the home-life so disrupted that it cannot be taken up with content. Perhaps it isn't possible to let one's thoughts play round a life about which one can make no plans.

They are adaptable, living for the minute—their present hope for the cup of tea, for the visiting day, for the concert; their future hope for the drying of the wound, for the day when the Sister's fingers may press, but no drop be wrung from the long scar.

Isn't it curious to wish so passionately for the day which may place them near to death again?

But the longing for health is a simple instinct, undarkened by logic.

Yet some of them have plans. Scutts has plans.

For a fortnight now he has watched for the post. "Parcel come for me, Sister? Small parcel?"

Or he will meet the postman in the corridor. "Got my eye yet?" he asks.

"What will it be like, Scutts?" we ask. "Can you move it? Can you sleep in it? Did he match your other carefully?"

"You'll see," he says confidently. "It's grand."

"When I get my eye...." he says, almost with the same longing with which he says "When I get into civies...."

Scutts is not one of those whose life is stopped; he has made plans. "When I get into civies and walk out of here...." His plans for six months' holiday "are all writ down in me notebook."

"But what shall you do, Scutts? Go to London?"

"London!... No towns fer me!"

He will not tell us what he is going to do. Secretly I believe it is something he wanted to do as a boy but thought himself a fool to carry out when he was a man: perhaps it is a sort of walking tour.

Among his eleven wounds he has two crippled arms. "I'm safe enough from death," he says (meaning France), "till it fetches me in a proper way."

Perhaps he means to live as though life were really a respite from death.

I had a day on the river yesterday.

"*I* seed yer with yer bit of erdy-furdy roun' yer neck an' yer little attachy-case," said Pinker.

"A nurse's life is one roun' of pleasure," said Pinker to the ward.

We had two operations yesterday—one on a sergeant who has won the D.C.M. and has a certificate written in gold which hangs above his bed, telling of his courage and of one particular deed; the other on a Welsh private.

I wonder what the sergeant was like before he won his D.C.M....

There is something unreal about him; he is like a stage hero. He has a way of saying, "Now, my men, who is going to volunteer to fetch the dinners?" which is like an invitation to go over the top.

The men gape when he says that, then go on with their cards. It is like a joke.

Before his operation he was full of partially concealed boastings as to how he would bear it, how he would "come to" saying, "Let me get up! I can walk...."

I felt a sneaking wish that he should be undone and show unusual weakness.

When the moment came he did as he had said he would do—he laughed and waved good-bye as he was wheeled away; and in the afternoon when I came on duty I found him lying in his bed, conscious, looking brown and strong and unconcerned.

But he can't let well alone....

As I passed up the ward to the bedside of the Welsh private I was called by the sergeant, and when I stood by his bed he whispered, "Is that chap making a fuss over there?"

"Evan?"

"Chap as has had an operation the same as me...."

"He's very bad."

"You don't find me making a fuss and my leg isn't half giving me something."

"We're not all alike, sergeant."

"Why should one make a fuss and another say nothing?"

"Is your leg hurting you a lot?"

"Yes, it is," and he screwed up his face into a grimace.

After all, he was a child. "Try to go to sleep," I said, knowing that it was his jealousy that was hurting him most.

I went to Evan.

He could do nothing with his pain, but in its tightest embraces, and crying, he lay with his large red handkerchief over his eyes.

"Oh, Evan...!" I said. I couldn't do anything either.

"Oh dear, dear, dear, dear, dear...." he wailed in his plaintive Welsh voice. "Oh, my dear leg, my poor leg...." He looked about nineteen. "Couldn't I lie on my side?"

"No, it would make it bleed."

"Would it?" He was so docile and so unhappy. The tears had run down and marked his pillow; I turned it, although the sergeant couldn't see.

"Will they give me something to make me sleep to-night?"

"Yes, Evan, at eight o'clock."

I said that because I was so sure of it, I had always seen it done. But oh, I should have made more sure...!

He built on it, he leant all his hopes upon it; his little clenched hands seemed to be holding my promise as firmly as though it had been my hand.

And Sister said, "No, no ... it would be better not." "Oh, Sister, why not...?" (I, the least of mortals, had made a promise belonging only to the gods....)

"Oh, Sister, why not?"

Her reason was a good one: "He will want it more later in the night, and he can't have it twice."

I ran back to tell him so quickly—but one can't run back into the past.

It is wonderful to talk to men affectionately without exciting or implying love. The Utopian dreams of sixteen seem almost to be realized!

When I sew splints they come and talk to me. Scutts will some-times talk for an hour. At first I was so proud that I dared hardly stir a finger for fear that I should frighten him away; now I am more sure of him. He never says "What?" to me, nor any longer jumps when I speak to him as though my every word must carry some command. When I sew splints and listen to Scutts or the old Scotch grocer or Monk—that squinting child of whom Pinker said, "Monk got a girl! He don' know what a girl is!"—I think, "We cannot all be efficient, but ... this serves some end."

For they are complaining that I am not efficient. At first it hurt my pride; but it depends upon the point of view. Does one go into a ward primarily to help the patients or to help the Sister? It is not always the same thing, but one must not question discipline....

To-day nine of the patients "went convalescent." They departed, hobbling and on stretchers, at two o'clock, with bursts of song, plastered hair, bright buttons, and not a regret. "You'll be able to hear a pin fall to-night, nurse," said one of them.

"I know we shall. And a tear too," I added.

But they won't listen to any such nonsense. They are going off to the little convalescent hospitals, they are going away to be treated like men; and I must laugh and shake hands and not dream of adding, "Perhaps we shall see you back again."

"No more route-marching...!" was the last cry I heard from the Nine.

How they hate route-marching—especially the City men, most especially Pinker! "March down the silly road," he grumbles, "sit on the silly grass and get heat-bumps."

Sometimes I think that sewing splints will be my undoing. If I listen much longer I shall see crooked.

To-day they had some small bottles of stout to help us say good-bye to the Nine.

Happiness is cheap. Last night at dinner a man said as he refilled his glass with champagne, "It makes me sad to think how much happi-ness there is in a bottle...."

The attack has begun.

"At 3.15 this morning ... on a front of two miles...."

So that is why the ward is so empty and the ambulances have been hurrying out of the yard all day. We shall get that convoy for which I longed.

When the ward is empty and there is, as now, so little work to do, how we, the women, watch each other over the heads of the men! And because we do not care to watch, nor are much satisfied with what we see, we want more work. At what a price we shall get it....

Scutts and Monk talk to me while I sew, but what about the Monks, Scutts, Gayners, whose wounds will never need a dressing or a tube—who lie along a front of two miles, one on his face, another on his back?

Since 3.15 this morning a lot of men have died. Thank God one cannot go on realizing death.

But one need not think of it. This is a ward; here are lucky ones. Even when I look at Rees, even when I look at the grocer, even when I look at the T.B. ward, I know that anything, *anything* is better than death. But I have known a man here and there who did not think so—and these men, close on death it is true, were like strangers in the ward.

For one can be close on death and remain familiar, friendly, comprehensible.

I used to think, "It is awful to die." But who knows what compliance the years will bring? What is awful is to die *young.*

A new V.A.D. came into the ward yesterday—a girl straight from home, who has never been in a hospital before.

Rees told me, "She turned her head away when she saw me arm."

"I did once, Rees."

He looked down at the almost unrecognizable twelve inches which we call "Rees's wound," and considered how this red inch had paled and the lips of that incision were drawing together. "'Tisn' no more me arm," he said at length, "than...." he paused for a simile. "'Tisn' me arm, it's me wound," he finally explained.

His arm is stretched out at right angles from his bed in an iron cradle, and has been for six months.

"Last night," he said, "I felt me arm layin' down by me side, an' I felt the fingers an' tried to scratch me knee. It's a feeling that's bin comin' on for some time, but last night it seemed real."

The pain of the dressing forces Rees's reason to lay some claim to his arm, but when it ceases to hurt him he detaches himself from it to such a point that the ghost-arm familiar to all amputations has arrived, as it were, by mistake.

The new V.A.D. doesn't talk much at present, being shy, but tonight I can believe she will write in her diary as I wrote in mine: "My feet ache, ache, ache...." Add to that that she is hungry because she hasn't yet learnt how to break the long stretches with hurried gnawings behind a door, that she is sick because the philosophy of Rees is not yet her philosophy, that her hands and feet grow cold and her body turns to warm milk, that she longs so to sit on a bed that she can almost visualize the depression her body would make on its counterpane, and I get a glimpse of the passage of time and of the effect of custom.

With me the sickness and the hunger and the ache are barely remembered. It makes me wonder what else is left behind.... The old battle is again in my mind—the struggle to feel pain, to repel the invading familiarity.

Here they come!

One convoy last night and another this morning. There is one great burly man, a sort of bear, whose dried blood has squeezed through bandages applied in seven places, and who for all that mumbles "I'm well" if one asks him how he feels.

Long before those wounds are healed he will diagnose himself better than that!

"I'm well...." That's to say: "I'm alive, and I have reached this bed, and this bit of meat, and this pudding in a tin!" He answers by his standards.

But in a few days he will think, "I am alive, but I might be better..."; and in a few weeks, "Is this, after all, happiness?"

How they sleep, the convoy men! Watching their wounds as we dress them, almost with a grave pleasure—the passports to this wonderful sleep.

Then when the last safety-pin is in they lie back without making themselves in the least comfortable, without drawing up a sheet or turning once upon the pillow, and sleep just as the head falls.

How little women can stand! Even the convoy cannot mend the pains of the new V.A.D. I dare not speak to her: she seems, poor camel, to be waiting for the last straw.

But when we wash the bowls together we must talk. She and I together this morning washed and scrubbed, rinsed, dried, and piled basins into little heaps, and while we washed we examined each other.

She is a born slave; in fact, I almost think she is born to be tortured. Her manner with the Sisters invites and entices them to "put upon" her. Her spiritual back is already covered with sores.

I suppose she is hungry for sympathy, but it isn't really a case in which sympathy can do as much as custom. I showed her the white butterflies, without supposing them to be very solid food.

She reminds me of the man of whom the Sister said, "He must stick it out." I might have pointed to the convoy and suggested comparisons; but one cannot rub a sore back.

Some one has applied the last straw in the night.

When I came on duty a brisk little war-hardened V.A.D. was brushing a pile of dust along the long boards to the door. The poor camel whose back is broken is as though she had never existed; either she is ill or she is banished.

Such is the secret diplomacy of these establishments that nothing is known of her except her disappearance—at least among those whom one can ask. Matron knows, Sister knows.... But these are the inscrutable, smiling gods.

There is only one man in the ward I don't much care for—a tall boy with a lock of fair hair and broken teeth. He was a sullen boy whose bad temper made his mouth repulsive. I say "was," for he is different now.

Now he is feeble, gentle, grateful, and he smiles as often as one looks at him.

Yesterday he went for his operation in the morning, and in the afternoon when I came on duty he was stirring and beginning to groan. Sister told me to sit beside him.

I went up to the little room of screens in which he lay, and taking a wooden chair, I slipped it in between the screen and the bed and sat down.

Is it the ether which rushes up from between his broken teeth?—is it the red glare of the turkey-twill screens?—but in ten minutes I am altered, mesmerized. Even the size of my surroundings is changed. The screens, high enough to blot out a man's head, are high enough to blot out the world. The narrow bed becomes a field of whiteness. The naked arm stretched towards me is more wonderful than any that could have belonged to a boy with dirty fair hair and broken teeth; it has sea-green veins rising along it, and the bright hairs are more silver than golden.

The life of the ward goes on, the clatter of cups for supper, the shuffling of feet clad in loose carpet-slippers, but here within he and I are living together a concentrated life.

"Oh, me back!"

"I know, I know...."

Do I know? I am getting to know. For while the men are drinking their cocoa I am drinking ether. I know how the waves of the pain come up and recede; how a little sleep just brushes the spirit, but never absorbs it; how the arms will struggle up to the air, only to be covered and enmeshed again in heat and blankets.

"Was it in me lung?" (He pronounces the "g"—a Lancashire boy....)

"The shrapnel?"

He nods. I hold up the piece of metal which has lain buried in him these past three weeks. It has the number 20 engraved on it. That satisfies him. The blood which has come from between his lips is in a bowl placed too high for him to see.

Through the crack in the screens the man in the bed opposite watches us unwinkingly.

Eight o'clock.... Here is Sister with the syringe: he will sleep now and I can go home.

If one did not forget the hospital when one leaves it, life wouldn't be very nice.

From pillar to post....

The dairyman, who has been gone to another hospital these five weeks, returned to-day, saying miserably as he walked into the ward, "Me 'ead's queerer than ever." His eyes, I think, are larger too, and he has still that manner of looking as though he thought some one could do something for him.

I can't—beyond raising the smallest of tablets to him with the inscription, "Another farthing spent...."

Waker had a birthday yesterday and got ten post cards and a telegram. But that is as nothing to another anniversary.

"A year to-morrow I got my wound—two o'clock to-morrow morning."

"Shall you be awake, Waker?"

"Yes."

How will he celebrate it? I would give a lot to know what will pass in his mind. For I don't yet understand this importance they attach

69

to such an anniversary. One and all, they know the exact hour and mi-nute on which their bit of metal turned them for home.

Sometimes a man will whisper, "Nurse...." as I go by the bed; and when I stop I hear, "In ten minutes it will be a twelvemonth!" and he fixes his eyes on me.

What does he want me to respond? I don't know whether I should be glad or sorry that he got it. I can't imagine what he thinks of as the minute ticks. For I can see by his words that the scene is blurred and no longer brings back any picture. "Did you crawl back or walk?"

"I ... walked." He is hardly sure.

I know that for some of them, for Waker, that moment at two o'clock in the morning changed his whole career. From that moment his arm was paralysed, the nerves severed; from that moment football was off, and with it his particular ambition. And football, governing a king-dom, or painting a picture—a man's ambition is his ambition, and when it is wiped out his life is changed.

But he knows all that, he has had time to think of all that. What, then, does this particular minute bring him?

They think I know; for when they tell me in that earnest voice that the minute is approaching they take for granted that I too will share some sacrament with them.

Waker is not everything a man should be: he isn't clever. But he is so very brave.

After his tenth operation two days ago there was a question as to whether he should have his pluggings changed under gas or not. The discussion went on between the doctors over his bed.

But the anæsthetist couldn't be found.

He didn't take any part in the discussion such as saying, "Yes, I will stand it...." but waited with interest showing on his bony face, and when they glanced down at him and said, "Let's get it through now!" he rolled over to undo his safety-pin that I might take off his sling.

It was all very fine for the theatre people to fill his shoulder chockful of pluggings while he lay unconscious on the table; they had packed it as you might stuff linen into a bag: it was another matter to get it out.

I did not dare touch his hand with that too-easy compassion which I have noticed here, or whisper to him "It's nearly over...." as the forceps pulled at the stiffened gauze. It wasn't nearly over.

Six inches deep the gauze stuck, crackling under the pull of the forceps, blood and puss leaping forward from the cavities as the steady hand of the doctor pulled inch after inch of the gauze to the light. And when one hole was emptied there was another, five in all.

Sometimes, when your mind has a grip like iron, your stomach will undo you; sometimes, when you could say "To-day is Tuesday, the fifth of August," you faint. There are so many parts of the body to look after, one of the flock may slip your control while you are holding the other by the neck. But Waker had his whole being in his hands, without so much as clenching them.

When we had finished and Sister told me to wipe the sweat on his forehead, I did so reluctantly, as though one were being too exacting in drawing attention to so small a sign.

I must say that the dairyman seems to me quite mad, and I only wonder how little it is noticed. He will sit in a chair beside Palmer for hours, raising and lowering his eyebrows and fitting imaginary gloves on to his fingers.

An inspecting general, pausing at his bed this morning, said: "A dairyman, are you? Frightened of horses, are you? Then what do you do about the cows?"

He was pleased with his own joke, and the dairyman smiled too, uncomprehendingly, his eyebrows shooting up and down like swallows' wings. Such jokes mean nothing to him; he is where no joke but his own will ever please him any more....

Palmer doesn't like sitting near him, but since it is too much trouble to move he allows it—poor Palmer, who has a piece of metal somewhere in his brain and is never seen without one long hand to his aching head. He said to me yesterday when I asked him which convalescent home he was going to, "It doesn't matter. We both go to the same kind before long...." jerking his thumb at the dairyman. As for the latter, there surely can be no escape, but for Palmer....

"They won't take it out; too risky. Seen my X-ray picture?"

"No."

"You look at it. Right in the middle of the brain. Seems funny that if I say I'm willing to risk it, why they shouldn't be."

"You're willing to risk it?"

"I'm only nineteen! What's the good of my head to me! I can't remember the name of the last hospital I was at...."

71

Ah, these hurried conversations sandwiched between my duties, when in four sentences the distilled essence of bitterness is dropped into my ear!

"Sister, what will they do with Palmer?"

"They are going to discharge him. They won't operate."

"But what will happen to him?"

"I don't know."

"But if he is willing to risk his life to save his brain, can they still refuse?"

"They won't operate."

Pinker is full of grains of knowledge. He has just discovered a wonderful justification for not getting up directly he is told off for a job.

"I never refuse a nurse," he said, as he thoughtfully picked over the potatoes ("Li'l men, li'l spuds!" he says, to excuse himself for taking all the sought-after small ones).... "I never refuse a nurse. But I like to finish me game of draughts first—like Drake."

Pinker notices everything. He took the grocer for a ride on the tram yesterday. "'E got so excited he got singing 'Tipperary,' an' the blood-vessels on his neck goin' fit to burst. Weren't he, Bill?"

He appealed to Monk, whose name is George.

(By the way, I wonder when people will stop calling them "Tommy" and call them "Bill." I never heard the word "Tommy" in a soldier's mouth: he was a red-coated man. "But every mate's called 'Bill,' ain't 'e, Bill?")

From the camp across the road the words of command float in through the ward window.

"Halt!" and "Left wheel!" and "Right wheel!..."

They float into the ward bearing the sense of heat and dust, and of the bumping of the saddle. The dairyman has perhaps put me a bit against the camp across the road.

When the dressings are finished and we scrub the enamel bowls in the annexe, one can see all the dairymen and all the plumbers, *chefs* and shopwalkers bumping up and down in a ring amid a cloud of dust, while the voice of the sergeant cries out those things that my dairyman used to think of in his sleep.

Then the jumps go up. "Left wheel!" "Right wheel!..." And now, "Cross your stirrups!" One out of every four of them is clinging, grabbing, swaying.

The seventh is off! It was a long fight.... He went almost round the horse's neck before he fell.

We must win the war, win the war, win the war!

Every sort of price must be paid, every Mud of curious coinage—the pennies and farthings of fear and despair in odd places, as well as the golden coin of life which is spent across the water.

All day long the words of command come over the ward window-sills. All day long they bump and shout and sweat and play that charade of theirs behind the guns.

All day long little men training to fill just such another hospital as ours with other little men.

But one does not say any longer, "What a strange thing is life!" for only in rare moments does the divine astonishment return.

THE
HAPPY
FOREIGNER

PROLOGUE

THE EVE

Between the grey walls of its bath—so like its cradle and its coffin—lay one of those small and lonely creatures which inhabit the surface of the earth for seventy years.

As on every other evening the sun was sinking and the moon, unseen, was rising.

The round head of flesh and bone floated upon the deep water of the bath.

"Why should I move?" rolled its thoughts, bewitched by solitude. "The earth itself is moving.

"Summer and winter and winter and summer I have travelled in my head, saying—'All secrets, all wonders, lie within the breast!' But now that is at an end, and to-morrow I go upon a journey.

"I have been accustomed to finding something in nothing—how do I know if I am equipped for a larger horizon!..."

And suddenly the little creature chanted aloud:—

"The strange things of travel,
The East and the West,
The hill beyond the hill,—
They lie within the breast!"

PART I.
THE BLACK HUT AT BAR

I. THE TRAVELLER

The war had stopped.

The King of England was in Paris, and the President of the United States was hourly expected.

Humbler guests poured each night from the termini into the overflowing city, and sought anxiously for some bed, lounge-chair, or pillowed corner, in which to rest until the morning. Stretched upon the table in a branch of the Y.W.C.A. lay a young woman from England whose clothes were of brand-new khaki, and whose name was Fanny.

She had arrived that night at the Gare du Nord at eight o'clock, and the following night at eight o'clock she left Paris by the Gare de l'Est.

Just as she entered the station a small boy with a basket of violets for sale held a bunch to her face.

"No, thank you."

He pursued her and held it against her chin.

"No, thank you."

"But I give it to you! I *give* it to you!"

As she had neither slept on the boat from Southampton nor on the table of the Y.W.C.A., tears of pleasure came into her eyes as she took them. But while she dragged her heavy kitbag and her suitcase across the platform another boy of a different spirit ran beside her.

"Mademoiselle! Mademoiselle! Wait a minute..." he panted.

"Well?"

"Haven't you heard ... haven't you heard! The war is over!"

She continued to drag the weighty sack behind her over the platform. "She didn't know!" howled the wicked boy. "No one had told her!"

And in the train which carried her towards the dead of night the taunt and the violets accompanied her.

At half-past two in the morning she reached the station of Bar-le-Duc. The rain rattled down through the broken roof as she crossed the lines of the platform on the further side, where, vaguely expecting to be met she questioned civilians and military police. But the pall of death that hung over Bar stretched even to the station, where nobody knew anything, expected anything, cared anything, except to hurry out and away into the rain.

She, too, followed at last, leaving her bag and box in the corner of a deserted office, and crossing the station yard tramped out in the thick mud on to a bridge. The rain was falling in torrents, and crouching for a minute in a doorway she made her bundles faster and buttoned up her coat. Roofs jutted above her, pavements sounded under her feet, the clock struck three near by. If there was an hotel anywhere there was no one to give information about it. The last train had emptied itself, the travellers had hurried off into the night, and not a foot rang upon the pavements. The rain ran in a stream down her cap and on to her face; down her sleeves and on to her hands.

A light further up the street attracted her attention, and walking towards it she found that it came from an open doorway above which she could make out the letters "Y.M.C.A."

She did not know with what complicated feelings she would come to regard these letters—with what gratitude mixed with irritation, self-reproach with greed.

Climbing the steps she looked inside. The hall of the building was paved with stone, and on a couple of dozen summer chairs of cane sat as many American officers, dozing in painful attitudes of unrest. By each ran a stream of water that trickled from his clothes, and the streams, joining each other, formed aimless rivers upon the floor.

The eye of a captain opened.

"Come in, ma'am," he said without moving. She wondered whether she should.

The eye of a lieutenant opened.

"Come in, ma'am," he said, and rose. "Take my chair."

"Could you tell me if there is any hotel?"

"There is some sort of a shanty down the street. I'll take you."

Further up the street a faint light shone under a slit between two boards. There was no door near it, no keyhole or shutter. The American thundered at the boards with a tin of jam which he took out of his pocket. The noise was monstrous in the blackness, but the town had heard noises more monstrous than that, and it lay in a barred and blind, unanswering stupor.

"God!" said the American, quickly angered, and kicked the board till the slit grew larger. The light went out.

"Some one is coming round to the door," said Fanny, in time to prevent the destruction of the board.

Higher up the street bolts were being withdrawn and a light fell upon the pavement.

"Who's there?" creaked a voice. The American moved towards the light.

"The hotel is shut to Americans," said the voice.

"The devil it is," shouted the American. "And why, then?"

"Man killed here last night," said the voice briefly. Fanny moved towards the light and saw an old man with a shawl upon his shoulders, who held a candle fixed in the neck of a bottle.

"I am English," she said to the old man. "I am alone. I want a room alone."

"I've a room ... If you're not American!"

"I don't know what kind of a hole this is," said the American wrathfully. "I think you'd better come right back to the 'Y.' Say, here, what kind of a row was this last night you got a man killed in?"

"Kind of row your countrymen make," muttered the old man, and added
"Bandits!"

Soothing, on the one hand, entreating on the other, the girl got rid of her new friend, and effected an entrance into the hotel. ("If hotel it is!" she thought, in the brief passage of a panic while the old man stooped to the bolts of the door.)

"I've got rooms enough," he said, "rooms enough. Now *they've* gone. Follow me."

She followed his candle flame and he threw open a door upon the ground floor.

"I've no light to give you."

"Yet I must have a light."

Grumbling, he produced half an inch of wax candle.

"Hurry into bed and that will last you. It's all I have."

The bed wore a coloured rug, bare and thin, an eiderdown, damp and musty. Spreading her wet mackintosh on the top she rolled herself up as well as she could, and developing a sort of warmth towards morning, slept an hour or two. The daylight showed her nothing to wash in, no jug, no basin, no bell to pull.

As no one would come to her, as there was nothing to be gained by waiting, she got up, and going into the hall, entered a dark coffee-room in which breakfast was served at its lowest ebb, black coffee, sugarless, and two pieces of dry bread.

Yet, having eaten, she was able to think: "I am a soldier of five sous. I am here to drive for the French Army." And her thoughts pleased her so well that, at the moment when her circumstances were in their state of least perfection, she exclaimed: "How right I was to come!" and set off down the street to find her companions.

A mile out of the town upon the banks of a tributary of the Meuse stood a deserted glass factory which had been converted by the French into a garage for a fleet of thirty cars. Above the garage was a large attic used as a dormitory for the mechanics, soldier-cooks, drivers and clerks. In a smaller room at the end slept the non-commissioned officers—the *brigadier* and the two *maréchaux des logis*.

A hundred yards from the factory, built upon the brink of the stream which was now in flood, and reached from the road by a narrow wooden bridge, stood a tarred hut of wood and tarpaulin. It was built upon simple lines. A narrow corridor ran down the centre of it, and on either hand were four square cells divided one from the other by grey paper stretched upon laths of wood—making eight in all. At one end was a small hall filled with mackintoshes. At the other a sitting-room.

This was the home of the women drivers attached to the garage. In one of these paper cells, henceforward to be her own, Fanny set up her intimate life.

* * * * *

Outside the black hut the jet-black night poured water down. Inside, the eight cubicles held each a woman, a bed, and a hurricane lantern. Fanny, in her paper box, listened to the scratching of a pen next door, then turned her eyes as a new and nearer scratching caught her ear. A bright-eyed rat stared at her through the hole it had made in the wall.

"Food is in!"

Out of the boxes came the eight women to eat pieces of dark meat from a tin set on the top of the sitting-room stove—then cheese and bread. The watery night turned into sleet and rattled like tin-foil on the panes.

"Where is Stewart?"

"She is not back yet."

Soon the eight crept back to their boxes and sat again by the lamps to read or darn or write. They lived so close to each other that even the most genial had learnt to care for solitude, and the sitting-room remained empty.

The noise of Stewart's feet sounded in the corridor. She swung a lantern in her hand; her face was shining, her hair streaming.

"Is there any food?"

"It's on the stove."

"Is it eatable?"

"No."

Silence for a while, and then one by one they crept out into the black mud beyond the hut to fill their cans with hot water from the cook-house—and so to bed, on stretchers slung on trestles, where those who did not sleep listened through the long night to those who slept too well.

"Are you awake?" came with the daylight. "Ah, you are washing! You are doing your hair!" There was no privacy.

"How cold, how cold the water, is!..." sighed Fanny, And a voice through the paper wall, catching the shivering whisper, exclaimed: "Use your hot-water bottle!"

"What for?"

"Empty it into your basin. If you have kept it in your bed all night you will find the water has the chill off."

Those who had to be out early had left before the daylight, still with their lanterns swinging in their hands; had battled with the cold cars in the unlighted garage, and were moving alone across the long desert of the battle-fields.

On the first morning she was tested on an old ambulance, and passed the test. On the second morning she got her first run upon a Charron car that had been assigned to her.

Driving into Bar-le-Duc in the early morning under a grey flood of rain she asked of a passer-by, "Which is the Rue Thierry?" She got no answer. The French, too poor and wet, did not trouble to reply; the Americans did not know. As she drove along at the side of the road there came a roar out of the distance, and a stream of American lorries thundered down the street. Men, women and children ran for their lives to gain the pavements, as the lorries passed, a mud-spout covered Fanny's face and hands, and dripped from her windscreen.

"Why do they drive like that?" she wondered, hunting blindly for her handkerchief, and mopping at her face. She thought there must be some desperate need calling for the lorries, and looked after them with respect.

When she had found her street, and fetched her "client," she drove at his order to Souilly, upon the great road to Verdun. And all day, calling at little villages upon the way, where he had business, she drove with the caution of the newcomer. It seemed to her that she had need for caution. She saw a Ford roll over, leave the road, and drop into the ditch. The wild American who had driven it to its death, pulled himself up upon the road, and limping, hailed a passing lorry, and went upon his way.

She saw a horse gallop out of a camp with a terrified Annamite upon its back. Horse and Annamite shot past her on the road, the yellow man's eyes popping from his head, his body slipping, falling, falling. When she would have slowed the car to watch the end of the flight her client cried to her: "Why do you wait?"

Enormous American guns, trailed behind lorries driven by pink-faced boys swayed from side to side on the greasy road, and threatened to crush her like an egg-shell.

Everywhere she saw a wild disregard for life, everywhere she winced before the menace of speed, of weight, of thundering metal.

In the late afternoon, returning home in the half-light, she overtook a convoy of lorries driven by Annamites.

Hooting with her horn she crept past three lorries and drew abreast of the fourth; then, misjudging, she let the tip of her low mudguard touch the front wheel of the foremost lorry. The touch was so slight that she had passed on, but at a cry she drew up and looked back. The lorry which she had touched was overhanging the edge of the road, and its radiator, striking a tree, had dropped down into the valley below. Climbing from her car she ran back and was instantly surrounded by a crowd of Annamites who chirped and twittered at her, and wrung their little hands.

"What can I do?..." she said to them aloud, in distress.

But they understood nothing, and seemed to echo in their strange bird language, "What can *we* do ... what can *we* do?..." ("And I..." she thought in consternation, "am responsible for this!")

But the last lorry had drawn alongside, and a French sergeant descended from it and joined the Annamites. He walked to the edge of the road, saw the radiator below upon a rock, and shrugged his shoulders. Catching sight of Fanny's face of horror he laughed.

"*Ne vous en faîtes pas, mademoiselle!* These poor devils sleep as they drive. Yes, even with their eyes open. We started nine this morning. We were four when we met you—and now we are three!"

On the third morning the rain stopped for an hour or two. Fanny had no run till the afternoon, and going into the garage in the morning she set to work on her car.

"Where can I get water?" she asked a man.

"The pump is broken," he replied. "I backed my car against it last night. But there is a tap by that broken wall on the piece of waste ground."

She crossed to the wall with her bucket.

Standing upon the waste ground was an old, closed limousine whose engine had long been injured past repair. One of the glass windows was broken, but it was as roomy and comfortable as a first-class railway carriage, and the men often sat in it in a spare moment.

The yard cleared suddenly for the eleven o'clock meal. As Fanny passed the limousine a man appeared at the broken window and beckoned to her. His face was white, and he wore his shirt, trousers, and braces. She stopped short with the bucket in her hand.

"On est delivré de cette bande!" he said, pointing to the yard, and she went a little nearer.

"Wait till I get my coat on," he said softly to her, and struggled into his coat.

He put both his hands on the window ledge, leant towards her, and said clearly: "Je suis le président Wilson."

"You are the President Wilson," she echoed, hunting for the joke, and willing to smile. He passed her out his water-bottle and a tin box. "You must fill these for me," he said. "Fill the bottle with wine, and get me bread and meat. Be quick. You know I must be off. The King expects me."

Where have you come from?"

"I slept here last night. I have come far. But I must be quick now, for it's late, and ... I believe in Freedom!" he finished emphatically.

"Well, will you wait till I have made you up a parcel of food?"

"Only be quick."

"Will you wait in the car? Promise to wait!"

"Yes. Be quick. Look sharp."

She put down her bucket and stretched up her hand for the bottle and the box. He held them above her a second, hesitating, then put them into her hand. She turned from him and went back into the yard. As she approached the door of the room where the men sat eating she looked round and saw that he was watching her intently. She waved once, soothingly, then slipped into the long room filled with the hum of voices and the smell of gravy.

"There is a poor madman in the yard," she whispered to the man nearest her. The others looked up.

"They've lost a man from the asylum. I heard in the town this morning," said one. "We must keep him here till we telephone. Have you told the brigadier, mademoiselle?"

"You tell him. I'll go back and talk to the man. Ask the brigadier to telephone."

"I'll come with you, mademoiselle," said another. "Where is he?"

"In the old limousine by the water tap. He is quiet. Don't frighten him by coming all together." Chairs and benches were pushed back, and the men stood up in groups.

"We will go round by the gate in case he makes a run for it. Better not use force if one can help it...."

Fanny and her companion went out to the car. "Where is my food and wine?" called the man.

"It's coming," answered Fanny, "they are doing it up in the kitchen."

"Well, I can't wait. I must go without it. I can't keep the King waiting." And he opened the door of the limousine. As he stood on the step he held a bundle of rusty weapons.

"What's that you've got?"

"Bosche daggers," he said. "See!" He held one towards her, without letting it go from his hand.

"Where did you find those?"

"On the battlefields." He climbed down the steps.

"Stay a moment," said Fanny. "I'm in a difficulty. Will you help me?"

"What's that? But I've no time...."

"Do you know about cars?"

"I was in the trade," he nodded his head.

"I have trouble ... I cannot tell what to do. Will you come and see?"

"If it's a matter of a moment. But I must be away."

"If you leave all those things in the car you could fetch them as you go," suggested Fanny, eyeing the daggers.

The man whistled and screwed up one eye. "When one believes in Freedom one must go armed," he said. "Show me the car."

Going with her to the car-shed he looked at the spark-plugs of the car, at her suggestion unscrewing three from their seatings. At the fourth he grew tired, and said fretfully: "Now I must be off. You know I must. The King expects me."

He walked to the gate of the yard, and she saw the men behind the gate about to close on him. "You're not wearing your decorations!" she called after him. He stopped, looked down, looked a little troubled.

She took the gilt safety pin from her tie, the safety pin that held her collar to her blouse at the back, and another from the back of her skirt, and pinned them along his poor coat. An ambulance drove quickly into the yard, and three men, descending from it, hurried towards them. At sight of them the poor madman grew frantic, and turning upon Fanny he cried: "You are against me!" then ran across the yard. She shut her eyes that she might not see them hunt the lover of freedom, and only opened them when a man cried in triumph: "*We'll* take you to the King!"

"Pauvre malheureux!" muttered the drivers in the yard.

Day followed day and there was plenty of work. Officers had to be driven upon rounds of two hundred kilometres a day—interviewing mayors of ruined villages, listening to claims, assessing damage caused by French troops in billets. Others inspected distant motor parks. Others made offers to purchase old iron among the villages in order to prove thefts from the battlefields.

The early start at dawn, the flying miles, the winter dusk, the long hours of travel by the faint light of the acetylene lamps filled day after day; the unsavoury meal eaten alone by the stove, the book read alone in the cubicle, the fitful sleep upon the stretcher, filled night after night.

A loneliness beyond anything she had ever known settled upon Fanny. She found comfort in a look, a cry, a whistle. The smiles of strange men upon the road whom she would never see again became her social intercourse. The lost smiles of kind Americans, the lost, mocking whistles of Frenchmen, the scream of a nigger, the twittering surprise of a Chinese scavenger.

Yet she was glad to have come, for half the world was here. There could have been nothing like it since the Tower of Babel. The country around her was a vast tract of men sick with longing for the four corners of the earth.

"Have you *got* to be here?" asked an American.

"No, I wanted to come."

The eye of the American said "Fool!"

"Are you paid to come here?" asked a Frenchman.

"No. In a sense, I pay to come." The eye of the Frenchman said, "Englishwoman!"

Each day she drove in a wash of rain. Each night she returned long after dark, and putting her car in the garage, felt her way up the inky road by the rushing of the river at its edge, crossed the wooden bridge, and entered the cell which she tried to make her personal haven.

But if personal, it was the personality of a dog; it had the character of a kennel. She had brought no furnishings with her from England; she could buy nothing in the town. The wooden floor was swamped by the rain which blew through the window; the paper on the walls was torn by rats; tarry drops from the roof had fallen upon her unmade bed.

The sight of this bed caused her a nightly dismay. "Oh, if I could but make it in the morning how different this room would look!"

There would be no one in the sitting-room, but a tin would stand on the stove with one, two, or three pieces of meat in it. By this she knew whether the cubicles were full or if one or two were empty. Sometimes the coffee jug would rise too lightly from the floor as she lifted it, and in an angry voice she would call through the hut: "There is no coffee!" Silence, silence; till a voice, goaded by the silence, cried: "Ask Madeleine!"

And Madeleine, the little maid, had long since gone over to laugh with the men in the garage.

Then came the owners of the second and third piece of meat, stumbling across the bridge and up the corridor, lantern in hand. And Fanny, perhaps remembering a treasure left in her car, would rise, leave them to eat, feel her way to the garage, and back again to the safety of her room with a tin of sweetened condensed milk under her arm. So low in comfort had she sunk it needed but this to make her happy. She had never known so sharp, so sweet a sense of luxury as that with which she prepared the delicacy she had seized by her own cunning. It had not taken her long to learn the possibilities of the American Y.M.C.A., the branch in Bar, or any other which she might pass in her travels.

Shameless she was as she leant upon the counter in some distant village, cajoling, persuading, spinning some tale of want and necessity more picturesque, though no less actual, than her own. Secret, too, lest one of her companions, over-eager, should spoil her hunting ground.

86

Sitting with her leather coat over her shoulders, happy in her solitude, she would drink the cup of Benger's Food which she had made from
the milk, and when it was finished, slide lower among the rugs, put out the
lights, and listen to the rustle of the rats in the wall.

"Mary Bell is getting married," said a clear voice in the hut.

"To the Wykely boy?" answered a second voice, and in a sudden
need of sound the two voices talked on, while the six listeners upon their
stretchers saw in the dark the life and happiness of Mary Bell blossom before them, unknown and bright.

The alarm clock went off with a scream at five.

"Why, I've hardly been asleep!" sighed Fanny, bewildered, and, getting up, she lit the lamp and made her coffee. Again there was not time to
make the bed. Though fresh to the work she believed that she had been
there for ever, yet the women with whom she shared her life had driven the
roads of the Meuse district for months before she came to them, and their
eyes were dim with peering into the dark nights, and they were tired past any
sense of adventure, past any wish or power to better their condition.

On and on and on rolled the days, and though one might add them
together and make them seven, they never made Sunday. For there is no
Sunday in the French Army, there is no bell at which tools are laid aside, and
not even the night is sacred.

On and on rolled the weeks, and the weeks made months, till all No-
vember was gone, and all December, and the New Year broke in fresh
torrents of rain.

Fanny made friends all day and lost them again for ever as she passed
on upon the roads. Sometimes it was a sentry beside whom her "clients" left
her for an hour while they inspected a barracks; sometimes it was an old
woman who called from a doorway that she might come and warm her
hands at the fire; sometimes an American who helped her to change a tyre.

There were times, further up towards Verdun, where there were no
old women, or young women, or villages, when she thought her friends were
mad, deranged, eccentric in their loneliness.

"My sister has a grand piano ..." said one American to her—opening
thus his conversation. But he mused upon it and spoke no further.

"Yes?" she encouraged. "Yes?"

He did not open his mind until she was leaving, when he said simply
to her: "I wish I was back home." And between the two sentences all the
pictures of his home were flowing in his thoughts.

An old woman offered her shelter in a village while her clients were busy with the mayor. In the kitchen there was a tiny fire of twigs.

American boys stamped in and out of the house, laughing, begging the daughter to sew on a button, sell them an egg, boys of nineteen and twenty, fair, tall, and good-looking.

"We shall be glad when they are gone," said the old woman looking at their gay faces. "They are children," she added, "with the faults of children."

"They seem well-mannered."

"They are beautiful boys," said the peasant woman, "and good-mannered. But I'm tired of them. Children are all very well, but to have your house full of them, your village, your family-life! They play all day in the street, chasing the dogs, throwing balls. When our children come out of school there's no holding them, they must be off playing with the Americans. The war is over. Why don't they take them home?"

"Good-day, ma'am," said a tall boy, coming up to Fanny. "You're sure cold. We brought you this." And he offered her a cup of coffee he had fetched from his canteen.

"Yes, they're good boys," said the old woman, "but one doesn't want other people's children always in one's life."

"Is this a park?" Fanny asked a soldier in the next village, a village whose four streets were filled with rows of lorries, touring cars and ambulances. On every car the iron was frail with rust, the bonnets of some were torn off, a wheel, two wheels, were missing, the side ripped open disclosing the rusting bones.

"Pardon, madame?"

"What are you doing here?"

"We are left behind from the Fourth Army which has gone up to Germany. I have no tools or I would make one car out of four. But my men are discouraged and no one works. The war is over.

"Then this is a park?"

"No, madame, it is a cemetery."

Months went by, and there came a night, as wet and sad as any other, when no premonitory star showed in the sky, and all that was bright in Fanny's spirit toned itself to match the monotonous, shadowless pallor about her.

She was upon her homeward journey. At the entrance to the hut she paused; for such a light was burning in the sitting-room that it travelled even the dark corridor and wandered out upon the step. By it she could see the beaded moisture of the rain-mist upon the long hair escaped from her cap.

A group of women stood within, their faces turned towards the door as she entered.

"Fanny...."

"What is it?"

"We are going to Metz! We are ordered to Metz!" Stewart waved a letter.

Was poverty and solitude at an end? They did not know it. In leaving the Meuse district did they leave, too, the boundless rain, the swollen rivers, the shining swamps, the mud which ebbed and flowed upon the land like a tide? Was hunger at an end, discomfort, and poor living? They had no inkling.

Fanny, indifferent to any change, hoping for nothing better, turned first to the meat tin, for she was hungry.

"Metz is a town," she hazarded.

"Of course!"

"There will be things to eat there?"

"No, very little. It was fed from Germany; now that it is suddenly fed from Paris the service is disorganised. One train crosses the devastated land in the day. I hear all this from the brigadier—who has, for that matter, never been there."

"Then we are going for certain?"

"We are sent for. Yes, we are going. We are to be attached to the Headquarters Staff. Pétain is there. It might even be gay."

Fanny laughed. "Gay!"

"Why not?"

"I was thinking of my one pair of silk stockings."

"You have silk stockings with you!"

"Yes, I ... I am equipped for anything."

There came a morning, as wet and sad as any other, when Stewart and Fanny, seated in the back of an ambulance, their feet overhanging the edge, watched the black hut dwindle upon the road, and wondered how any one had lived there so long.

PART II. LORRAINE

II. METZ

With its back to the woods and hills of Luxembourg, with its face to the desolation of Northern France, the city of Metz stood at the entry of Lorraine like the gate to a new world.

The traveller, arriving after long hours of journey through the battle-fields, might sigh with relief, gape with pleasure, then hurry away down deflagged streets, beneath houses roped with green-leafed garlands, to eat divinely at Moitrier's restaurant, and join the dancing in the hall below.

Not a night passed in Metz without the beat of music upon the frosty air. It burst into the narrow streets from *estaminets* where the soldiers danced, from halls, from drawing-rooms of confiscated German houses where officers of the "Grand Quartier Général" danced a triumph. Or it might be supposed to be a triumph by the Germans who stayed in their homes after dark. They might suppose that the French officers danced for happiness, that they danced because they were French, because they were victorious, because they were young, because they must.

It was not, surely, the wild dancing of the host whose party drags a little, who calls for more champagne, more fiddles?

In the centre of the city of Metz sat the Maréchal Pétain, and kept his eye upon Lorraine. He was not a man who cared for gaiety, but should the Lorraines be insufficiently amused he gave them balls—insufficiently fed, he sent for flour and sugar; all the flour and sugar that France could spare; more, much more, than Paris had, and at his bidding the cake-shops flowered with *éclairs, millefeuilles, brioches, choux à la crême*, and cakes more marvellous with German names.

France, poor and hungry, flung all she had into Alsace and Lorraine, that she might make her entry with the assuring dazzle of the benefactress. The Lorraines, like children, were fed with sugar while the meat shops were empty—were kept dancing in national costume that they might forget to ask for leather boots, to wonder where wool and silk were hiding.

Fêtes were organised, colours were paraded in the square, torchlight processions were started on Saturday nights, when the boys of the town went crying and whooping behind the march of the flares. Artists were sent for from Paris, took train to Nancy, and were driven laboriously through hours of snow, over miles of shell-pitted roads, that they might sing and play in the theatre or in the house of the Governor. To the dances, to the dinners, to the plays came the Lorraine women, wearing white cotton stockings to set off their thick ankles, and dancing in figures and set dances unknown to the officers from Paris.

The Commandant Dormans, head of all motor transport under the Grand Quartier Général, having prepared his German drawing-room as a ballroom, having danced all the evening with ladies from the surrounding hills, found himself fatigued and exasperated by the side of the head of Foreign Units attached to the Automobile Service.

"I thought you had Englishwomen at Bar-le-Duc," he said to the latter.

"I have—eight."

"What are they doing at Bar-le-Duc? Get them here."

"Is there work, sir?"

"Work! They shall work from dawn to sunset so long as they will dance all night! Englishwomen do dance, don't they?"

"I have never been to England."

"Get them here. Send for them."

So through his whim it happened that six days later a little caravan of women crossed the old front lines beyond Pont-à-Mousson as dusk was falling, and as dark was falling entered the gates of Metz.

They leant from the ambulance excitedly as the lights of the streets flashed past them, saw windows piled with pale bricks of butter, bars of chocolates, tins of preserved strawberries, and jams.

"Can you see the price on the butter?"

"Twenty-four...."

"What?"

"I can't see. Yes.... Twenty-four francs a pound."

"Good heavens!"

"Ah, is it possible, éclairs?"

"Eclairs!"

And with exclamations of awe they saw the cake shops in the Serpenoise.

German boys cried "American girls! American girls!" and threw paper balls into the back of the ambulance.

"I heard, I heard...."

"What is it?"

"I heard German spoken."

"Did you think, then, they were all dead?"

"No," but Fanny felt like some old scholar who hears a dead language spoken in a vanished town.

They drove on past the Cathedral into the open square of the Place
du Theâtre. Half the old French theatre had been set aside as offices for the
Automobile Service, and now the officers of the service, who had waited for
them with curiosity, greeted them on the steps.

"You must be tired, you must be hungry! Leave the ambulance where
it is and come now, as you are, to dine with us!"

In the uncertain light from the lamp on the theatre steps the French
tried to see the English faces, the women glanced at the men, and they
walked together to the oak-panelled Mess Room in a house on the other side
of the empty square. A long table was spread with a white cloth, with silver,
with flowers, as though they were expected. Soldiers waited behind the
chairs.

"Vauclin! That *foie gras* you brought back from Paris yesterday...
where is it, out with it? What, you only brought two jars! Arrelles, there's a
jar left from yours."

"Mademoiselle, sit here by Captain Vauclin. He will amuse you. And
you, mademoiselle, by me. You all talk French?"

"And fancy, I never met an Englishwoman before. Never! Your responsibility is terrible. How tired you must be!... What a journey! For to-
night we have found you billets. We billet you on Germans. It is more comfortable; they do more for you. What, you have met no Germans yet? They
exist, yes, they exist."

"Arrelles, you are not talking French! You should talk English. You
can't? Nor I either...."

"But these ladies talk French marvellously...."

Some one in another house was playing an ancient instrument. Its
music stole across the open square. Soldiers passed singing in the street.

A hundred miles ... a hundred years away ... lay Bar-le-Duc, liquid in mud, soaked in eternal rain. "What was I?" thought Fanny in amazement. "To what had I come, in that black hut!" And she thought that she had run down to the bottom of living, lain on that hard floor where the poor lie, known what it was to live as the poor live, in a hole, without generosity, beauty, or privacy—in a hole, dirty and cold, plain and coarse.

She glanced at her neighbour with wonder and appreciation, delight and envy. There was a light, clean scent upon his hair. She saw his hands, his nails. And her own.

A young Jew opposite her had his hair curled, and a faint powdery bloom about his face.

("But never mind! That is civilisation. There are people who turn from that and cry for nature, but I, since I've lived as a dog, when I see artifice, feel gay!")

"You don't know with what interest you have been awaited."

"We?"

"Ah, yes! And were you pleased to come?"

"We did not know to what we were coming!"

"And now?..."

She looked round the table peacefully, listened to the light voices talking a French she had never heard at Bar.

"And now?..."

"I could not make you understand how different...." (No, she would not tell him how they had lived at Bar. She was ashamed.) But as she was answering the servant gave him a message and he was called away. When he returned he said: "The Commandant Dormans is showing himself very anxious."

The Jew laughed and said: "He wants to see these ladies this evening?"

"No, he spares them that, knowing of their journey. He sends a message by the Capitaine Châtel to tell us that the *D.S.A.* gives a dance tomorrow night. The personal invitation will be sent by messenger in the morning. You dance, mademoiselle?"

"There is a dance, and we are invited? Yes, yes, I dance! You asked if I was happy now that I am here. To us this might be Babylon, after the desert!"

"Babylon, the wicked city?"

"The gay, the light, beribboned city! What is the 'D.S.A.'?"

"A power which governs our actions. We are but the C.R.A.... the regulating control. But they are the Direction. 'Direction Service Automobile.' They draw up all traffic rules for the Army, dispose of cars, withdraw them. On them you depend and I depend. But they are well-disposed towards you."

"And the Commandant Dormans is the head?"

"The head of all transport. He is a great man. Very peculiar."

"The Capitaine Châtel?"

"His aide, his right hand, the nearest to his ear."

Dinner over, the young Jew, Reherrey, having sent for two cars from the garage, drove the tired Englishwomen to their billets. As the cars passed down the cobbled streets and over a great bridge, Fanny saw water gleam in the gulf below.

"What river is that?"

"The Moselle."

A sentry challenged them on the far side of the bridge. "Now we are in the outer town, the German quarter."

In a narrow street whose houses overhung the river each of the section was put down at a different doorway, given a paper upon which was inscribed her right to billets, and introduced in Reherry's rapid German to her landlady.

Fanny in her turn, following the young man through a dark doorway, found herself in a stone alley and climbed the windings of a stairway. A girl of twelve or thirteen received her on the upper landing, saying "Guten Abend," and looking at her with wonder.

"Where is your mother?" said Reherry.

"She is out with my eldest sister."

"What is your name?"

"Elsa."

"Then, Elsa, look after this lady. Take her to her room, the room I saw your mother about, give her hot water, and bring her breakfast in the morning. Take great care of her."

"Jawohl, mein Herr."

Reherry turned away and ran down the stairs. Elsa showed Fanny to a room prepared for her.

"You are English?" said Elsa, and could not take her eyes off her.

"Yes, I am English. And are you German?" (Question so impossible, so indiscreet in England...)

"I am real German, from Coblentz. How did you come here, Fräulein?"

"In a car."

"But from England! Is there not water?"

"I crossed the water in a ship, and afterwards I came here in a car."

"You have a motor car? But every one is rich in England."

"Oh, not very..."

"Yes, every one. Mother says so."

The girl went away, then brought her a jug of hot water.

"I hope," said Fanny, venturing upon a sea of forgotten German, "I hope
I haven't turned you or your sister out of this room."

"This is the strangers' room," said Elsa. "I thank you."

When she had gone, Fanny looked round the room. It was too German to be true. The walls were dark red, the curtains dark red, the carpet, eiderdown, rep cover of the armchair, plush on the photograph frames, embroidered mats upon the washstand, tiles upon the stove, everything a deep, dark red. Four mugs stood upon the mantelpiece, and ... she rubbed her eyes ... was it possible that one had an iron cross upon its porcelain, one the legend "Got mit uns," the third the head of the Kaiser, the fourth the head of the Kaiserin? "That is too much! The people I shall write to won't believe it!"

Her bed was overhung by a large branch of stag's horn fixed upon the wall.

She felt the bed, counted the blankets, found matches on the mantelpiece, a candle in the candlestick, room in the stove to boil a kettle or a saucepan. Hot water steamed from her jug, a hot brick had been placed to warm her bed, a plate of rye bread cut in slices and covered with a cloth was upon the table.

Foreign to her own, the eyes which had rejoiced in this room ... yet the smile of German comfort was upon it.

She lay down beneath the branching antlers, and smiled before she went to sleep: "One pair of silk stockings ... to dance in Babylon ..."

* * * * *

In the morning a thin woman dressed in black brought her breakfast—jam, rye bread, coffee and sugar.

95

"Guten Morgen," said the woman, and looked at her curiously. But Fanny couldn't remember which language she ought to talk, and fumbled in her head so long that the woman went away.

She dressed and went out, meeting Stewart by her doorway. Together they crossed the bridge, the theatre square, and went towards the Cathedral with eager faces. They did not look up at the Cathedral, at the statute of old David upon which the Kaiser had had his own head carved, and upon whose crossed hands the people had now hung chains fastened with a padlock—they did not glance at the Hôtel de Ville in the square beyond, but, avoiding the tram which emerged from the narrow Serpenoise like a monster that had too long been oppressed, they hurried on up the street with a subdued and hungry gaiety.

There was a Need to be satisfied before anything could be seen, done, or said. A Need four years old, now knocking at the doors of heaven, howling to be satisfied.

Before the windows of a shop they paused, but Stewart, standing back and looking up the street, said: "There is a better further on!" and when they had gone on a few paces Fanny whispered, hurrying, "A better still beyond!" At the third shop, the Need, imperative, royal, would wait no longer, and drove them within.

"How many?" asked the saleswoman at the end of ten minutes.

"Seven *éclairs* and a cream bun, said Stewart.

"Just nine *éclairs*," said Fanny.

"Seventeen francs," said the woman without moving an eyelash.

This frenzy cooled, their pockets lighter, they walked for pleasure in the town. The narrow streets streamed with people—French soldiers and officers, Lorraine women in the costumes of pageantry, and German children who cried shrilly: "Amerikanerin, Amerikanerin!"

An English major passed them. They recognised his flawless boots before they realised his nationality. And, following his, the worst boots in the world—worn by a couple of sauntering Italian officers, gay in olive and silver uniform. German men in black slouch hats hurried along the streets.

It had been arranged that they should eat their meals in a room overlooking the canal, at the foot of the Cathedral—and there at eleven o'clock they went, to be a little dashed in spirit by the reappearance of the Bar-le-Duc crockery.

The same yellow dish carried what seemed the same rationed jam; the square blocks of meat might have been cooked in the Bar cook-hut, and brought with them over the desert; two heavy loaves stood as usual on the wooden table. The French Army ration was the same in every town.

"Mesdames," said the orderly assigned to them, "there are two sous-officers without who wish to speak with you."

"Let them come in."

Two blue figures appeared in the doorway and saluted. The first brought a card of invitation from the Commandant Dormans. The second was the brigadier from the garage with a list of the cars assigned to the drivers.

"Perhaps these ladies would come down and try their cars after lunch?" he suggested, and lunch being over they walked with him through the winding streets. At the gates of a great yard he paused and a sentry swung them open. Behind the gates lay a sandy plain as large as a parade ground, which, except for gulleys or gangways crossing it at intervals, was packed from end to end with row after row of cars; cars in the worst possible condition, torn, twisted, wheelless, cars with less dramatic and yet fatal injuries; some squatting backwards upon their haunches, some inclined forwards upon their knees—one, lately fished up from a river, had slabs and crusts of ice still upon its seats—one, the last dragged in at the tail of a breakdown lorry, hung, fore-wheels in the air, helpless upon a crane. Here, in the yard, was nothing but broken iron and mouldering carriage work—the cemetery of the Transport of the Grand Quartier.

Lining all one side of the yard ran a shed, closed and warmed and lighted, where living cars slept in long rows mudguard to mudguard, and bright lamps facing outward.

As the Englishwomen walked in a soft rustle could be heard up and down the lighted shed, for each half-hidden driver working by his car turned and shot a glance, expectant and mocking, towards the door.

"Ben quoi, i'paraît qu'c'esst vrai! Tu vois!"

"Qu'est-ce qu'il dit, c'ui-là?"

"C'est les Anglaises, pardi!"

"Tu comprends, j'suis contre tout ca. I'y a des fois ou les femmes c'est bien. Mais ici ..."

"Tu grognes? On va r'devenir homme, c'est tres bien!"

"C'est idiot! Qu'est-ce qu'elles vont faire ici!"

"On dirait—c'est du militarisme francais!"

"Le militarisme francais j'm'en f——! Tu verra, cela va faire encore du travail pour nous."

"Attends un peu!"... And murmurs filled the shed—glances threaded the shadows, chilling the spirit of the foreign women adventuring upon the threshold.

"Four Rochets," said the *brigadier*, consulting his paper, "two Delages, two FIATS ... Mademoiselle, here is yours, and yours. The Lieutenant Denis will be here in a moment. He fears the Rochets will be too heavy for you, but we must see."

The lieutenant who had been at dinner the night before entered the shed, greeted them, and turned to Stewart. "That car is too heavy for your strength, mademoiselle. It is not a car for a lady."

"I like the make," she said stiffly, conscious of the ears which listened in the shed.

"See if you can start her now, mademoiselle," said the *brigadier*, arranging the levers.

There was a still hush in the shed as Stewart bent to the handle. Fanny, standing by the Rochet which had been assigned to her, felt her heart thumping.

("Tu vas voir!" whispered the little soldiers watching brightly from behind the cars. "Attends, attends un peu! Pour les mettre en marche, les tacots, c'est autre chose!")

Stewart, seizing the handle, could not turn it. In the false night of the shed the lights shone on polished lamps, on glass and brass, on French eyes which said: "That's what comes of it!"—which were ready to say—"March out again, Englishwomen, ridiculous and eager and defeated!"

Fanny, looking neither to right nor left, prayed under her breath — "Stewart, Stewart we can never live in this shed if you can't start her. And if you can't, nobody else can...."

There was a spurt of life from the engine as it back-fired, and Stewart sprang away holding her wrist with the other hand. The lieutenant, the brigadier, and a driver from a car near by crowded round her with exclamations.

"You advanced the spark too much," said the driver to the *brigadier*. "*Tenez*! I will retard it."

"She shan't touch the car again." said the lieutenant. "It is too heavy."

"Leave the controls alone," said Stewart, scowling at the driver. "Give me room ..." She caught the handle with her injured hand, and with a gasp, swung the Rochet into throbbing life.

There was a murmur of voices down the shed, and each man with a slight movement returned to the work he had been doing; the polishers polished, the cleaners swept, and a little chink of metal on metal filled the garage. The women were accepted.

The day had vanished. Cars, yard and garage sank out of sight. Out in the streets the lamps woke one by one, and from the town came shouts and the stamp of feet marching. It was Saturday night and a torchlight procession of soldier and civilians wound down the street. The band passed first, and after it men carried fire-glares fastened upon sticks.

The garage gates turned to rods and bars of gold till the light left them, and the glare upon the house-fronts opposite travelled slowly down the street.

Fanny slipped out of the yard and crept along behind the flares like a shadow on the pavement. At the street corner she passed out on to the bridge over the Moselle, and leant against the stonework to watch the plumes of fire as they glittered up the riverside upon the tow-path. The lights vanished, leaving the darkness so intense that she could only feel her way over the bridge by holding to the stonework with her hand. A sentry challenged her and when she had passed him she had arrived at the door of her German lodging.

Climbing the stairs a slow breeze of excitement filled out the sails of her spirit. "My silk stockings ... my gold links, and my benzene bottle!" she murmured happily. Now that of all her life she had the slenderest toilet to make—three hours was the time she had set aside for it!

III. JULIEN

Earth has her usual delights—which can be met with six days out of the seven. But here and there upon grey earth there exist, like the flying of sunlight, celestial pleasures also—and one of these is the heaven of success. When, puffed-up and glorious, the successful creature struts like a peacock, gilded in a passing radiance. And in a radiance, in a magic illumination, the newcomers danced in the drawing-room of the Commandant Dormans, and tasted that which cannot be found when sought, nor held when tasted.

Old tapestries of tropical foliage hung around the walls, dusk upon one wall, dawn upon another. Trees climbed from floor to ceiling laden with lime-coloured flowers, with birds instead of fruits upon the branches.

When at a touch the yellow dust flew out under the lamplight it seemed to the mazy eye of the dancer that the trees sent up a mist of pollen and song.

In this happy summer, Fanny, turning her vain ear to spoken flattery, her vain eye to mute, danced like a golden gnat in fine weather.

The Commandant Dormans spoke to her. If he was not young he had a quick voice that was not old. He said: "We welcome you. We have been waiting for you. We are glad you have come."

Faces surrounded her which to her fresh eyes were not easy to read. Names which she had heard last night became young and old men to her — skins red and pale and dark-white—eyes blue and olive and black—gay, audacious and mocking features. She was dazzled, she did not hurry to understand. One could not choose, one floated free of preference, all men were strangers.

"One day I shall know what they are, how they live, how they think." But she did not want that day to come.

The Commandant Dormans said: "You do not regret Bar-le-Duc?"

"No, no, no."

"I hear you are all voracious for work. I hear that if you do not drive from morning to night we cannot hope to keep you with us!"

Denis said to her: "Be careful of him! He believes there is no end to the human strength."

She replied joyously: "There is no end to our strength!"

When she had eyes to see, to watch, to choose, she found that there was in the room a man who was graceful and young, whose eyes were a peculiar shape, who laughed all the time gently as he danced. He never looked at her, never came near her. This young man was indifferent to her, he was indifferent to her ... Soon he became a trouble and a pleasure to her. With whom was he dancing now ... and now? Who was it that amused him? His eyes and his hair were bright ... but there were many around her whose eyes and hair were as bright. Before she had seen that young man laugh her pleasure had been more complete.

While she was talking to Denis a voice said to her: "Won't you dance with me?"

Looking up she saw who it was. His mouth smiled, his eyes were clever and gay.

The moment she danced with him she began to grow proud, she began to find herself. Someone whispered to her: "The section must leave at such and such an hour...."

She thought in a flash: "For me the section is dissolved ... I am I, and the others are the others!"

The evening wore on. The musicians flagged and took up their courage again. It was late when Stewart, touching Fanny's arm, showed her that they were almost the only two women in the room.

"Where are the others?"

"In the hall, putting on their coats. We are all going."

"Aren't they in a hurry?"

"They have had orders, which were brought up just now, for runs early to-morrow morning. But you and I have nothing, and Denis has asked us ... if you are quick you can slip away ... to have supper with him at Moitriers."

"Well?"

"We can. The others go home in two cars which have been sent for us. No one will know that we are not in the other car. I'm so hungry."

"So am I, starving. Very well."

They joined the others, put on their coats, hunted ostentatiously for their gloves, then slipped ahead down the dark stairway into the square below. Denis joined them.

"Splendid. I have my car round that corner. It will be only a matter of half an hour, but if you are both as hungry as I you will welcome it. Everything was finished upstairs, every crumb and cake. We must get a fourth. Who shall I get?"

"Any one whom you would like to bring," said Stewart. "I don't think I have mastered the names yet. I really don't mind."

"And you, mademoiselle?"

"Nor I either," said Fanny, sniffing at the frosty air, at the fresh night.

"Whom you like!"

"Then I won't be a moment. I'll bring whom I can."

"Monsieur!"... as he reached the corner. He turned back.

"There is an artillery captain ... in a black uniform with silver."

"An artillery captain ..." he paused enquiringly.

"In black and silver. There was no other in the room."

"Oh, yes, there were two in black and silver!"

"Tall, with ..."

"Ah, tall! The other is very short ... The tall one is the Commandant's aide, Captain Châtel. He may not be able.... But I will see!" He disappeared again.

When he returned he had the young man beside him.

"One moment," said Châtel, as they walked towards the car; "who asked for me, the girl with the fair hair, or with the dark?"

"With the fair."

Moitriers was closed when they reached it, and they drove on to the only other place where food could be bought past the hour of midnight—the station buffet.

Pushing past the barriers at the entrance to the station they entered a long corridor filled with heavy civilian life. Men and women lay, slept and snored upon the stone ledges which lined the side of the tunnel, their bags and packets stacked around them. Small children lay asleep like cut corn, heads hanging and nodding in all directions, or propped against each other in such an intricate combination that if one should move the whole sheaf of tired heads slipped lower to the floor.

Further on, swing doors of glass led to a waiting-room, and here the sleeping men and women were so packed upon the ground and around the little tables that it was difficult to walk between them. Men sat in groups of nine or ten around a table meant for four each with his head sunk down between his hands upon the marble surface. On one table a small child wrapped in shawls lay among the circle of heads, curled like a snail, its toe in its father's ear. At each end of the room stood soldiers with fixed bayonets.

Denis paused at the entrance. "Walk round here," he said, "there is a gangway for the sentry."

"If we talk too loud," said Fanny, "we shall wake them."

"They must soon wake in any case. It must be near the time for the train. You know who they are?"

"Who?"

"Germans. Expelled from Metz. They leave in batches for Germany every night—by a train that comes in and goes out at some horrible hour."

Passing through more glass doors they came to an inner room where, behind a buffet, a lady in black silk served them with beer and slices of raw ham and bread.

The four sat down for a moment at a little table—Denis talking of the system by which the outgoing Germans were nightly weeded from those who had permission to remain behind in Metz. Julien Châtel joined in the conversation. He spoke with the others but he glanced at Fanny. For the briefest of seconds he thought as he looked at her face that he saw a new interest smile upon it. He did not know that his own face wore the same look. His look said as he looked at her: "You, you, you!" At one moment she thought: "Am I pretty?" At the next she was content only to breathe, and thought no more of herself. She took in now his eyes which seldom rested on her, now a movement of his lips which made her feel both happy and miserable, and suddenly she learnt how often his finger traced some letter upon his cheek.

These things were important. They were like the opening sentences of a great play to which one must listen, absorbed, for fear of misunderstanding all the story.

It was not long before they rose, threaded their way back between the sleeping Germans, regained the car, and drove down the silent streets towards the Cathedral.

"Have you seen it?" said Julien in a low voice, addressing her directly.

"The Cathedral?"

"Yes. I want to show it to you. Will you meet me there to-morrow at three?"

(The others talked and smiled and knew nothing. Whoever has a secret is stronger than they who know nothing. Fanny thought: "My companions, to be as you are is not to exist! Whatever you feel, you are feeling nothing ...")

"Will you?"

"Yes," she answered, and joined her hands tightly, for this was where the play really began.

* * * * *

The sun shone gaily. Here was no mud, no unhappiness, here were no puzzled women, and touching mayors of ruined villages, but instead gay goblin houses, pointed churches like sugar cake, the old French theatre with its stone garlands glittering in the sun; sun everywhere, streaming over the Place du Théâtre, over women shaking coloured rags from the windows, women washing linen by the river; everything that had been wet was drying, everything that had savoured of tears and age and sadness was burning up under the sun, and what moisture remained was brighter than jewels.

"Suppose he never came!"

"Why, then, be ready for that. Very likely he wouldn't come. Very likely he would think in daylight—' She is not a woman, but an English Amazon...'" Fanny glanced down at her clothes regretfully. She was ill-equipped for an assignation.

"At least I might have better gloves," she thought, and walked into a small shop which advertised men's clothes in German across the window. She bought yellow washing-leather gloves at twenty-eight francs a pair, and would have paid a hundred had the salesman insisted.

And now with yellow gloves, silk stockings, shining shoes and a heart as light as a leaf upon a wind she walked towards the Cathedral.

"He won't come. He won't be there...." She pushed at the east door.

He was under a Madonna, his black and silver hat in his hand, his eyes critical and pleased as he walked to meet her. They sat down together on a seat, without speaking. Then, each longing for the other to speak — "You have come...." he said first. (His face was oval and his hair was shining.)

"Yes," she nodded, and noticed a peculiar glory in the Cathedral. The dark cave shone as white flesh and youth can shine through the veils of a mourner.

They no longer lived their own separate lives; they had come together at each other's call.

"I thought you wouldn't come."

"Why, why did you think that?"

Little questions and little answers fell in a sudden rain from their lips. Yet while Fanny spoke he did not seem to know what she said, and answered at random, or sometimes he did not answer at all, but smiled.

Afraid of the fragile avowal of silence, evading it, she found little words to follow one another. But he answered less and less, and smiled at her, till his face was full of this smile. So then she said: "We'll go out and walk by the river," and he rose at once and followed her among the forest of wooden chairs. They forgot that he was to have shown her the Cathedral. In all its length she never saw one statue except the first Madonna, not one stone face but his young face with the cold light upon it, his hands as white as stones, as long and fine as any of the carved fingers which prayed around them.

They walked together down the winding path below the bridge to the very edge of the Moselle, which lay in light winter sunlight, its banks buried in shrubberies of green.

Mont St. Quentin, conical, covered with waving trees, shone like a hill in summer, and beyond it the indigo forest of every Lorraine horizon floated indefinitely like a cloud.

A young doctor lounged beside them, putty-coloured under his red plush cap. "Why are all doctors plain in France?" she laughed.

"Hush!" He wound his hand round and round like the player of a barrel -organ. "I have to stop you when you say silly things like a phonograph, at so much a metre."

So he believed he might tease her.... Delighted, she stopped by the bank of the river and stared into the water. The sun ran over her shoulders and warmed her hands. The still shine of the river held both their eyes as movement in a train holds the mind.

"I am enjoying my walk," he said. He did not mean it like that, or as a compliment to her. When it was said he thought it sounded banal, and was sorry. "What a pity!"

But she was not critical because she was looking for living happiness, and every moment she was more and more convinced that she would get it. But when he asked her her name and she repeated it, it sounded so much like an avowal that they both turned together down the tow-path with a quick movement and spoke of other things, for they were old enough to be afraid that the vague happiness that fluttered before them down the path would not be so beautiful when it was caught. And at this fear she said distinctly to herself: "In love!" and wondered that she had not said it before.

Coming back to him with her words, she then began to wound and to delay him. "You mustn't be late for your office...."

"When shall I see you again?"

They dropped into a long silence. She summoned her coquetry that she called pride. The blue, blue forest at the edge of her sight tilted a little like a ship, the watery hill-country rolled towards it in mysterious kilometres.

"It is beautiful," she said clumsily, avoiding his question, ignoring it. "Yet when I go there it is always more beautiful on the next hill.'

"I must hurry," he said at once, "I shall be late at my office."

"Where is your office?"

He looked round vaguely. "There in that group of pines." They walked towards it, they were almost at the door, but he would not repeat his question. Would he not at the last moment? No. Had it not then been clear that the living happiness was at her lips? No. Could he let her go, could it have been a failure? He was holding out one of the stone hands. He was going.

She looked up and the sun was streaming in his eyes, blinding him, and without seeing her he stared into the darkness that was her face. "I have so enjoyed my walk," he said. "Thank you for coming."

All her face said "Oh!" in a hurt, frightened stare, but the sun only came round the edges of her hair and cap and left the panic in a shifting darkness. He was gone.

She went back to her street. Reaching the big, populous house she followed the corridor that led from the stone courtyard, climbed to the first floor and opened the door of her own room. A bitter disillusion ran through her. The close-packed furniture seemed to say indifferently, "There's not much room for you!" and she knew quite well as she sat down on the bed that it was not her room at all, but had been as public to the birds of passage as the branch of a tree to the birds of the air.

"I did so little. I did so little. It was such a little mistake!" Self-pity flooded her.

"And why did he ask me to come to the Cathedral if such a little thing, such a little thing...." Indignation rose.

"Things don't crumble like that, don't vanish like that!" She stared, astonished, at the scenes she had left behind her, the shining of the dark Cathedral, the ripple on the Moselle. "But they do, they do, they do...."

Down in the street her own name caught her ear, and she went to the window.

"Are you there, are you there?" cried the voice.

Hanging waist-deep out of the window she received her orders for the next day.

"I came down to tell you now," said the girl below on the pavement. "I thought you might have things to do to the car. You must be at the Hôtel Royal, near the station, at half-past six to-morrow morning."

"Have you any idea whom I'm to take? Or where?"

"I don't know where, but the man is a Russian colonel."

She drew her head back through the window, and the gay tumble of the street gave way to the impersonal, heavy room. Cramming her oil-stained overall into her haversack, she put on her leather coat and went up to the garage.

The sun had disappeared. A cold wind struck the silk-clad ankles.

IV. VERDUN

"Come in," she said in English, lifting her head and all her mind and spirit out of the pit of the pillow.

Feet came further into the room and a shivering child held a candle in her face. "Halb sechs, Fräulein," it said. But the Fräulein continued to stare at him. He thought she was not yet awake—he could not tell that she was counting countries in her head to find which one she was in—or that she was inclining towards the theory that she was at school in Germany. He was very cold in his shirt and little trousers, and he pulled at her sheets. "Fräulein!" he said again with chattering teeth, and when she nodded more collectedly the little ghost slipped out relieved by the door. "Russian colonel ... I must get up. Fancy making that boy call me! Why couldn't someone older ... I must get up."

He had left the electric light burning in her room, but out in the corridor all was black and hushed as she had left it the night before when she had gone to bed. Behind the kitchen door there was a noise of water running in the sink. She opened the door, and there was the wretched child again, still in his shirt, rinsing out her coffee-pot by the light of one candle. Well, since he was doing it ... Poor child! But she must have her coffee. By the time she was dressed he tapped again and brought in the tray with coffee, bread and jam on it. Setting it down, he looked it over with an anxious face. "Zucker," he said, and disappeared to fetch it. She filled her thermos bottle with the rest of the coffee which she could not finish, and put two of the slices of grey bread into the haversack, then crept downstairs and out into the black street where the gas lamps still burnt and the night sentry still paced up and down in the spectral gloom. Over the river hung a woolly fog, imprisoning the water; but as she crossed the bridge she noticed where its solidity was incomplete and torn, and into the dark water which lay at the bottom of such crevasses a lamp upon the bridge struck its arrowed likeness. It was a good seven minutes' walk to the garage, and she tried to get warm by running, but the ice crackling in the gutters and between the cobble stones defied her, and her hands ached with cold though she put them in turn right through her blouse against her heart to warm them as she ran. Fetching her car she drove to the Hôtel Royal, and settled down to wait.

A porter came out and swept the steps of the hotel, and a puff of his dust caught her in the face. He laid a fibre mat on each stone step, and clipped them with little metal clips.

"Are you for us?" asked a *sous-lieutenant*, looking first up and down the empty street and then at the car. He had blue eyes and a long, sad moustache that swept down the lower half of his face and even below his chin, making him look older than he should.

"I am for a Russian colonel," she said, liking his mild face.

"That's right. Yes, a Russian colonel. Colonel Dellahousse. But can you manage by yourself? Can you really? I will tell him...."

He disappeared up the steps and through the swing door of the hotel. A moment later he was out again.

"He will come to you himself, he will see you. But we want to go to Verdun! Could you drive so far? You could? Yes, yes, perhaps. Yet here he comes...."

In dark civilian clothes the Russian came down the hotel steps. He was tall, serious, upright, rich. His face beneath his wide, black hat was grave and well cared for. The sombre glitter of his eye was grave, his small dark beard shone in the well-controlled prime of its growth. From the narrow line of white collar to the narrower thread of French watchchain—from the lean, long feet to the lean, white hands she took him in, and braced herself, adjusted herself, to meet his stately gravity. If there was something of the Mephistopheles in fancy dress about him, it was corrected by his considerate expression.

"Have you had breakfast?" he began, speaking French with a softly nasal accent.

"How kind of you to think of it! Yes, thank you, monsieur."

"I have to go to Verdun," he put it to her. "I have business there." It was as though he expected that she would let him off without difficult explanations, would exclaim: "There is some mistake! Some other car, some other driver is intended for your work!"

But she remained silent except for a smile of acknowledgment, and with a sigh he summoned the lieutenant and went back into the hotel. In a few minutes the Frenchman came out again. "Monsieur Dellahousse would like to know if you know the way?" he inquired.

"He doesn't want to take me? Isn't that it?" asked Fanny, smiling but anxious.

"He is a little doubtful," admitted the lieutenant. "You must excuse...."

"Perhaps I appear flippant to him. But I am grave, too, grave as he, and I long to go, and the car and I, we are trustworthy. I do, indeed, know the way to Verdun."

He went in again, and for answer the porter brought out the bags, and Colonel Dellahousse followed, carrying a sealed black bag with care under his arm. She was sure he had said to the Frenchman: "But what sort of a woman is she? One does not want to have difficulties." And as sure, too, that the other had answered: "I know the English. They let their women do this sort of thing. I think it will be all right."

She no longer felt defiant towards the spoken and unspoken criticism she met everywhere: "What kind of women can these be whose men allow them to drive alone with us for hours, and sometimes days?" but had begun to apologise for it even to herself, while it sometimes caused her bewilderment.

She drove them back through the waking town and out by the Verdun gates, and soon up on to the steep heights above the town among frozen fields and grasslands white with frost. The big stone tombs of 1870 stuck out of a light ground fog like sails upon a grey sea, and it was not long, at Jeandelize, before the 1914 graves began, small isolated wooden crosses. They touched the brink of the battlefields; a rain of dead gunfire began along the sides of the road, shell-holes with hairy edges of dried thistles and, at the bottom of each, green moss stiffened with ice. The road grew wilder and wilder and took on the air of a burnt-out moor, mile after mile of grey, stricken grass, old iron, and large upturned stones. Wherever a pair of blasted trees was left at the road's side a notice hung in mid-air, on wires slung from tree to tree across the road.

"Halt—Autos!" shouted the square, black, German orders from the boards which swung and creaked in the wind.

"Nach Verdun," said the monster black arrows painted on trees and stone, pointing, thick, black and steady, till it seemed that the ghost of the German endeavour still flung itself along the road. "Nach Verdun! Nach Verdun!" without a pause, with head down. "Nach Verdun," so that no one might go wrong, go aside, go astray, turn back against the order of the arrow. Not an arrow anywhere answered "Nach Metz."

For miles and miles nothing living was to be seen, neither animal, nor motor, nor living man; only the stray fires of the Chinese fluttered here and there like blue and red marsh fires a mile or so back from the main road. Once as she flew along she shied like a horse and twisted the wheel as a wild

110

screaming and twittering rose at the side of the car, and glancing back she saw three figures wriggle and laugh in mockery and astonishment. They had risen round the embers of a dead fire, and stood swaying on their feet and showing white teeth in orange faces. One had the long hair of a woman flapping about his ears.

They reached Etain, and turned the sharp corner in the street lined with hollow houses, passed under a tunnel of thick camouflage, leafy as an arbour, mouldy as the rags upon a corpse, and came on the first pill-boxes of the Hindenburg line.

Another twelve miles and the twin towers of Verdun appeared over the brow of a hill.

"I thought it but dust!" exclaimed the Russian. "I thought it a ruin; it is a town!"

"Wait, wait till you get nearer...."

Then down the last long hill and over the paved Route d'Etain into the suburbs of Verdun. As they neared it the town began to show its awful frailty—its appearance of preservation was a mockery. Verdun stood upright as by a miracle, a coarse lace of masonry—not one house was whole.

"Stop!" ordered the Russian, and at the foot of the steep, conical hill which wore Verdun upon its crest they stopped and stared. The town was poured over the slopes of the hill as though a titanic tipcart had let out its rubbish upon the summit. Houses, shops and churches, still upright, still formed Verdun, kept its shape intact, unwilling that it should fall to dust while these deadly skeletons could keep their feet. Light glared through the walls, and upon the topmost point of all the palace of the bishop was balanced, its bones laced against the sky. The Russian, who had stood up in the car, sat down. "Now go on...."

The streets which circled the base of the hill had been partially cleared of fallen rock and stonework, and the car could pick its way between the crazy shop-fronts, where notices of vanished cobblers, manicurists, butchers, flapped before caverns hollowed by fire, upon fingers of stone already touched by moss.

Here and there soldiers moved in bands at their work of clearing. But the black hat, the drab coat of the civilian had long been left behind —and here the face of a woman was unknown as the flying dragons of the world's youth.

Now and then with a crash the remains of a house fell, as the block of stonework which alone supported it was disarranged by the working soldiers.

"Where am I to go?" asked Fanny, as the street wound round the base of the hill.

"I will climb over beside you and direct you," said the French lieutenant, and dropped into the front seat.

"Where do these soldiers sleep? Not among these ruins?"

A block of masonry fell ahead of them and split its stones across the street.

"Be careful! You can get round by this side street. Up here.... In these ruins. No living soul can sleep in Verdun now."

"Where, then?"

"Don't you know? They sleep *beneath* Verdun, in this hill around which we are circling. I am looking for the entrance."

"Inside this hill? Under the town?"

"But you've heard of the *citadelle?*"

"Yes, but... this hill is so big."

"There are fifteen kilometres of tunnel in this hollow hill, and hundreds of steps lead up to the top by the palace, where there is a defence of barbed wire and guns. Look, here is the entrance."

They left the car. Before them was a small dark hole in the side of the hill, an entrance not much higher than a man, into which ran a single rail line of narrow gauge. A sentry challenged them as they walked towards him.

Entering the hill they found themselves in a tunnel lit by electric bulbs which hung in a dotted line ahead of them.

"Wait!" ordered the deep voice of the Russian, and he strode from them into the depths of the tunnel with the Eastern swing of Ali Baba entering his cave.

Fanny stood by the mild lieutenant, and they waited obediently.

"I must tell you a secret," he said to her. "Monsieur Dellahousse is very glad to be here. He said this morning: 'The Governor has sent me a woman to break my neck!'"

"But he took me...."

"Could he refuse you?—For he felt that it was a glove of challenge thrown down by the Governor of Metz. They do not get on together.... He took you with dignity, but he was convinced that he placed himself in the jaws of death."

"When do we go back? We cannot now be in Metz before dark."

"But haven't they told you? Never warned you? How monstrous! We are staying here."

"And I return alone?"

"No, you stay too. You are lent to us for five days. They should have told you!"

"Oh, I stay too. In this tunnel, here! How odd, how amusing!"

"Monsieur Dellahousse has gone to ask the Commandant of the *citadelle* to house us all. Here he comes."

The Russian returned under the chain of lights. "Follow me," he said, and led them further into his cavern.

They followed him like children, and as they advanced the lieutenant whispered: "We are now well beneath the town. It lies like a crust above our heads. Exactly beneath the palace you will see the steps go up...."

"What is the railway line for?"

"Bread for the garrison. There are great bakeries in the *citadelle*."

Further and further still.... Till the Russian turned to the right and took a branching tunnel. Here, lining the curve of the stone wall were twenty little cubicles of light wood, raised a few inches from the moist floor, and roofless except for the arch of the tunnel that ran equally above them all. These were the rooms assigned to the *officers de passage*, officers whom duty kept for a night in Verdun. Each cubicle held a bed, a tin basin on a tripod, a minute square of looking-glass, a chair and a shelf, and each bore the name of its temporary owner written on a card upon the door.

"Twenty ... twenty-one ... and twenty-two," read the Russian from a paper he carried, and threw open the door of twenty-two.

"This is yours, mademoiselle"; he bowed and waved her toward it. Fanny entered the room, which, from his manner, might have been the gilded ante-chamber of his Tzar.

She heard him enter his own room, and through the partition the very sighing of his breath was audible as it rustled upon his lips! He tried to give her the illusion of privacy, for, wishing to speak to her, he left his room again to tap at her door, though his voice was as near her ear whether at door or wall.

"I hope you are content, mademoiselle?" he said through the wood-work.

"Delighted, monsieur."

"You will sleep here," he continued, as though he suspected her of sleeping anywhere but there, "and dine with us in the officers' mess at seven. Until then, please stay in the *citadelle* in case I need you."

She heard his footsteps go up the corridor, the lieutenant following him. "I will unpack," she thought, and from her knapsack drew what she had by chance brought with her. Upon the shelf she arranged a tin of *singe*—the French bully beef—a gilt box of powder, a toothbrush, a comb, a map, a packet of letters to be answered, and a magneto spanner.

There was an hour yet before dinner and she wandered out into the corridors to explore the *citadelle*. A soldier stood upon a ladder changing the bulb of an electric light.

Catching sight of her he hurried from his ladder, and passing her with a stiff face, saluted, and disappeared.

Soon she began to think that this was the busy hour in the fortress: the corridors rustled gently, the unformed whispering of voices echoed behind her. The walls seemed to open at a dozen spots as she walked on, and little men with bright, grave faces hurried past her about their duties.

"Perhaps they are changing the guard...."

Yet a face which had already passed her three times began to impress its features upon her, and she realised suddenly that it was curiosity, not duty, that called the soldiers from their burrows. The news was spreading, for out of the gloom ahead fresh parties of onlookers appeared, paused disconcerted as she wished them "good evening," nodded or saluted her in haste, then hurried by.

An officer with grizzled hair stepped into the passage from a doorway.
As she neared him she saw he wore the badges of a commandant.

"Who is this?" he asked in a low voice of the soldier who followed at his heels.

"J'n'en sais rien, mon commandant," The soldier stiffened as a watchdog who sees a cat.

Fanny hastened nearer. "I drive a Russian officer," she explained. "I hope I have your permission to stay here."

"Ah!" exclaimed the officer, looking at her in surprise. "Colonel Dellahousse told me 'a driver'; he did not add that the driver was a lady. Where have they put you? Not in the cubicles of the *officiers de passage*? No, no, that must be changed, that won't do. Come, you shall sleep in the room next to the bishop's room, as he is absent. It is in my corridor."

Fanny followed him, and noticed that the corridor was now clear of
soldiers. The commandant paused before a door decorated with flags and
led her into another corridor lined with cubicles much larger than those she
had seen at first.

"Open number seven."

The soldier took his bunch of keys and opened the door.

"Now fetch mademoiselle's effects from the other corridor. Which
number was your room, mademoiselle?"

"Twenty-two. But I can fetch them ... I have really nothing."

The soldier withdrew.

"He will get them. You dine with us, I hope, to-night at seven. Are
you
English, mees?"

"Yes, English—with the French Army. I am really so grateful...."

"The other room was not possible. I like the English, mees. I have
known them at my home near Biarritz. You and I must talk a little. Do you
care to read?"

"Oh, yes, if I get time...."

"Any books you may want please take from my sitting-room, number
sixteen in this corridor. *Tenez!* I have an English book there—'The Light that
Failed'—I will get it for you."

"Oh! I have read ... But thank you."

"De rien, de rien! I will get it now." He hastened up the corridor and
returned with the book in his hand.

The soldier, too, returned, bearing the seven objects which had accompanied her travels.

"You will clean mademoiselle's shoes, brush her uniform, and bring
her hot water when she needs it," ordered the commandant, and the soldier
saluted impassively—a watch-dog who had been told that it was the house-
cat after all.

Left alone, she searched all her pockets for some forgotten stick of
chocolate, and finding nothing, sat down upon the bed to wait hungrily till
seven. The air in the tunnels was heavy and dry, and throwing off her tunic
she lay down on the bed and slept until footsteps passing her door awoke
her.

She became aware that the inhabitants of her corridor were washing
their hands for dinner, and sitting up sleepily found that it was already seven.
In a few minutes she hurried from her room and out into the main tunnel,

glad to get nearer the fresh air which filtered in through the opening at the far end.

Reaching a door which she had noticed before, marked "*popote*," she paused a second, listening to the hum of voices within, then pushed at the door and entered.

Instantly there was a hush of astonishment as seventy or eighty officers, eating at a long trestle table, sharply turned their heads towards her, their forks poised for a second, their hands still. Then, with a quick recovery, all was as before, and the stream of talk flowed on.

The first section of the table was reserved for strangers passing through Verdun, and here sat a party of young Russian officers in light blouse-tunics, an American or two, and a few French officers. At the next section sat the officers of the *citadelle*, a passing general, and at the left hand of the commandant, Monsieur Dellahousse and the mild lieutenant.

Overhead the stone roof of the tunnel was arched with flags, and orderlies hurried up and down serving the diners.

Fanny, halfway up the long table, wavered in doubt. Where, after all, was she supposed to sit? At the top section, as a guest—or, as a driver, among the whispering Russians at the "stranger" section? Her anxiety showed in her face as she glanced forwards and backwards and an orderly hurried towards her. "Par ici, mademoiselle, par ici!" and she followed him towards the head of the table. Her doubts dissolved as she saw the gap left for her by the friendly arm of the lieutenant, and, arrived at the long wooden bench upon which they sat, she bowed to the commandant, and lifting one leg beneath her skirt as a hen does beneath its feathers, she straddled the difficult bench and dropped into position.

"Beer, mademoiselle? Or red wine?" asked the Russian, suddenly turning to her; and the commandant, released from his conversation, called out gaily: "The mees will say 'water'—but one must insist. Take the wine, mees, it is better for you." The idea of water had never crossed Fanny's mind, but having decided on beer she changed it politely to red wine, which she guessed to be no other than the everlasting *pinard*.

"I know them...." continued the commandant, smiling at the general. "I know the English! My home is at Biarritz and there one meets so many."

And this old man thus addressed, a great star blazing on his breast, and tears of age trembling in his blue eyes, lifted his hand to attract her attention, and said to Fanny in gentle English: "Verdun honours a charming guest, mademoiselle."

"*Verdun ... honours....*" His words lingered in her ear. She a guest, *she* honoured ... *here*!

116

Up till now the novelty of her situation had engrossed her, the little soldiers watching in the tunnels, the commandant so eager to air his stumbling English, these had amused her.

And when she had perceived herself rare, unique, she had forgotten why she was thus rare, and what strange, romantic life she meddled in.

Here in this womanless region, in this fortress, in this room, night after night, month after month, the commandant and his officers had sat at table; in this room, which, unlike the tomb, had held only the living, while the dead and the threatened-with-death inhabited the earth above.

They had finished dinner and Monsieur Dellahousse signalled to Fanny that she might rise. She rose, and at the full sight of her uniform he remembered her duties and said stiffly: "Be good enough to wait up till ten to-night. I may need you."

They passed out again down the length of the tables. Near the door the Russian paused to speak with his countrymen, who rose and stood respectfully round him. Fanny and the lieutenant went on alone to the corridor.

"You have travelled with him before?" she asked.

"Oh, yes. I am lent to him to help him through the country. He is on a tour of inspection for the Red Cross; he visits all the camps of Russian prisoners liberated from Germany."

"But are there many round Verdun?"

"Thousands. You will see to-morrow. And be prepared for early rising. If he doesn't send for you by ten to-night I will tell the orderly to let you know the hour at which you will be wanted to-morrow morning. The car is all ready to start again?"

"I am going out to her now."

He turned away to join the Russian, and Fanny passed the sentry at the tunnel's mouth, and stood in the road outside.

Verdun by night, Verdun by starlight, awaited her.

Up the slopes of the hill, every spar, brick and beam, carried its bristle of gold. At her own head's imperceptible movement flashes came and went between the ribs of the Bishop's Palace. The sentry by the tunnel stood between the upper and the underground:—with his left eye he could watch the lights that strung back into the hollow hill, with his right, the smiling and winking of the stars in the sky.

"Fait beau dehors." His voice startled her. She turned to him, but he stood immobile in the shadow as though he had never spoken. She could not be sure that he had indicated to her that every man has his taste and his choice.

She set to work on her car which stood in the shelter of an archway opposite, and for half an hour the sky trembled unregarded above her head. When she had finished she stood back and gazed at the Rochet with an anxious friendly enmity—the friendship of an infant with a lion. "The garage is eighty miles away," she sighed, "with its friendly men who know all where I know so little.... Ah, do I know enough? What have I left undone?" For she felt, what was the truth, that the whole expedition depended on her, that the stately Russian had perhaps never known what it was to have a breakdown—that in Moscow, in Petrograd, in his faraway life, he had sat in town cars behind two chauffeurs, unaware of the deadly traps in rubber and metal.

V. VERDUN

Night was the same as day in the tunnels; the electric light was always on, and with the morning no daylight crept in to alter it. The orderly called her at half-past six and she took her "clients" to a barracks in the suburbs of Verdun, where Russian prisoners "liberated" from Germany crowded and jostled to see her from behind the bars of the barrack square, like wild animals in a cage. Armed sentries paced backwards and forwards across the gateway to the yard. As it came on to snow a French soldier came out of a guardroom and invited her in by the fire.

Inside, the rest of the guard huddled about the stove, and behind them a Russian prisoner with a moon face swept up the crumbs from their last meal.

"Why do Americans guard the gate?" she asked, "since you are a French guard?"

"Because we don't shoot with enough goodwill," grinned a little man.

"But who do you want to shoot?"

"Those fellows!" said the little man, slapping the moon-faced Russian on the thigh. "We used to guard the gates a week ago. But the Russians were always escaping, and not enough were shot as they got over the wall. So they said: 'The Americans are the types for that!' and they put them on to guard the gates. Look outside! You are having a success, mademoiselle!"

Hundreds of Russians stood about together outside, in strange, poor, scraped-together clothes, just as they had come from Germany, peering at Fanny in silence through the open doorway.

"But I thought these were *liberated* prisoners from Germany?"

"Don't ask me!" said the little man disgustedly. "I wish to heaven they were all back in Germany. Look at me! I've fought in the Somme, the Aisne, and Verdun, and now at the end of the war I'm left here to look after these pigs!"

A sergeant entered. "A man to take the prisoner in the fourth cell up to the doctor," he said sharply.

"It's not my turn," said the little man, aggrieved that the eye of the sergeant should so rest on him. "It's yours!" he said to the man on the bench beside him. "It's yours!" replied this man to the next.

"Yes, it's Chaumet's! Yes, it's Chaumet's, *va-t'en!*" they all said, and a man with a cast in his eye got up slowly, grumbling, and turned towards the door.

"Here, dress yourself!"

"What, to take a ... to the doctor?"

He pulled his belt and gun off the rack with an ill-will and disappeared, buckling it on.

"You have Russians in cells, too?"

"Those who won't work, yes. On bread and water. That one has been on bread and water for five days. In my opinion he'll die."

"But why won't they work?"

"Work! He won't even clean his own cell out! They say it's because they are Bolshevists, but I don't know about that. I talk a little Russian, and I think they are convinced that if they make themselves at all useful to us we shall never send them home. Some of them think they are in Germany still. They're an ignorant lot."

An American came in rather hesitatingly, but without nodding to the French.

"We've got bacon-chips in our camp," he said, addressing Fanny directly. "I don't like to bring them in here, but if you'd just step across ... it isn't a stone's throw."

She did not like to desert the French, but she was sick with hunger, and rose. She knew she would have nothing from the guard-house meal, for they probably had the same ration as she—one piece of meat, two potatoes, and one sardine a man.

After all, food was more important than sentiment, and she followed him out of the hut.

"You won't get anything from those skinflints," said the American, "so we thought you'd better come and have some chips."

"Because they have nothing to give," she answered, half inclined to turn back. The American barracks were opposite, and in the yard, under a shelter of planks, the men were eating round a complicated travelling kitchen on wheels. "They have all the latest, richest things," thought Fanny, jealous for the French, antagonistic, yet hungry. But when she was among the Americans, they were simple and kind to her, offering her a great tray of fried bacon chips, concerned that she should have to eat them with her hand, washing out their tin mugs and filling them with coffee for her, making her sit on a barrel while she ate. "It's only that they are so different," she thought. "So different from the French that they can never meet without hurting and jarring each other."

Russians slouched about in the snow, washing the pans. When they had finished eating the Americans called to the Russians to eat what remained of the bacon chips. Watching them eat with the hunger of animals, they said:

"They starve them in the French barracks. We give them food here, or they'd sure die."

"They give them what they can in the French barracks; the soldiers don't get a ration like this, you know, even for themselves."

"Their fault for not kicking up a shindy," said the free-born Americans.
"We wouldn't stand it."

"You have no idea of poverty."

Food was even lying in the snow. A soldier cook thrust his head out of a hut, crying: "Any one want any more chips?"

She knew that it was probably true what the Frenchman had said, that the Americans shot the Russians as lightly as if they were sparrows. Yet here they wept over the French ration that kept the Russians hungry, though alive and well. What a curious mixture of sentiment and brutality they were....

She pulled out her cigarette case and offered a cigarette to a man standing near her. He took it and answered in a thick, lisping Jewish accent, soft and uniformed: "I don't smoke, ma'am. But I'll keep it as a souvenir give to me by the only lady I've seen in three months."

"That's really true? You haven't seen a woman for three months?"

"No, ma'am. Not a one. It must seem strange to you to hear us say that.
Just as though you were a zebra."

"There's some one over by your car," said the sentry, who had no idea of silence at his post. She got up quickly and flew back to the other barracks, jumping the deep pools of water and mud and the little heaps of soiled snow, started up the car and drove back to the *citadelle* for lunch.

At one-thirty they started out again, to chase over the grey downs in search of Russian camps folded away in small depressions and hollows, invisible from the main roads.

And thus, day after day, for five days, she drove him from morning to evening, from camp to camp around Verdun, until they had seen many thousands of Russians. Sometimes the French lieutenant came with them, and once or twice the Russian gravely invited him to sit in front with the driver. Then they would talk together a little in English, and once he said: "Would you like me to tell you something that will surprise you and interest me?"

She looked round.

"Your employer," he said, smiling gently over the expression, "is jealous of you."

She did not know what to make of this.

"He dislikes it intensely when you talk to the commandant of the *citadelle*."

"But...."

"He does not think you exclusive enough, considering you, as he does, as *his woman*."

"But, why...."

"Yes, of course! But you ought to realise that you are the only woman for miles around, and you belong to us!"

"You too?"

"Well, yes. I have something the same feeling. But his is stronger because his nature is Oriental. He thinks: 'This woman is a great curiosity, therefore a great treasure; and this treasure belongs to me. I brought her here, I am responsible for her, she obeys my orders.'"

"But does he tell you all this, or do you guess it?"

"We talk of this and that."

That night in the mess-room the Russian leant across the table to Fanny.

"What is man's mystery to a woman if she lives surrounded by him?"

"Oh, but that's not necessary ... mystery!"

"It *is* necessary to love."

"Colonel Dellahousse," explained the lieutenant, smiling very much, "does not believe that you can love what you know."

The Russian nodded. "Love is based on a fabulous belief. An illusory image which fills the eyes of people who are unused to each other. This poor lady will soon be used to everything."

Fanny, who felt momentarily alarmed, suddenly remembered Julien.

"When do we go back?" she asked absently.

The sympathetic eyes of the lieutenant seemed to understand even that, and he smiled again.

They left next day, after the midday meal.

Before lunch she met a soldier, who stopped her in one of the branching corridors.

"You are going," he said. "I have a little thing to ask."

She waited.

"Mademoiselle, it would not incommode you, it is such a little thing. Think! We have not seen a woman here so long."

Still she waited; and he muttered, already abashed:

"One kiss would not hurt you, mademoiselle."

"Let me pass...." she stammered to this member of the great "monastery."

He wavered and stood aside, and she went on up the corridor vaguely ashamed of her refusal.

* * * * *

"We go now," said the Russian, rising from the luncheon table. "Are you satisfied with your experience, mademoiselle?"

"My experience?"

"Verdun. This life is strange to you. I have seen you reflective. Now, if you will go out to the car you shall go back to your civilised town where the Governor so dislikes me, and you shall see your women friends again! But we are not coming all the way with you."

"No?"

"No, we stay at Briey. You return from Briey alone."

They set out once more upon the roads which ran between the dead violence of the plains—between trenches that wandered down from the side of a sandy hillock, by villages which appeared like an illusion upon the hillside, fading as they passed and reforming into the semblance of houses in the distance behind them.

The clouds above their heads were built up to a great height, rocky and cavernous; crows swung on outspread wings, dived and alighted heavily on the earth like fowls. They came behind the old German lines, and the road changing led them through short patches of covering woods filled with instruments. Depôt after depôt was piled between the trees and the notices hanging from the branches chattered antique directions at them. "The drinking trough—the drinking trough!" cried one, but they had no horse to water. "Take this path!" urged another, "for the...." but they flew by too fast to read the end of the message, while the path pursued them a little way among the pines, then turned abruptly away. "Do not smoke here ... *Nicht rauchen*," "NICHT RAUCHEN," "*Rauchen streng verboten*," cried the notices, in furious impotent voices. The wood chattered and spat with cries, with commands for which the men who made them cared no longer. The hungry noses of old guns snuffed at the car as it rolled by, guns dragging still upon their flanks the torn cloak of camouflage—small squat guns which stared idly into the air, or with wider mouths still, like petrified dogs for ever baying at the moon—long slim guns which lay along the grass and pushing under-growth—and one gun which had dipped forward and, fallen upon its knees, howled silenced imprecations at the devil in the centre of the earth.

When they had passed the shattered staging of the past they came out upon the country which had been occupied by Germans but not by war-fare. Here the fields, uncultivated, had grown wild, but round the sparse villages little patches of ground had been dug and sown. Not a cow grazed anywhere, not a sheep or a goat. No hens raced wildly across village streets. Far ahead on the white ribbon of road a black figure toiled in the gutter, and Fanny debated with herself: "Might I offer a lift?"

Looking ahead she saw no village or cottage within sight, and with a murmured apology to the Russian she pulled up beside the old woman whom she had overtaken.

"Where are you going?"

"To Briey."

"We, too. Get in, madame."

The Russian made no comment. The old crone, knuckled, hard-breathing, climbed in, holding uncertainly to the windscreen and pulling af-ter her her basket and umbrella.

"Cover yourself, madame," ordered Fanny, as to a child, and handed her a rug.

"I have never been in an auto before," whispered the old creature against a wind which made her breathless. "I have seen them pass."

"You are not afraid?"

"Oh, no!"

"Cover yourself well, well."

Gallant old women, toiling like ants upon the long stretches of road, who, suddenly finding themselves projected through the air at a pace they had never experienced in their lives before, would say not a word, though

the colour be whipped to their cheeks and their eyes rained tears until, clinging to the arm of the driver: "Stop here, mademoiselle!" they would whisper,
expecting the car to rear and stop dead at their own doorstep; and finding
themselves still carried on, and half believing themselves kidnapped: "Ah,
mademoiselle, stop, stop...."

They slipped down into the pit of Briey where the houses cling to the
sides of a circular hollow, and drew up by a white house which the Frenchman indicated.

The old woman searched, trembling and out of breath for her handkerchief, and wiped her streaming eyes; then, as she climbed out backwards,
with feet feeling for the ground—"What do I owe you, mademoiselle?"

"Ah, nothing, nothing."

"*Mais si*! I am not at all poor!" and leaving a twopence-halfpenny
piece on the seat, she hurried away.

Colonel Dellahousse came to the side of the car and thanked Fanny
ceremoniously. "And if I do not see you again, mademoiselle," he said, "remember what I say and go back to your home before the pleasure of life is
spoilt for you."

"Good-bye, good-bye," said the French lieutenant.

Soon after she had left Briey snow began to fall. A river circled at the
foot of a hill, and she followed its windings on a road which ran just above
it. Night wiped out the colours on the hills around her, until the moon rose
and they glowed again, half trees, half light. She climbed slowly up to a plateau not a dozen miles from Metz.

* * * * *

An hour later, the car put away in the garage, Fanny was tapping at
the window of the bath house in the town. The beautiful fat woman who
prepared the baths answered her tap. "Fräulein," said Fanny, "would it matter if I had a bath? Is it too late? I'll turn it on myself and dry it afterwards."

What did the woman mind if Fanny had a bath? Fat and beautiful,
she had nothing left to wish for, and contentedly she gave her the corner
room overlooking the canal and the theatre square, wishing her a good-night
full of German blessings. The water ran boiling out of the tap, and the
smoke curled up over the looking-glass and the window-sill.

When the bath was full to the brim she got in, lay back, and pulled
open the window with her toe. The beautiful French theatre, piebald with
snow and shadow, shone over the window-sill. The Cathedral clock struck
out ten chimes, whirling and singing over her head, the voices of the little
boys died down, the last had thrown his last snowball and gone to bed. The

steam rose up like a veil before the window, and once again, between the grey walls of her bath—so like her cradle and her coffin—she meditated upon the riches and treasure of the passing days.

"And yet," echoed the thoughts in that still water travelling still, "to travel is not to move across the earth."

Peering back into the past, frowning in the effort to string forgotten words together, Fanny whispered upon the surface of the water:

"The strange things of travel,
The East and the West,
The hill beyond the hill—"

But the poem was shattered as the voice of the bath woman called to her through the door.

"You are well, Fräulein?"

Fanny turned in her bath astonished. "Why, yes, thank you! Did you think
I was ill?"

"I didn't know. I daren't go to bed till I see you out, for last week we had a woman who killed herself in here, drowned in the water. I have just remembered her."

"Well, I won't drown myself."

"I can never be sure now. She gave me such shock."

"Well, I'm getting out," said Fanny.

"What?"

"I'm getting out. Listen!" And naked feet padded and splashed down upon the cork mat. "Now go to bed. I promise you I have no reason to drown myself."

VI. THE LOVER IN THE LAMP

"How do you know you will meet him?" said the cold morning light; and when she walked in it the city looked big enough to hide his face. In the first street a girl said the name of Julien without knowing what it was she said. But only a child shrieked in answer from a magic square of chalk upon the pavement.

"You've been away for days and days," said her companions at the garage, to show that they had noticed it. "Where have you been?"

The garage faded. "Verdun," she said; and Verdun lacy and perilous, hung in her mind.

"Whom did you take?"

She struggled with the confusing image of the Russian. Before she could reply the other said: "There's to be an inspection of the cars this morning. You'll have to get something done to your car!"

Outside in the yard the sun was gay upon the thinly frosted-stones, but in the shadow of the garage the glass and brass of seventy or eighty cars glowed in a veiled bloom of polish. Only the Rochet-Schneider, which had been to Verdun, stood unready for the inspection, coated from wheel to hood with white Meuse mud. There was nothing to be done with her until she had been under the hose.

Out in the street, where the hose was fastened to the hydrant, the little pests of Metz clustered eagerly, standing on the hose pipe where the bursts were tied with string, and by dexterous pressure diverting the leaks into gay fountains that flew up and pierced the windows opposite. As the mud rolled off under the blast of the hose and left the car streaky and dripping, the little boys dipping their feet into the gutters and paddled.

Soaked and bareheaded, Fanny drove the clean car slowly back into the garage and set her in her place in the long line.

Stewart, beside her, whispered, "They've come, they've come! They're starting at the other end. Four officers."

Fanny pulled her tin of English "Brasso" from a pocket-flap, and began to rub a lamp. At the far, far end of the long shed four men were standing with their backs to her, round a car. The globed lamp was tricky, and the chamois-leather would slip and let her bark her knuckle on the bracket. But the glow, born in the brass, grew clearer and clearer, till suddenly, stooping to it, she looked into a mirror and saw all the garage behind her and the long rows of cars bent in a yellow curve, and little men and oily women walking incredibly upon the rounded ball of the world. They hung with their feet on curving walls running and walking without difficulty, blinking, moving, talking in a yellow lake of brass.

Julien, Dennis and two others, stopping at car after car, came nearer and nearer. And Julien, holding the inspection, nodded gravely to their comments, searching car after car with his eyes as he walked up the garage, until they rested on the head and the hair of the girl he knew; then he paused, three cars from her, and watched the head as it hung motionless, level with the lamp she had just turned into a mirror.

And within the field of her vision he had just appeared. He paused, fantastic, upon the ball of the world, balanced amazingly with his feet on the slope of a golden corridor, and, hypnotised, she watched his face, bent into the horn of a young moon—Julien, and yet unearthly and impossible. There were his two hands, lit in a brassy fire, hanging down his sides, and the cane which he held in his left went out beyond the scope of the corridor. The three others hung around him like bent corn. She watched these yellow shades, as tall as ladders, talk and act in the little theatre of the lamp…. He was coming up to her, he became enormous, his head flew out of the top of the world, his feet ran down into the centre of the earth. He was effacing the garage, he had eaten up the corridor and all the cars. He must be touching her, he must have swallowed her too, his voice in her ear said: "You'd gone for ever…."

"I … I had gone?" She drew her gaze out of the mirror.

The world outside let him down again on to his feet, and he stood beside her and said gently in her ear: "Will you meet me again in the Cathedral at four to-day?" She nodded, and he turned away, and she saw that he was so unknown to her that she could hardly tell his uniformed back from the backs of those about him.

To meet this stranger then at four in the Cathedral she prepared herself with more care than she would have given to meet her oldest friend. The gilded day went by while she did little things with the holy air of a nun at her lamp—polishing her shoes, her belt, her cap badge, sitting on her bed beneath the stag's horn, an enraptured sailor upon the deck of the world. Around the old basin on the washstand faded blue animals chased each oth-

128

er and snapped at ferns and roses: she lifted the jug and drowned the beasts in water, and even to wash her hands was a rite which sent a shower of thoughts flying through her mind. How many before her had called this room a sanctuary, a temple, and prepared as carefully as she for some charmed meeting in the crannies of the town? This room? This "corridor." The passengers, travellers, soldiers, who had used this bed for a night and passed on, thought of it only as a segment in the endless chain of rooms that sheltered them. Bed, washstand, chair, table, rustled with history. Soldiers resting from the battle out there by Pont-à-Moussons, kissing the girl who lived in the back room, waking in the morning as darkly as she, leaving the room to another. Soldiers, new-fledged, coming up from Germany, trembling in the room as they heard the thunder out at Pont-à-Moussons. An officer—that ugly, wooden boy who stared at her from the wall above the mantelpiece. (What a mark he had left on the household that they should frame him in velvet and keep him staring at his own bed for ever!) She all but saw spirits—and shivered at the procession of life. Outside in the street she heard a cry, and her name called under the window. How like the cry that afternoon a week ago which had sent her to Verdun! Standing in the shadow of the curtain she peered cautiously out.

At sight of her, a voice cried up from the street: "There is a fancy dress dance next Tuesday night! I'm warning every one; it's so hard to get stuffs." The voice passed on to the house where Stewart lived.

("How nice of her!") This was a good day. ("What shall I wear at the dance?") There, about the face of the clock, windless and steady, hung the hours. Not yet time to start, not yet.

Through the lace of the curtain and the now closed window, the shadows hurried by upon the pavement, heads bobbed below upon the street.

Oh Dark, and Pale, and Plain, walking soberly in hat and coat, what sign in these faces of the silver webbery within the brain, of the flashing fancies and merry plans, like birds gone mad in a cage! The tram, as antique as a sedan chair, clanked across the bridge over the river, and changing its note as it reached firmer land, roared and bumbled like a huge bee into the little street. Stopping below her window it was assailed by little creatures who threw themselves as greedily within as if they were setting out upon a wild adventure.

"All going to meet somebody," said Fanny, whose mind, drowned in her happiness, took the narrowest view of life. But for all their push and hurry the little creatures in the glass cage were forced to unfold their newspapers and stare at each other for occupation while the all-powerful driver and *Wattmann*, climbing down from the opposite ends of the car, conferred together in the street. "It's waiting for the other tram!" And even as she said it, she found the clock behind her back had leapt mysteriously and slyly forward. "I'll take the other...." And, going downstairs, she stood in the shelter of her doorway, out of the cold wind that blew along the street. The delay of the other car brought her well up to her hour. "I'll even be a little late," she thought, proud of herself.

"Don't talk to the *Wattmann*," said the notices in the tramcar crossly to her in German as she slipped and slid upon its straining seats. "Don't spit, don't smoke ... don't...." But she had her revenge, for across all the notices *her* side of the war had written coldly: "You are begged, in the measure possible to you, to talk only French."

When they got into the narrow town the tramcar, mysteriously swelling, seemed to chip the shop windows and bump the front doors, and people upon the pavement scrambled between the glass of the tram and the glass of the big drapery shop.

They met, as it were, in the very centre of a conversation. "I never know where you are," he complained, as though this trouble was so in his thoughts that he must speak of it at once, "or when I shall see you again." She smiled radiantly, busier with greeting, less absorbed than he.

"You may go away and never come back. You go so far."

She went away often and far. But that was his trouble, not hers. He, at least, remained stationary in Metz. She was full of another thought—the vagueness, the precariousness of the chance that even in Metz had brought them together.

"How lucky...."

"How lucky what?"

How lucky? How lucky? He begged, implored, frowned, tried to peer. He would not let her rest. "Why should you hide what you think? I don't like it."

Oh, no, he did not like it. No one likes to get hint of that fountain of talk which, sweet or bitter, plays just out of reach of the ear, just behind the mask of the face.

"How lucky that you held the inspection!" had all but stolen from her lips. But this implied too clearly that it was lucky for somebody—for her, for him. And how could she say that? Her thoughts were so far in advance of her confessions. A dozen sentences rose to her lips, all too clear, too intimate. So she became silent before the things that she could not say.

"Of what are you thinking?"

Extortionate question. ("Am I to put all my fortune in your hand like that? Am I to say, 'Of you, of you'?") For every word she said aloud she said a hundred to herself; and after three words between them she had the impression of a whole conversation.

"One must arrange some plan," he said, pursuing his perplexity, "so that I know when you go, and when you come back. I can't always be holding inspections to find out."

"It was for that *that* you held the inspection?"

"Why, of course, of course!"

"But entirely to find out?" (divided between the desire to make him say it again and the fear of driving his motives into daylight).

"I didn't know what to do. I couldn't telephone and ask whether your car had returned."

Wonderful and excellent! She had had the notion while she was at Verdun that something might be rolling up to her account in the bank at Metz, and now he was giving her proof after proof of the accumulation.

But from the valley of vanity she suddenly flew up to wonder. "He does that for me!" looking at herself in the mirror of her mind. "He does it for me!" But of what use to look at the daylight image of herself—the khaki figure, the driver? "For he must be looking at glory as I do." The Russian said: "Love is an illusory image." "Isn't it strange how these human creatures can cast it like a net out of their personality?..." Vanity, creeping above love, beat it down like a stick beats down a fire; it was too easy to-day; he gave her nothing left to wish for; the spell over him, she felt, was complete, and now she had nothing else to do but develop her own. And this she had instantly less inclination to do. But, guided by his bright wits, he too withdrew, let the tacit assumption of intimacy drop between them, and their walk by the Moselle was filled by her talk of the Russian prisoners and Verdun.

She glanced at him from time to time, and would have grown more silent, but by his light questions he kept her talking briskly on, offering her no new proof, until she grew unsure and wondered whether she had been mistaken; and, the hour striking for her supper in the town, she went to it, filled anew with his charm and her anxiety. Other meetings came, when, thrilling with the see-saw of belief and doubt, they watched each other with absorbed attention, and in their fragile and unconfessed relationship sometimes one was the victor and sometimes the vanquished. Yet what was plain to the man who swept the mud from the streets was not plain to them.

"Does he love me already?"

"Will she love me soon?"

131

When they saw other couples by the banks of the Moselle, Reason in a convinced and careless voice said: "That is love!" But on coming towards each other they were not sure at all, and each said of the other: "To-morrow he may not meet me...." "To-morrow she will say she is busy and it will not be true!"

When Fanny said, "He may not meet me," she was mad. How could he fail to meet her when the rolling hours hung fire and buzzed about his head like loaded bees, unable to proceed; when in a lethargy of vision he signed his name at the bottom of the typewritten sheet, saying confusedly, "What does she think? Does she think of me?"

When at last they met under the shadow of the Cathedral they would exclaim in their hearts: "What next?" and hurry off by the Moselle, looking into the future, looking into the future, and yet warding it off, aware of the open speech that must soon lie between them, and yet charmed by the beautiful, the merciful, the delay. And going home, each would study the hours they had spent together, as a traveller returned from wonderful lands pores over the cold map which for him sparkles with mountains and rivers.

That very Saturday night after the early supper in their room in the town, she had gone out to the big draper's shop which did not close till seven, almost running into Reherrey on the pavement.

"I'm going to Weile," he said.

"I'm going there myself."

"To get your dress?"

"Yes."

They went into the large, empty shop together, to be surrounded at once by a group of idle girls.

"Stuffs ..." said Fanny, thinking vaguely.

"Black bombazine," said Reherrey, who had finished his thinking.

Fanny followed Reherrey to a newly-polished counter, backed by rows of empty shelves. They had no black bombazine.

"Black tulle," said Reherrey, with his air of cool indifference, "black gauze, black cotton..."

It had to be black sateen in the end. "Now you!" said Reherrey, when he had bought six yards at eight francs a yard.

"White ... something ... for me."

There was white nothing under sixteen francs a yard. "But cheap, cheap, CHEAP stuff," she expostulated—"stuff you would make lampshades of, or dusters. It's only for a fancy dress." The idle little girls assumed a special air. Fanny looked round the shop in desperation. It was like all the shops in Metz—the window dressed, the saleswomen ready, the shelves scrubbed out and polished, the lady waiting at the pay desk—but the goods hadn't come!

Here and there a shelf held a roll or two of some material, and eventually Fanny bought seven yards of white soft stuff at seven francs a yard.

"White," said Reherrey, with a critical look; "how *English*!"

Fanny had an idea of her own.

"*Wo*," she said heavily to Elsa's mother still later in the evening, "*ist eine Schneiderin?*"

"A dressmaker who speaks French...."

Elsa took her out into the dark street again, and in at a neighbouring archway, till at the back of deep courtyards they found a tiny flat of a little old lady. "Like this," explained Fanny, drawing with her pencil.

"Why, my mother had a dress like that!" said the little lady, pleased. "Before the last war." She nodded many times. "I know how to make a crinoline. But when do you want it?"

"For Tuesday night."

"Ah, dear mademoiselle! How can I! To-day is Saturday. I have only to-day and Monday. Unless.... Are you a Catholic?"

"No."

"Then you can sew on Sunday. You can do the frills."

All Sunday Fanny sewed frills under the stag's horn, and when she went to meet Julien in the late afternoon, she had the frills still in a parcel. "What is that?" he asked, as she unfolded the parcel in the empty Cathedral, and began to thread her needle.

"My dress for the dance."

"What is it going to be?"

"Frills. Hundreds of frills." She shook her lap a little, and yards and yards of white frills leapt on to the floor in a river.

"Those flowers you bought, look, you have never put them in water!"

He shook his head, and leaning from his chair, stretched out his arm for the parcel of white paper. "They are dying. Smell them! They yield more scent when they die." She sat holding the flowers near her face, and not thinking of him very distinctly, but not thinking of anything else.

"But they won't last."

"They will last this visit. I'll get new ones."

"Oh, how extravagant you are with happiness!..."

They looked startled and became silent. For every now and then among their talk some sentence which they had thought discreet rang out with a clarity which disturbed them.

Between them there had been no avowal, and neither could count on the other's secret. She was not sure he loved her; and though he argued, "Why should she come if she does not care?" he watched her sit by him with as little confidence, with as much despair, as if she sat on the other side of the Atlantic Ocean. "Is it raining again? How dark it gets. I must soon go." She made gaps in and scattered that alarming silence in which the image of each filled and fitted into the thoughts of the other like an orange into its close rind. Yet so dark and perfect is the mask of the face, so dull the inner ear, that each looked uncertainly about, half deaf to the song which issued so plainly from the other, distracted by the great gaps in the music.

"Won't you stay with me till you have sewn to the end of that frill?"

She sat down again without a word. And, greedy after his victory, he added: "But I oughtn't to keep you?"

"I want to stay, too."

The frill flowed on with the beat of the Cathedral clock, and came to an end.

"Now I must go. It's supper—supper in the garage."

He walked with her almost in silence down the Cathedral steps and to the door of the house in the dark street by the river.

"You do say good-bye so curiously," he remarked, "so suddenly. Perhaps it's English."

"Perhaps it is," she agreed, disappearing into the house.

"What have you got there?" said her companions in the lighted room upstairs.

"My dress for the dance." But she did not open the parcel to show them the charmed frills. ("How is it they don't know that I left him in the street below?") She looked at the seven travellers who met each night round the table for dinner, overcome with the mystery of those uncommunicating, shrouded heads. "What have they all been doing?"

"Has every one had runs?"

"Yes, every one has been out. What have you been doing?"

"I haven't left Metz to-day," she replied, giddy with the isolation and the silence of the human mind.

VII. THE THREE "CLIENTS"

"What!" cried Fanny on Monday morning, staring at the brigadier and at the pink paper he offered her.

"At once, at once, mademoiselle. You ought to have been told last night. You must go back for your things for the night and then as quickly as you can to the Hôtel de l'Europe. I don't know how many days you'll be, but here is an order for fifty litres of petrol and a can of oil, and Pichot is getting you two spare tubes...."

She stared at him in horror a moment longer, then took the pink order and disappeared through the dark garage door. Her mind was in a frenzy of protestation. She saw the waiting cars which might have gone instead, the drivers polishing a patch of brass for want of something to do, and accident, pure accident, had lighted on *her*, to sweep *her* out of Metz, away from that luminous personality which brooded over the city like a sunset, out into the nondescript world, the cold *Anywhere*. White frills and yards of bleached calico lying at the dressmaker's cried out to her to stay, to make some protest, to say something, anything—that she was ill—and stay.

She splashed petrol wastefully into the tank, holding the small blue tin with firm hands high in the air above the leather strainer and the funnel.

"And if I said—(it is mad)—if I said, 'I am in love. *I can't go*. Send some one who is not in love!'" She glanced down from her perch on the footboard at the olive profile bent over the next car. The driver was sitting on his step with his open hand outstretched to hold a dozen bright washers which he was stirring with his forefinger. The hand with the washers sank gently to rest on his knee, and he sighed as he ceased stirring, and looked absently down the garage, his mystical cloak of bone and skin shrouding his thoughts. Idle men all down the garage hung about the cars, each holding within him some private affection, some close hope, something which sent a spurt of dubious song out of his mouth, or his eyes, wandering sightless, down the shed.

The tank, resenting her treatment, overflowed violently and drenched her skirt and feet.

"Are you ready, mademoiselle?"

"Coming. Where are the tubes?"

"I have them."

She drove through the yard, down the street, and hurried over the bridge to her room. Nightgown, toothbrush, comb, sponge, and powder—hating every hour of the days and nights her preparations meant.

At the Hôtel de l'Europe, three men waited for her with frowns, loaded with plaid rugs, mufflers, black bags, and gaping baskets of food, from which protruded bottles of wine. It was, then, to be one of those days when they lunched by the wayside in the bitter cold.

She drew up beside them. A huge man with an unclean bearskin coat and flaccid red cheeks told her she was very late. She listened, apologising, but intent only on her question.

"And could you tell me—(I'm so dreadfully sorry, but they only told me very late at the garage)—and would you mind telling me which day you expect to get back?"

He turned to the others.

"It depends," said a dry, dark man with a look of rebuke, "on our work.
To-morrow night, perhaps. Perhaps the next morning."

"Where shall I drive you?"

"Go out by Thionville. We are going up the Moselle to Trèves."

Anxious to dispose of such a mountain of a man, it was suggested that the Bearskin should climb in beside the driver. Instantly Fanny was smothered up as he sat down, placing so many packages between himself and the outer side of the car that he sank heavily against her arm, and the fur of his coat blew into her mouth.

In discomfort she drove them from the town, brooding over her wheel, unhappily on and on till Metz had sunk over the edge of the flat horizon. The weary way to Thionville unfurled before them, furnaces to the left and flat grass prairie to the right—little villages and clustering houses went by them, and Thionville itself, with its tramlines and faint air of Manchester, drew near. Beyond Thionville the road changed colour abruptly, and stretched red and gravelly before them. The frost deepened, the wheels bit harder on the road surface, the grass-fields sparkled with a brittle light, and scanty winter orchards sprang up beside the road, which narrowed down and became a lane of beautiful surface. Not for long, however, for the surface changed again, and long hours set in when the car had to be held desperately with foot and hand brake to save the springs, and the accelerator could only be touched to be relinquished.

Fanny, hardly sad any more, but busy and hungry, secretly lifted the corner of her sleeve to peer at her wrist-watch, and seeing that it was half-past twelve, began to wonder how soon they would decide to sit down by the roadside for their lunch. She fumbled in the pocket of the car, but the last piece of chocolate had either been eaten or had slipped down between the leather and the wood. She could bring up nothing better than an old postcard, a hairpin, and a forgotten scrap of chamois-leather.

At last they stopped for lunch, choosing a spot where a hedge rose wirily against the midday sky, and spread the rugs on the frozen grass. The sudden cessation of movement and noise brought a stillness into the landscape; a child's voice startled them from the outskirts of a village beyond, and the crackle of a wheelbarrow that was being driven along the dry road.

The third man, who had blackberry eyes, and glasses which enlarged them, made great preparations over the setting of the meal. They had forgotten nothing. When they sat down, the Bearskin upon the step of the motor, the others cross-legged upon the ground, each man had a napkin as big as a sheet spread across the surface of his coat and waistcoat, and tied into the band of the overcoat at the side. Bottles of red wine, and a bottle of white to finish with, lay on a cloth spread upon the grass. Bread, cheese, sausage, *pâté*, and a slab of chocolate; knives, forks and a china cup apiece. Fanny, who had taken her own uneatable lunch from the garage, was made to eat some of theirs. They were on a high, dry, open plateau of land, and the winter sun, not strong enough to break the frost, faintly warmed their necks and hands and the round bodies of the bottles.

It was not unpleasant sitting there with the three white-chested strangers, watching the sky through the prongs of the bare hedge, spreading *pâté* on to fresh bread, and balancing her cup half full of red wine among the fibres and roots of the grass.

"Now that I have started I am well on my way to getting back," she thought, and found that within her breast the black despair of the morning had melted. She watched her companions for amusement.

The Bearskin, cumbrous, high-coloured, and blue-eyed, looked like an innkeeper in an English tavern. When he took off his cloth hood she thought she had never seen anything so staring as the pink of his face against the blue of his cap; but when the cap came off too for a second that he might stir his forehead with his finger, the blaze and crackle of his red hair beneath was even more ferocious. Yet he seemed intimidated by his companions, and kept silence, eating meekly from his knife, and spreading his napkin with care to the edge of his knees.

The little man with warm black eyes and the colder, thinner man talked appreciatively together.

"*Hé!* The *pâté* is not bad."

"Not bad at all. And you haven't tried the cheese?"

"No, no. I never touch cheese before the wine; it's a sin. Now the bottle is all warmed. Try some."

"What is your father?" said the little man suddenly to Fanny.

"He is in the army."

"You have no brother—no one to take care of you?"

"You mean, because I come out here? But in England they don't mind; they think it interesting for us."

"Tiens!"

They obviously did not believe her, and turned to other subjects. But the Bearskin began to move uncomfortably on the step of the car, and, bending forward to attract their attention, he burst out:

"But, don't you know, mademoiselle is not paid!"

The others reconsidered her.

"How do you live then, mademoiselle? You have means of your own? You do not buy your clothes yourself? Your Government gives you those, and that fine leather coat?"

"I bought it myself," said Fanny, and caused a sensation.

Immediately they put out their delicate hands, and fingers that loved to appraise, to feel the leather on the lapel.

"How soft! We have no leather now like that in France! How much did that cost? No, let me guess! You never paid a sou less than—Well, how much?"

The Bearskin, who had sat beside her all the morning, and had now turned her into an object of interest, took a pride in Fanny.

"The English upbringing is very interesting," he said, pushing back his cap and letting out the flame of his hair. "The young ladies become very serious. I have been in England. I have been in Balham."

But though, owing to the leather coat, the others seemed to consider that they had an heiress amongst them, they would not let the big Bearskin be her *impresario* or their instructor.

"Divorce is very easy in England," said the thin man solemnly, and turned his shoulder slightly on the Bearskin, as though he blamed him for his stay in Balham.

When the lunch was over and the last fragment of *pâté* drawn off the last knife upon the crust of bread that remained, Fanny's restless hopes turned towards packing up; but she counted without the white wine and the national repose after the midday meal. They washed their cups with care under the outlet tap of the radiator, and, wiping them dry to the last corner, sat back under the hedge to drink slowly.

All this time a peculiar quality had been drawing across the sun. It grew redder and duller, till, blushing, it died out, and Fanny saw that the morning frost had disappeared. Out to the left a mauve bank of cloud moved up across the sky like the smoke from a titanic bonfire, and, with the first drift of moisture towards them, the four shivered and rose simultaneously to pack the things and put them in the car.

As Fanny stooped to wind up the handle the first snowflake, soft and wet and heavy, melted on her ear.

"It won't lie," said the Bearskin. "Shall we draw up the hood?"

They drew it up, but the thin man, huddling himself in the corner of the back seat, insisted on "side-curtains as well."

"Then I'm sorry. Will you get out? They are under the seat."

"Oh, never mind, my dear fellow," said Blackberry-Eyes.

"No, no. One ought to keep the warmth of food within one."

And the other got out, and stood shivering while the Bearskin and Fanny pulled rugs and baskets and cushions out into the road that they might lift the back seat and find the curtains.

"Oh, how torn!" exclaimed the thin man bitterly, as he saw her drape the car with leather curtains whose windows of mica had long since been cracked and torn away. The snow was hissing on the radiator and melting on the road, and there seemed no wind left anywhere to drive the weight of the mauve cloud further across the sky. It hung solid and low above them, so that between the surface of the earth and the floor of the sky there was only a foggy tunnel in which the road could be seen a few yards ahead.

As they drove forward the windscreen became filmed with melting snow. Fanny unscrewed it and tilted it open, and the Bearskin fumbled unhappily at his collar to close every chink and cranny in his mossy hide.

They were climbing higher and higher across an endless plateau, and at last a voice called from the back, "We must look at the map." It was a

139

voice of doubt and distrust that any road could be right road which held so much discomfort.

Fanny stopped and pulled her map from behind her back, where she was keeping it dry. "It's all right," she showed them, leaning over the back and holding the map towards them. Then she discovered that the back seat was empty, and her clients were huddled among the petrol tins and rugs upon the floor.

"You must be miserable! It's so much colder in the back. See, here's the big road that we must avoid, going off into Luxembourg, and here's ours, running downhill in another mile."

They believed her, being too cramped and miserable to take more than a querulous interest. In another half-hour the snow ceased, and as they glided down the long hill on the other side of the plateau in a bed of fresh, unruffled wool, the sun struck out with a suddenness that seemed to tear the sky in two, and turned the blue snow into a sheet of light which stretched far below them into a country of pine woods and pits of shadow. Down, down they ran, till just below lay a village—if village it was when only a house or two were gathered together for company in the forest.

The snow seemed to have lain here for days, for the car slipped and skidded at the steep entrance, where the boys of the village had made slides for their toboggans. A hundred feet from the first house a triumphal arch was built of pine and laurel across the road. On it was written in white letters "Soyez le Bienvenu." All the white poor houses glittered in the snow with flags.

A stream crossed the village street, and a file of geese on its narrow bridge brought her to a standstill.

"What are the flags for?" she asked of an old man, pressing back into a safety alcove in the stone wall of the bridge.

"We expect Pétain here to-day. He is coming to Thionville."

"But Thionville is forty miles away—"

"Still, he might pass here—"

Running on and on through forest and hilly country, they left the snow behind them, and slipped down into greener valleys, till at last they came upon a single American sentry, and over his head was chalked upon a board: "This is Germany."

They pulled up. Germany it might be—but the road to Tréves? He did not know; he knew nothing, except that with his left foot he stood in Germany, and with his right in France.

VIII. GERMANY

Over the side of the next mountain all Hans Andersen was stretched before them—tracts of little country, little wooden houses with pointed roofs, little hills covered with squares of different coloured woods, and a blue river at the bottom of the valley, white with geese upon its banks. They held their open mouths insultedly in the air as the motor passed. The narrow road became like marble, and the car hissed like a glass ball rolled on a stone step. On every little hill stood a castle made of brown chocolate, very small, but complete with turrets. Young horses with fat stomachs and arched necks bolted sideways off the road in fear, followed by gaily painted lattice-work carts, and plunged far into the grassland at the side. Old women with coloured hoods swore at them, and pulled the reins. Many pointed hills were grey with vine-sticks, and on the crest of each of these stood a small chapel as if to bless the wine. The countryside was wet and fresh—white, hardly yellow—with the winter sun; moss by the roadside still dripped from the night, and small bare orchard trees stood in brilliant grass."Look! How the grass grows in Germany!"

"Ah, it doesn't grow like that in the valley of the Meuse—"

Every cottage in every village was different; many wore hats instead of roofs, wooden things like steeples, with deep eaves and carved fringes, in which were shadowy windows like old eyes. Some were pink and some were yellow.

Soon they left the woods and came out upon an open plateau surrounded by wavy hills with castles on them. In the middle of the plateau was a Zeppelin shed which looked like the work of bigger men than the crawling peasants in the roads. One side of the shed was open, and the strange predatory bird within, insensible to the peering eye of an enemy, seemed lost in thought in this green valley. The camp of huts beside it was deserted, and there seemed to exist no hand to close the house door. They rose again on to a hillside, and on every horizon shone a far blue forest faint like sea or cloud.

Nearer Tréves the villages were filled with Americans—Americans mending the already perfect roads, and playing with the children.

"This is a topsy-turvy country, as it would be in Hans Andersen," thought Fanny. "I thought the Germans had to mend the broken roads in France!"

They stayed that night in the Porta-Nigra hotel, which had been turned
into an Allied hostel. The mess downstairs was chiefly filled with American officers, though a few Frenchmen sat together in one corner. The food was American—corn cakes, syrup, and white, flaky bread.

"Well, what bread! It's like cake!"

"Oh, the Americans eat well!"

"I don't agree with you. They put money into their food, and they eat a lot of it, but they can't cook.

"Isn't it astonishing what they eat! It's astonishing what all the armies eat compared with our soldiers."

"Now this cake-bread! I should soon sicken of it. But *they* will eat sweets and such things all day long."

"Well, I told you they are children!"

"The Americans here seem different. They behave better than those in
France."

"These are very *chics types*. Pershing is here. This is the Headquarters Staff."

"Yes, one can see they are different."

"It appears they get on very well with the Germans."

"Hsh—not so loud."

After dinner they strolled out into the town. The Bearskin was very anxious to get a "genuine iron cross."

He was offered iron crosses worked on matchboxes, on cigarette lighters, on ladies' chains.

"But are they genuine?"

He did not know quite what he meant.

"I don't suppose them to be taken from a dead man's neck, but are they genuine?"

In the streets the Germans sold iron crosses from job lots on barrows for ten francs each.

"But I will get one cheaper!" said the Bearskin, and clambered up the steps into shop after shop. He found an iron cross on a chain for seven francs. No one knew what the mark was worth, and the three men, with the German salesman, bent over the counter adding and subtracting on paper.

"How can a goblin countryside breed people who sell iron crosses at ten francs each?" wondered Fanny.

There was a notice on the other side of the street, "Y.M.C.A., two doors down the street on your left," and the thin man stood in the door of the shop beside Fanny and pointed to it.

"Couldn't you go there and get me cigars? They will be very cheap. Have you money with you?"

"I'll try," said Fanny, "I've money. We can settle afterwards," inwardly resolving to get as many cigarettes as she could to take back for the men in the garage. She crossed the street, but looked back to find the thin man creeping after her. She waited for him, irritated.

"Go back. If the American salesman sees you he'll know it's for the French, and he won't sell."

"Tiens?"

"He knew that quite well," she thought impatiently to herself, "or he wouldn't have asked me to buy for him."

The thin man turned back to the cover of the shop like an eager little dog which has jumped too quickly for biscuit and been snubbed.

She went down the street and into the Y.M.C.A.

Instantly she was among three or four hundred men, who stood with their backs to her, in queues up the long wooden hall. Far ahead on the improvised counter was a *guichet* marked "Cigars." She placed herself at the tail of that queue.

"Move up, lady," said the man in front of her, moving her forward. "Say here's a lady. Move her up."

Men from the other queues looked round, and one or two whistled slyly beneath their breath, but her own queue adopted her protectingly, and moved her up to their head, against the counter.

It was out of the question to get cigars now. She had become a guest, and to get cigars would imply that she was not buying for herself, but to supply an unknown man without. And the marks on her uniform showed that the unknown was French.

"One carton of Camels, please," she said, used to the phraseology.

"Take two if you like," said the salesman. "We've just got a dump in."

She took two long cardboard packets of cigarettes, and put down ten francs.

143

"Only marks taken here," said the salesman. "You got to make the change as you come in."

"Oh, well—I'll—"

"Put it down. Put it here. We don't get a lady in every day."

He gave her the change in marks, which seemed countless.

"I'm sure you've given me too much!"

"Oh no. Marks is goin' just for love in this country. Makes you feel rich!"

As she emerged from the hall with her two long cartons under her arm she found the thin man, the Bearskin and Blackberry-Eyes standing like children on the doorstep.

It was too much—to give her away like that.

Other Americans, coming out, looked at them as a gentleman coming out of his own house might look at a party of penguins on his doorstep.

Fanny swept past her friends without a glance and walked on up the street with her head in the air. They turned and came after her guiltily. When they caught her up in the next street, she said to the thin man, "I asked you not to come near while I was buying—"

"Have you got cigars, mademoiselle?"

"No, I couldn't. Why did you come like that? Now I can go in no more.
You'd only to wait two minutes."

They looked crestfallen, while she held the cigarettes away from them as a nurse holds sweets from a naughty child.

"I could only get two packets. I can give you one. I'm sorry, but I promised to get cigarettes for some people in Metz."

The thin man brightened, and took the big carton of Camels with delight.

"They're good, those!" he said knowingly to the others. "How much were they, mademoiselle?"

"Five francs twenty the carton."

"Is it possible? And we have to pay...."

By his tone he made it seem a reflection on the Americans. Why should a country be so rich when his had been devastated, so thinned, so difficult to live in? Fanny thought of the poor huddled clients who had sat on the floor of the car during the snowstorm. It had been a bitter journey for them.

144

After all—those rich, those pink and happy Americans, leather-coated down to the humblest private, pockets full of money, and fat meals three times a day to keep their spirits up—why shouldn't they let him have their cigarettes?

"You can have this carton, too, if you like," she said, offering it. "I'll manage to slip in to-morrow morning."

He thanked her, delighted, and they went back to the hotel.

The problem of the kindness of the Americans, and her frequent abuse of it to benefit the French, puzzled her.

"But, after all, it's very easy to be kind. It's much easier to be kind if you are American and pink than if you are French and anxious."

Another difference between the two nations struck her.

"The Americans treat me as if I were an amusing child. The French, no matter how peculiar their advances, always, always as a woman."

Next morning, when she got down to breakfast at eight, she found that the three Frenchmen had already gone out about their work.

"Perhaps I shall get home to-night, after all," she prayed. She sat in the hotel and watched the Americans, or wandered about the little town until eleven. The affair with the cigars was suitably arranged. The hall was nearly empty when she went in, and the few men who stood about in it did not disarm her with special kindness. On getting back to the hotel she found the Bearskin pushing breathlessly and anxiously through the glass doors.

"Monsieur Raudel has left his cigarettes in his bedroom," he said, "unlocked up. He is anxious so I have come back."

"Well, tell him that if he—tell him quite as a joke, you know—that if I can get home—"

(Something in his little blue eye shone sympathetically, and she leant towards him.) "Well, I'll tell *you*! There is a dance to-night in Metz, and I am asked. And tell him that I have bought two boxes of cigars for him!"

The Bearskin, enchanted, promised to do his best.

By half-past twelve the three were back at lunch in the hotel. Over the coffee Monsieur Raudel looked reflectively at his well-shaped nails.

"Well, mademoiselle, so this is what it is to have a woman chauffeur—"

Fanny looked up nervously, regretting her confidence in the Bearskin.

"Apart from the pleasure of your company with us, we get cheap cigars, and you get your dance, so every one is pleased."

"Oh!" She was radiant. "But you haven't hurried too much? Are we really starting back?"

Monsieur Raudel, who was a new man when he wasn't cold, reassured her, and soon they were all packed in the Renault, and running out of Tréves.

IX. THE CRINOLINE

That same night as dusk fell she shook the snow from her feet and clothes and entered the dressmaker's kitchen. Four candles were burning beside the gas, and the tea-cups lay heaped and unwashed upon the dresser."Good-evening, good-evening," murmured a number of voices, German and French, and the old dressmaker, standing up, her face haggard under the gas, took both Fanny's hands with a whimper:

"It will never be done! Oh, dear child, it will *never* be done!"

The crinoline which they were preparing lay in white rags upon the table.

"Oh, Elsa, that is good! Are you helping too?" Elsa had brought three of her friends with her, and the four bright, bullety heads bent over the long frills which moved slowly through their sewing fingers. "*Good* Conquered Children!" They were sewing like little machines.

"The Fräulein Schneiderin," explained Elsa, "is so upset."

And this was evident and needed no explaining. The little lady twisted her fingers, grieved and scolded, snatching at this and that, and rapping with her scissors upon the table as though she were going to wear the dress herself.

"Mademoiselle, I had to get them." She nodded towards the busy Conquered Children, apologising for them as though she feared Fanny might think she had done a deal with the devil for her sake.

"Here are my frills," said Fanny, bringing from her pocket two paper parcels, one of which she laid in mystery upon the table, the other opened and shook out her two long frills. She drew off her leather coat and sat down to sew.

"Oh, how calm you are!" burst out the dressmaker. "How can you be so calm? It won't be finished."

"Yes, yes, yes. It's only half-past five. Can I have a needle?"

"My mother had a dress like this before the last war." (This for the fiftieth time.) "And will your *amoureux* be there?" she asked with the licence of the old.

"Well, yes," said Fanny smiling, "he will."

"And what will he wear?"

"Oh, it's a secret. I don't know. But I chose this particular dress because it is so feminine, and it will be the first time he has seen me in the clothes of a woman."

"Children, hurry, hurry!" cried the dressmaker, in a frenzy of sympathy. "Minette, get down!" She slapped the grey cat tenderly as she lifted him off the table. "Tell them in their language to hurry!" she exclaimed. "*I* never learnt it!"

But, after the breath of excitement, followed her poor despair, and she dropped her hands in her lap. "It will never be done. I can't do it."

"Look, my dear, courage! The bodice is already done ... Have you had any tea?"

"The children ate. I couldn't. I am too excited. But you are so calm. You have no nerves. It isn't natural!"

Yet she ate a little piece of cake, scolding the cat and the children with her mouth full, prowling restlessly above their bent heads as they sewed and solidly sewed.

At the end of an hour and a half the nine frills were on the skirt, the long hoops of wire had been run in, and the hooks and eyes on the belt.

Often the door opened and shut; visitors came and went in the room; the milk woman put her head in, crying: "What a party!" and left the tiny can of milk upon the floor: Elsa's mother came to call her daughter to supper, but let her stay when she saw the dress still unfinished. Now and then some one would run out of the flat opposite, the flat above or the flat next door and, popping a head in at the door, wish them good luck. All the building seemed to know of the crinoline that was being made in the kitchen.

"You do not smoke a pipe?..." said the dressmaker softly, with appreciation.

"But none of us do!"

"Oh, pardon, yes! I saw it yesterday. A great big girl dressed like you with her hands in her pockets and a pipe in her mouth. It made an effect on me—you can hardly believe how it startled me! I called Madame Coppet to see."

"I know it wasn't one of us. And (it seems rude of me to say so) I even think the woman you saw was French."

"Oh, my dear, French women never do that!"

"Well, they do when they get free. They go beyond us in freedom when they get it The woman you saw (I have seen her, too) works with the men, shoulder to shoulder, eats with them, smokes with them, drinks with them, drives all night and all day, and they say she can change a tyre in two minutes.

"There was a woman, too, who drove a lorry between Verdun and Bar-le-Duc, not a tender, you know, but a big lorry. She wore a bit of old ermine round her neck, knickerbockers, and yellow check stockings. One could imagine she had painted her face by the light of a candle at four in the morning. She never wore a hat, and her short yellow hair stuck out over her face which was as bright as a pink lamp shade."

"Terrible."

"She may have been, but she worked hard! She was always on that road. Or she would disappear for days with her lorry and come back caked in rouge and mud. I wish I could have got to know her and heard where she went and the things that happened to her."

"But, my dear, I keep thinking what a strange life it is for you. Are you always alone on your car?"

"Always alone."

"You are with men alone then all the time?"

"All the time."

"Well, it's more than I can understand. It's part of the war."

Elsa bent across the table and picked up the folded bodice, murmuring that it was done. The dressmaker rose, and reaching for the hooped skirt, held it up between her two arms. It was a thrilling moment. Fanny, too, rose. "Put it on a dummy," she commanded. Candles were placed around the dummy, who seemed to step forward out of the shades of the kitchen, and offer its headless body to be hooked and buttoned into the dress. All the room stood back to look and admire. "Wie schön!" said Elsa's shiny-headed friends, peering with their mouths open.

"Ah, dear child, you were so calm, and now it is done!" said the old dressmaker.

The dress stood stiffly glittering at them, white as snow, the nine frills pricking away from the great hooped skirt.

Fanny picked up the brown paper parcel she had laid on the dresser, taking from it a bottle of blue ink, a bottle of green, and a paint brush, and diluted the inks in a saucer under the tap. There was awe in the kitchen as she held the brush, filled with colour, in the air, and began to paint blue flowers on the dress.

At the first touch of the brush the old dressmaker clasped her hands. "What is she doing, the English girl! And we who have kept it so white…."

"Hush," said Fanny, stooping towards the bodice, "trust me!"

The children held their breath, except Elsa, who breathed so hard that Fanny felt her hair stir on her neck. She covered the plain, tight- waisted bodice with dancing flowers in blue and green.

On the frills of the skirt a dozen large flowers were painted as though fallen from the bodice. Soon it was done.

"Like that! In five minutes!" groaned the dressmaker, troubled by the peculiar growth of the flowers.

"Let it dry," said Fanny. "I'll go home and start doing my hair. Elsa will bring it round when it's dry."

The old woman held out both her hands, in a gesture of mute congratulation and fatigue.

"Now rest," said Fanny. "Now sleep—and in the morning I will come and tell you all about it," and ran out into the snow.

* * * * *

The top hook of the bodice would not meet. With her heart in her mouth, with despair, she pulled. Then sat down on the bed and stared blankly before her.

"Then if *that* won't meet, all, all the dress is wasted. I can't go. No, right in the front! There is nothing to be done, nothing to be done!" She sat alone in the room, the five candles she had lighted guttering and spilling wax. She was in the half-fastened painted bodice and a fine net petticoat she had bought at Nancy. Even the green silk bedroom slippers were on, tied round her ankles with ribbons, the only slippers she had found in Metz, and she had searched for them for hours.

The room was icy cold, and the hand of the clock chasing towards the hour for the dance. Should she go in uniform? Not for the world.

She would not meet him, and it seemed as though there could be no to-morrow, and she would never meet him again in this world. This meeting had had a peculiar significance—the flouncy, painted dress, the plans she had made to meet him for once as a woman. Shivering, and in absurd anguish she sat still on the bed.

150

"Oh, Elsa, Elsa, look!" Better the child than no one, and the shiny head was hanging round the door. ("Wie schön!")

"But it isn't *schön*! Look! It won't meet!"

"Oh!..." Elsa's eyes grew round with horror, and she went to fetch her mother. "Tanzen!" They talked so much of "tanzen" in that household. The thin mother was all sympathy, and stood in helpless sorrow before the gap in the bodice.

"What's all this?" and *der Vater* stood in the doorway, heavy as lead, and red as a plum.

"Give her a bunch of flowers," he said simply, and as if by accident, and "Oh!..." said Elsa's mother, and disappeared. She came back with three blue cotton cornflowers out of Elsa's hat, and the gap in the bodice was hidden.

* * * * *

He was not there. Her eyes flew round the room, searching the shadows in the corners, searching the faces. In the bitterness of dismay she could not fully enter the door, but stood a little back, blocking the entrance, afraid of the certainty which was ready for her within; but others, less eager, and more hurried, pressed her on, drove her into the centre of the room, and with a voice of excitement and distress chattering within her, like some one who has mislaid all he has, she shook hands with the eighteenth-century general who shrouded the personality of the Commandant Dormans.

At first she could not recognise any one as she looked round upon Turks, clowns, Indians, the tinselled, sequined, beaded, ragged flutter of the room, then from the coloured and composite clothing of a footballer, clown or jockey grinned the round face and owlish eyes of little Duval, who flew to her at once to whisper compliments and stumble on the swelling fortress of her white skirt. She realised dimly from him that her dress was as beautiful as she had hoped it might be, but what was the use of its beauty if Julien should be missing? And, looking over Duval's head, she tried to see through the crowd.

Suddenly she saw him, dressed in the white uniform of a Russian, standing by a buttress of the wall. His uniform had a faint yellowish colour, as if it had been laid away for many years against this evening's dance; the light caught his knees and long boots, but the shadow of the buttress crept over his face, turned from her towards a further door. On his head he wore a white hat of curling sheep's wool, which made him seem fantastically tall.

When Fanny had surveyed him, from the tip of his lit hat to his lit feet, she was content to leave him in his shadowed corner, and turned willingly to dance with Duval. The little man offered an arm to hold her, and, as

151

he came nearer to her, his feet pressed the bottom ring of wire about her skirt, and the whole bell of flowers and frills swung backwards and stood out obliquely behind her.

Presently the Jew boy, Reherrey, detached himself from the others and came out to stand by her and flatter her. He had wound the black stuff that he had bought three days before so cleverly round his slim body that he seemed no fatter than a lacquered hairpin. The cynical flattery of this nineteen-year-old Jew, the plunging admiration which Duval breathed at her side, the attentive look in the bright eyes of the Commandant Dormans, who had come near them and stood before her, filled her with joy. She looked about her, bright rat, tiny and enormous in her own sight, aware now of her outer, now of her inner life, and sipped her meed of success, full of the light happiness fashioned from the admiration of creatures no bigger than herself. She laughed at one and the other, bending towards them, listening to what they had to say, without denying, without doubts, with only triumph in her heart; and, the group shifting a little, a voice was able to say secretly at her ear, "You look beautiful, but you are not exclusive...." Her sense of triumph was not dimmed because her quick ear caught jealousy shading the reproach in his voice.

She did not answer him, except to look at him; but they seemed to forgive each other mutually as the figure of yellowish-white moved close enough to tilt the bell skirt and take the figure of bluish-white into his arms and dance with her. Calico and sheep's wool and painted flowers went down the room under the low gas brackets, and her eyes, avoiding his, looked out from a little personal silence into the far-off whirl of the room, and heard the dimmed music and the scrape of feet.

For him the world was a pale dumb-show, and she the absorbing centre. For her the world without was lit equally with his personality, the glamour of which hung over all the scenes before her eyes with the weight of the sky over the land. So long as he lit the horizon the very furthest object in it wore a shaft of his light upon its body.

They danced on, not wearing away the shining boards with their feet half so much as they wore away the thin ice above the enchanted lake.

The Commandant Dormans crossed the room to them.

"She must be drawn. She must go for her portrait. Spare me your partner.
Mademoiselle, we have an artist, a *poilu*, drawing some of the dresses. Will you come with me and sit for yours?"

She went into the little room and stood for the drawing; the door shut on her, and she and the artist faced each other. Through the door the music came softly, and as she stood, hands resting without a breath's stir on fold, on frill, head bent and wandering eyes, the artist with twitching face and moving hand looked up and down, up and down, and she sank, swaying a little upon her rooted feet, into a hypnotised tranquillity. She did not care what the man put upon the white paper with his flying hands; he might draw the flowers upon her skirt, but not the tall blooming flowers within her, growing fabulously like the lilies in a dream. Her thoughts went out to meet the waves of music floating through the door; her rooted body held so still that she no longer felt it, and her spirit hung unbodied in an exaltation between love which she remembered and love which she expected. No one came through the door; they left her in silence, enclosed in the cell of the room and of her dreams, and she was content to stand without movement, without act or thought. The near chair, the wall hard by, the golden room which she had just left so suddenly were alike to her; her eyes and her imagination were tuned to the same level, and there was no distinction between what was on her horizon and beyond it. Across the face of the artist the scenes in the room behind her passed in unarrested procession, and the voice of an illusory lover in her ear startled her by its clearness. The music wandered about the room like visible movement, and the artist, God bless him, never opened his mouth between his shower of tiny glances.

"Finished, mademoiselle!" and he held the drawing towards her as he leant back with a sigh. He had made too many drawings that evening, and any talent he had hung in his mind as wearily as a flag in an airless room. With an effort she broke her position and moved towards him, taking up the drawing in her hand with a forced interest. "Yes, thank you, thank you," she said, and he took it back and laid it with the pile he had made. "You don't like it? But I'm so tired. Look at these others I did earlier in the evening...."

But while she bent over them the door burst open and Dormans came in, followed by Duval and Dennis. "Is it finished? Let me look! Yes, yes, very good! Quite good!" They were pleased enough, and drew the artist away with them to the buffet.

Suddenly Julien was with her and had closed the door. He was hurried, excited, and it seemed as though he said what he could no longer contain, as though the thought biggest in his mind broke in a bound from him. He was white and he exclaimed: "It's terrible how *much* you could hurt me if you would!"

He seemed to close his eyes a little then and lean his head towards her. She looked at the drooping, half-lit head, and she knew that she had him without fear of escape. Knew too, that the moment was brief. Their recent, undeclared silence brooded as though still with them, half regretful and departing angel. "You will have other beauties," she said to her heart, "but none like this silence."

They were breathless. The ice had gone from the lake and the ship had not yet set sail. In a dream she moved down to the beach. She saw him open his eyes and stare at her incredulously. "I am going to break this beauty," she breathed alone, and put out her hand and launched the ship. He was by her side, the silence broken, the voyage begun.

X. FANNY ROBBED AND RESCUED

Clouds, yellow, mauve and blue, hung ominously over the road to Nancy. The valley was filled with shades, but the road itself gleamed like a bleached bone in a ditch. Seated upon the dashboard of her wounded car, Fanny had drummed her heels for warmth since morning, and seemed likely soon to drum them upon a carpet of snow. Beneath the car a dark stream of oil marked the road, and the oil still dripped from the differential case, where the back axle lay in two halves.

"I will telephone to your garage," her "client" had promised, as he climbed on to a passing lorry and continued his journey into Nancy. With that she had to be content, while she waited, first without her lunch, and then without her tea, for the breakdown lorry which his telephone message would eventually bring to her aid. Now it was nearly four o'clock. She had been hungry, but was hungry no longer. The bitter cold made her forehead ache, and though every moment the blue and mauve shades thickened upon the sky no flake of snow had fallen.

Only last night, only twenty-four hours ago, she had been preparing for the dance; and only last night she had said to Julien ... What had she said to Julien? What had he said to her? Again she was deep in a reverie that had lasted all day, that had kept her warm, had fed her.

She was almost asleep when a man's voice woke her, and she found a car with three Americans drawn up beside her.

"I guess this is too bad," said the man who had woken her. "We passed you this morning on our way into Nancy, and here you are still looking as though you had never moved. 'Ain't you had any food since then?"

"I haven't been so very hungry."

"Not hungry? You're sure past being hungry! Lucky we've got food with us in the car. Pity we've got to hurry, but here's sandwiches and sandwiches, and cakes and candy, and bits of bunstuff, and an apple. And here's a cheese that's running out of its wrappin'. When's your show coming to fetch you? 'Ain't you coming home along with us?"

"They won't be long now. Oh, you are good...." Fanny's hunger revived as she took the food, and now she was waiting ungratefully for them to be gone that she might start on her heavensent meal.

"Good-bye, ma'am," they cried together.

"Good-bye," she waved, and as their car passed onwards she climbed up on to the mudguard and spread the rug over her knees.

The slow night grew out of nothing, expanded, and nearly enveloped the slopes of the hill below. The wind dropped in the cloudy, heavy twilight, and the papers of the sandwiches did no more than rustle upon her knees. Not prepared yet to light her car lamps, Fanny laid her torch upon her lap, and its patch of white light lit her hands and the piles of bread, cake, and fancy buns.

Across the road in the deeper gloom that dyed the valley and spilt over its banks, a head rustled in the ragged border of twig and reed, and eyes watched the brightly-lighted meal which seemed to hang suspended above the vague shape of the motor car.

With a sense of being perfectly alone, walled round by the gathering dusk, Fanny made a deep inroad upon her sandwiches and cake, finishing with the apple, and began to roll up what remained in case of further need, should no one come to fetch her.

She reflected that her torch would not last her long and that she ought to put it and light her head and tail lamps instead, but, drowsy with pleasure in her lonely dinner, she sat on, prolonging the last moments before she must uncurl her feet and climb down on to the ground. The torch slipped from her knee on to a lower fold of the rug, lighting only the corner of a packet in which she had rolled the cake.

Suddenly, while she watched it, the gleam of the corner disappeared. She stared at the spot intensely, and saw a hand, a shade lighter than the darkness, travel across the surface of the rug, cover with its fingers the second parcel and draw it backwards into what had now become dense night. Her skin stirred as though a million antennae were alive upon it; she could not breathe lest any movement should fling the unknown upon her; her eyes were glued to the third packet, and, in a moment, the hand advanced again. With horror she saw it creep along the rug, a small brown, fibrous hand, worn with work. The third packet was eclipsed by the fingers and receded as the others had done, but as it reached the edge of the rug, overflowing horror galvanised her into movement, and catching the corners of the rug she threw it violently after the package and over the hand, at the same moment jumping from her seat and on to the footboard, to grope wildly for the switch. Her heart was leaping like a fish just flung into a basket, and every inch of her body winced from an expected grasp upon it. She flung herself over the side and into the seat of the car, found the switch and pushed it.

A dozen Chinese at least were caught in the two long beams that flew out across the darkness. For a second their wrinkled faces stared, eyes blinked, and short, unhollowed lips stretched over yellow teeth, then, with a flutter of dark garments, the Chinese started away from the fixed beams and were gone into the shadow. Except for the sudden twitter of a voice, the spurt of a stone flung up against the metal of the car, they melted silently out of sight and hearing. Sick with panic, Fanny leant down upon her knees and covered her head with her two arms, expecting a blow from above. Seconds passed, and ice-cold, with one leg gone to sleep, she lifted her head, switched off the lights and stared into the night. She could see nothing, and gradually becoming accustomed to the darkness, she found that they had completely disappeared. The rug, too, had gone, and all three packets of sandwiches. Cautiously, with trembling legs, she stepped upon the footboard.

Something hit her softly upon the forehead, but before she had time to suffer from a new fear her eye caught the glitter of a flake of snow in its parachute descent across the path of her lamps. "They hate snow...." she whispered, not knowing whether it was true. She tried to picture them as a band of workmen, who, content with their little pillage, were now far from her on their way to some encampment.

Finding the torch still caught between the mudguard and the bonnet, she prowled round the car, flashing it into corners and pits of darkness. There was no sign of a lurking face or flutter of garment.

Snow began to fall, patting her noiselessly on her face and hands, and curling faster and faster across the lights. In twenty minutes the road around her was lightened, and cones of delicate softness grew between the spokes of the wheels.

Climbing down again from her perch, Fanny went to the back of the car, and, taking from beneath the seat her box of tools, she groped in the hollow under the wood and pulled out an iron bar, stout and slightly bent, with a knob at one end—the handle of the wheel jack.

* * * * *

Far away, in what seemed another world, equally blind, snowy and obscure, but divided from this one by fathoms of frozen water, a car was coming out from Pont-à-Moussons on to the main Nancy road. Its two head-lamps glowed confusedly under the snow that clung to them, and the driver, his thick, blue coat buttoned about his chin, leant forward peering through the open windscreen, stung, blinded, and blinking as the flakes drove in.

The head-lamps swept the road, the range of the beams reaching out and climbing the tree trunks in sheltered spots, or flung back and huddled about the front wheels when a blast of fresh snow was swept in from the open valley on the left.

"We must be getting to Marbashe?"

"Hardly yet, *mon capitaine*. It was unlucky the *brigadier* should be at Thionville. I could have mended the spring on the lorry myself, but it wants two men to tow in the car."

"This is Marbache!"

In the shelter of the hamlet the lights leapt forward and struck a handful of houses, thickened and rounded with snow. Almost immediately darkness swallowed them up, and a drift of snow flung up by the wind burst in powder over the bonnet and on to the glass.

"The plain outside. Now we go down a long hill. We turn sharp to the right here."

The car entered a tunnel of skeleton trees through which the flakes drained and flickered, or broke in uneven gusts through the trunks. The left lamp touched a little wooden hut which stood blinkered and deserted. Just beyond it was a sharp turn in the road.

"What's that?"

A pale light hung in the dark ahead of them.

"Is it a car? No."

"Yes, lamps. With the beam broken by the snow."

"Go slow."

For fear of blinding the driver of a lighted vehicle which might, after all, be moving, one of the men put out his hand and switched off the head-lights, and the car glided forward on its own momentum.

Thus they came upon Fanny, in the hollow torn by the lamps out of an obscurity which whirled like a dense pillar above her, seated on her mud-guard, blanched and still as an image, the iron bar for a weapon in her right hand, the torch ready as a signal in her left.

"Julien!"

"Well, yes, my poor child!" And she saw the man behind him, and laughed.

"Help me down. Within and without I am set in plaster."

"You look like a poor, weather-chipped goddess, or an old stone pillar with a face."

158

"Be careful, that leg will not stand.... Oh, look, look how the snow clings. It's frozen on my lap."

"We must be quick. Everything must be quickly done, or we shall all stay here."

"Oh, I don't care about that now!"

"What have you got in your hand? Give it to me."

"That's a weapon. I almost needed it. Where is the lorry?"

"The garage was empty. The *brigadier* was at Thionville. The lorry had a spring broken."

"And they told you?"

"I did not call at the 'C.R.A.' office till late in the day, or you would have been fetched long ago. Come along! Have you got your things together? We must take them back in the other car. And the magneto too."

"We're to leave the car after all my guarding care?"

"No; here's Pichot volunteered to take your place."

"Has he got food with him and rugs. My rug has gone...."

"He has everything. Come along! Let's put everything of value into the other car."

When they had finished the night air was clear of snowflakes; hill, road and valley were lit by the pallor of the fallen snow.

Fanny followed Julien to the other car. He swung the handle and jumped into the driving seat. "Come...." he said, and held out a hand.

"Good-night, Pichot. We'll send for you early in the morning."

"Good-night, *mon capitaine*. Good-night, mademoiselle."

They moved forward, and the moon like a wandering lamp lit their faces.

"Blow out, old moon!" said Julien, turning his silvered face and hair up to the sky. The moon flew behind a cloud.

"Quick!" he said.

"What?"

... and kissed her. The jacks and tyres and wheels and bolts fluttered out of Fanny's head like black ravens and disappeared. They flew on, over the bridge at Pont-à-Moussons, up the shining ruinous street.

"Crouch lower!" said Julien. "If any one wanted to, they could count your eyelashes from the windows."

"Ah, yes, if there was any one to count...." She glanced up at the fragmentary pronged chimneys, the dark, unstirring caves of brick.

Soon the church clocks of Metz rang out, quarrelling, out of time with one another.

"Do you know this isn't going to last?" said Julien suddenly, as if the clocks had reminded him.

She turned swiftly towards him.

"The Grand Quartier is moving?"

"Ah, you knew? You had heard?"

"No, no," she shook her head. "But do you think I haven't thought of it? I keep thinking, 'We can't stay here for ever. Some end will come.' And then—'It will come this way. The Grand Quartier will go.'"

"But you are going with it."

"Julien! Is that true?"

"Certain. It was settled to-day. We are actually leaving in three days for Chantilly; and you, with all the garage, all the drivers, and the offices of the 'C.R.A.' are to be at Précy-sur-Oise, five miles away."

"But you are at Précy too?"

"No, I have to be at Chantilly. And worse than that ... The bridge over the Oise at Précy is blown up and all cars have to come sixteen miles round to Chantilly by another bridge. I am in despair about it. I have tried every means to get Dormans to fix upon another village, but he is obstinate, and Précy it must be for you, and Chantilly for me. But don't let's think of it now. Wait till you've eaten and are warm, and we can plan. Here are the gates!"

He handed out the paper pass as a red light waved to and from upon the snow. First the Customs-men, Germans still, in their ancient civic uniform. "Nothing to declare?" Then the little soldier with the lantern in his hand: "Your pass, *ma belle!*" As he caught sight of Julien, "Pardon, mademoiselle!" Lastly, up the long road into the open square by the station, down the narrow street, splashing the melted snow-water against the shop windows, and under the shadow of the cathedral.

"Put the car away and come and dine with me at Moitriers."

She looked at him astonished. "The car? Whose car is it? Does it belong to our garage?"

"It will in future. It arrived last night, fresh from Versailles. I am arranging with Dennis for you to take it over to-morrow."

Her eyes sparkled. "A beautiful Renault! A brand new Renault!..."

He laughed. "Hurry, or you will faint with hunger. Put it away and come, just as you are, to Moitriers, up into the balcony. I am going there first to order a wonderful dinner."

In a quarter of an hour they were sitting behind the wooden balustrade of the balcony at Moitriers—the only diners on the little landing that overhung the one fashionable restaurant in Metz. It was a quarter to nine; down below, the room, which was lined with mirrors set in gilt frames, was filled with light; knives and forks still tapped upon the plates, but the hour being late many diners leant across the strewn tablecloths and talked, or sat a little askew in their chairs and listened. A hum filled the warm air, and what was garish below, here, behind the balustrade, became filtered and strained to delicate streaks and bars of light which crossed and recrossed their cloth, their hands, their faces—what was noisy below was here no more than a soft insect bustle, a murmurous background to their talk.

The door of the balcony opened behind them, and Madame Berthe, the proprietress herself, moved at their side; her old-fashioned body, shaped like an hour-glass, was clothed in rucked black silk, which flowed over her like a pigment; flowed from her chin to the floor, upon which it lay stiffly in hills and valleys of braided hem. Her gay gold tooth gleamed, and the gold in her ears wagged, as she fed them gently on omelette, chicken and tinned peas, and a *soufflé* ice.

They talked a little, sleepy after the wind, smiling at each other.

"Don't you want more light than that?" said Madame Berthe, coming in again softly with the coffee.

Fanny shook her head. "Not any more than this."

Then they were left alone, stirring the coffee, gazing down between the wooden columns at the diners below.

"Of what are you thinking?" she asked, as a sigh escaped her companion.

"The move to Chantilly. I am so loth to break up all this."

"Break up?"

"Ah, well, it changes, doesn't it? Even if it is no longer the same landscape it changes!"

After a silence he added: "How fragile it is!"

"What?"

"You!" He covered her hand with both his. "You! What I think you are, and what you think I am. Love and illusion. Too fragile to be given to us with our blunders and our nonsense."

She watched him, silent, and he went on:

"I don't understand this life. That's why I keep quiet and smile, as you say I do. There are often things I don't say when I smile."

"What things?"

"Oh, I wonder how much you believe me. And I listen to that immense interior life, which talks such a different language. I *hate* to move on to Chantilly."

Suddenly she recognised that they were at a corner which he had wanted her to turn for days. There had been something he had hinted at, something he wanted to tell her. He chafed at some knowledge he had which she did not share, which he wanted her to share.

Once he had said: "I had letters this morning which worried me...."

"Yes?"

"One in particular. It hurt me. It gave me pain."

But she had not wanted to ask what was in the letter. Then he had grown restless, sighed and turned away, but soon they had talked again and it had passed.

And now to-night he said:

"Look how detached we are in this town, which is like an island in the middle of the sea. We behave as though we had no past lives, and never expected any future. Especially you."

"Especially I?"

"You behave as though I was born the day before you met me, and would die the day after you leave me. You never ask anything about me; you tell me nothing about yourself. We might be a couple of stars hanging in mid air shining at each other. And then I have the feeling that one might drop and the other wouldn't know where to look for it."

But after a little silence the truth burst out, and he said with despair: "Don't you want to know *anything* about me?"

(Yes, that was all very well. She did, she did. But not just this that was coming!)

And then he told her....

* * * * *

"What is she like ... Violette?"

"Fair."

After several low questions she seemed to stand between them like a child, thin and fair, delicate and silent, innocently expecting to be spared all pain.

"No, she doesn't go out very much. She stays indoors and does her hair, and her nails, and reads a little book."

"And have you known her for a long time?"

"A long time...."

After this they pretended that she did not exist, and the little wraith floated back to Paris from which she had come, suddenly, on days when she had written him certain letters which had brought tears into his eyes.

XI. THE LAST NIGHT IN METZ: THE JOURNEY

Fanny turned again to seek the lights of the town and the dagger points of the churches that climbed against the sky upon the hill be-hind her, but all that met her eyes was the blanket of wet darkness, and the shimmer of the snowflakes under the lamps.

She slipped through the garage gates, touching the iron bars ... "almost for the last time."

"But what does it matter? All towns are the same and we sing the same song in each and wear the same coloured feathers." She stirred the snow in the yard with her foot. "An inch already and the Renault has so little grip upon the snow. Shall we be able to start to-morrow?"

Then she set out to look for a heap of snow chains which she had noticed before in a corner of the yard. Not far from her another little torch moved in the darkness, and under its downward ray she caught sight of a khaki skirt and a foot. "Someone else has thought of chains, too! And there are so few!" She clicked off her light and moved stealthily along the forest of cars, her fingers sweeping blankets of snow from the mudguards. Passing the first line of corpse-cars she saw the light again. "She's in the wrong place!" she thought, and hurried on. "Those bags of chains are just behind the Berliet they brought in backwards." Behind the Berliet little mounds showed in the snow. She stooped over them, shading her light with her knees, and dug in the light powder with her hand, pulling out a small canvas bag which she dusted and beat with her fingers.

"Are you looking for chains?" she called to the other light, her bag safely in her arms.

"Yes."

"They are here. Here! In this corner!"

"Who are you?" cried the voice.

But she slipped away in silence to the garage door; for on this last black and white night in Metz she longed to creep about unspoken to, unquestioned. A little soldier sat on guard by a brazier of glowing charcoal near the door. She nodded to him as she moved down the long line of cars to her own.

There it stood, the light of the brazier falling faintly upon it, the two points of the windscreen standing up like the ready ears of an interested dog, the beautiful lines of its body, long bonnet and mudguards stretched like a greyhound at a gallop, at rest until the dawn. She flung the bag of chains inside, and, patting the bonnet, slipped away and out into the street without attempting to try the fit of the chains upon the wheels.

She slept a last night in the dark red German room three streets away—first making a little tour of the walls in her nightgown, the candle flame waving from her hand, the hot wax running in a cascade over her fingers—and looked at the stag's horn fastened to the bracket and the cluster of Christmas postcards pinned to the wall.

The postcards arrested her attention, and a light darted in her mind. They were dark postcards, encrusted with shiny frosting, like the snow outside. Little birds and goblins, a wreath of holly, and a house with red mica windows were designed on them. She put out a finger and gently touched the rough, bright, common stuff; standing opposite them, almost breathless with a wave of memory. She could see herself no taller than the nursery fireguard, with round eyes to which every bright thing was a desire. She could feel herself very small amid the bustle and clatter of Christmas, blowing dark breath marks against the bright silver on the table, pulling the fringe round the iced cake, wetting her finger and picking up "hundreds and thousands" with it from a bag.

These postcards now in front of her were made by some one with the mind of a child. It struck and shook her violently with memory to see them. "That's why the Germans write good fairy stories!" she thought, and her eyes passed to the framed photographs that hung near the postcards, pictures of soldiers in uniform, sitting at a table with the two daughters of the house. But these wooden faces, these bodies pressing through unwieldy clothes seemed unrelated to the childish postcards.

She went contentedly to her bed, the room, bare of all her belongings, except the one bag that stood, filled and open, upon the table; sleeping for the last time in the strange bed in the strange town which she might never see again. It was time indeed to go.

For days past civilians had crept through the gates of Metz, leading old horses, drawing ramshackle carts filled with mattresses, faded silk chairs, gilt ormolu stands, clocks and cloaks and parrot cages; all the strange things that men and women use for their lives. The furniture that had fled in other carts from villages now dust upon a dead plain was returning through all the roads of France, repacked and dusted, to set up the spirit of civilian life again.

It was time to go, following all the other birds of passage that war had dragged through the town of Metz—time to make way for the toiling civilian with his impedimenta of civilisation.

In the morning when she opened her eyes the room was darker than usual, and the opening of the window but the merest square of light. Snow was built up round the frame in thick rolls four inches high.

She dressed hurriedly and rolled up the sleeping-sack with her few last things inside it. Out in the street the snow was dry and thick and beautifully untrodden. The garage gates looked strange, with a thick white banner blown down each side of the pillars. She looked inside the garage shed. Yes, all the cars had gone—hers stood alone, the suitcases inside, tyres pumped stiff and solid, the hood well buckled back.

"Mademoiselle hasn't gone with the convoy?" said the *maréchal des logis*, aghast.

"Oh, I'm separate," she laughed.

"But the convoy is gone."

"I know it. But I'm not with them. It's an order. I'm going alone."

"*Bien*. But do you know the route?"

"I'm not going by it."

He laughed, suddenly giving up all attempt at responsibility, and bent to catch her starting handle.

"Oh, don't worry."

"Yes, it's your last day, I may as well help you to go away."

The engine started easily and she drove out of the garage into the yard, the wheels flying helplessly in the snow, and flinging up dry puffs like flour. "Haven't you chains?" said the *maréchal des logis*. But she smiled and nodded and could not wait. "Good-bye—good-bye to all the garage," she nodded and waved. The sun broke out from behind a cloud, her brass and glass caught fire and twinkled gaily, the snow sparkled, the gate-posts shone at her. She left the garage without a regret in her heart, with not a thought in her head, save that in a minute she would be safe, no accident could stop her, she would be abroad upon the magic, the unbelievable journey.

* * * * *

They were in a small circular room, shaped like an English oasthouse, its roof running upwards in a funnel to meet the sky. At the apex was a round porthole of thick glass to let in the light, but as this was supporting several feet of snow the lighting of the room was effected only by a large oil-lamp which stood on the blackened table in the centre. An old woman came forward into the light of the lamp. Her eyes were fine and black—her mouth was toothless and folded away for ever, lost in a crevice under her nose. When she smiled the oak-apples of her cheeks rose up and cut the black eyes into hoops.

"We are on a long journey, madame, to Chantilly. We are cold; can we have coffee?"

She drew out chairs and bade them sit, then placed two tall glasses of coffee in the ring of light from the lamp, sugar melting in a sandy heap at the bottom of each.

"What an odd shape your house is!" said Julien, looking round him.

"It's very old, like me. And the light is poor. You have to know it to get used to it," she replied.

"You've only that one window?" He stared up the funnel to where he could see the grey underside of the cone of snow.

"But I can make that one better than it is; and then the lady can see herself in this little glass!" The old woman moved to the side of the wall where a rope hung down. "*Elle a raison*; since she has a gentleman with her! I was the same—and even not so long ago!"

She put up her thin arm and gave the rope a long pull. She must have been strong, for the skylight and all its burden opened on a hinge, and the snow could be seen sliding from it, could be heard in a heavy body rumbling on the roof. She closed the skylight, and now a wan light filtered down the funnel and turned their faces green. It was like life at the bottom of a well, and they felt as though the level of the earth was far above their heads, and its weighty walls pressing against their sides.

"But why is it built this way?"

"Many houses are," said the old woman with a shrug. "It's old, older than my mother." She sat down beside them. "Soldiers have been drunk in here many times in the war," she said. "And in the old war, too. But I never saw one like you." She pinched Fanny's sleeve. "Fine stuff," she said. "The Americans are rich!"

"I'm not American."

"Rich they are. But I don't care for them. They have no real feeling for a woman. You are not stupid, *ma belle*, to get a Frenchman for a lover."

"Don't make him vain."

"It is the truth. He knows it very well. Why should he be vain? An American loves a pretty face; but a Frenchman loves what is a woman." She rose and lifted the lamp, and let its ray search out a corner of the room wherein the great bed stood, wooden and square, its posts black with age, its bedding puffed about it and crowned with a scarlet eiderdown as solid and deep as the bed itself.

"A fine bed; an old bed; it is possible that you will not believe me, but I shared that bed with a bishop not two years ago."

Fanny's eyes were riveted on the bed.

Julien laughed. "In the worst sense, mother?"

"In the best, my son," bragged the old woman, sliding a skinny finger to the tip of her nose. "You don't believe me?"

Coming nearer, she stood with the lamp held in her two hands resting on the table, so that she towered over them in fluttering shawl and shadow.

"He arrived in the village one night in a great storm. It was past the New Year and soldiers had been coming through the street all day to go up to the lines beyond Pont-à-Moussons. I've had them sleeping in here on the floor in rows, clearing away the table and lying from wall to wall so thick that I had to step on them when I crossed the room with my lamp. But that night there were none; they were all passing through up to the front lines, and though the other end of the village was full, no one knocked here. There was snow as there is to-day, but not lying still on the ground. It was rushing through the air and choking people and lying heavy on everything that moved outside. That glass of mine up there was too heavy for me to move so I let it be. A knock came at the door in the middle of the night, and when I got up to unbar the door there was a soldier on the doorstep. I said: 'Are you going to wake me up every night to fill the room with men?' And he said: 'Not to-night, mother, only one. Pass in, monsieur.'

"It was a bishop, as I told you. *Un éveque.* A great big man with a red face shining with the snow. If he had not been white with snow he would have been as black as a rook. He stamped on the cobbles by the door and the snow went down off him in heaps, and there he was in his beautiful long clothes, and I said to myself: 'Whatever shall I do with him? Not the floor for such a man!' So there we were, I in my red shawl that hangs on the hook there, and he in his long clothes like a black baby in arms, and his big man's face staring at me over the top.

"'I can't put you anywhere but in my bed,' I told him. I told him like that, quickly, that he might know. And he answered like a gentleman, the Lord save his soul: 'Madame, what lady could do more!'

"'But there's only one bed' I told him (I told him to make it clear), 'and I'm not young enough to sleep on the floor.' Not that I'm an old woman. And he answered like a gentleman, the Lord save him...."

"I will tell *you* the end," said the old woman, drawing near to Julien as he took some money from his pocket to pay for the coffee.

Two hours later they drew up at a *café* in the main square at Ligny.

Within was a gentle murmur of voices, a smell of soup and baking bread; warm steam, the glow of oil lamps and reddened faces.

Sitting at a small table, with a white cloth, among the half-dozen American soldiers who, having long finished their lunch, were playing cards and dominoes, they ordered bread-soup, an omelette, white wine, brille cheese and their own ration of bully beef which they had brought in tins to be fried with onions.

A woman appeared from the door of the kitchen, carrying their bowl of bread-soup. Across the plains of her great chest shone a white satin waistcoat fastened with blue glass studs, and above her handsome face rose a crown of well-brushed hair dyed in two shades of scarlet. A little maid followed, and they covered the table with dishes, knives and forks, bread and wine. The woman beamed upon Fanny and Julien, and laying her hand upon Fanny's shoulder begged them not to eat till she had fetched them a glass of her own wine.

"You bet it's good, ma'am," advised a big American sergeant at a table near them. "You take it."

She brought them a wine which shone like dark amber in a couple of glasses, and stood over them listening with pleasure to their appreciation while each slight movement of her shoulders sent ripples and rivers of heaving light over the waistcoat of satin.

The butter round the omelette was bubbling in the dish, the brille had had its red rind removed and replaced by fried breadcrumbs, the white wine was light and sweet, and with the coffee afterwards they were given as much sugar as they wished.

"I have seen her before somewhere," said Julien, as the scarlet head receded among the shadows of the back room. "I wonder where?"

"One wouldn't forget her."

"No. It might have been in Paris; it might have been anywhere."

The little maid was at his elbow. "Madame would be glad if you would come to her store and make your choice of a cigar, monsieur."

"Well, I shall know where I met her. Do you mind if I go?"

He followed the girl into the back room. Fanny, searching in her pocket for her handkerchief, scattered a couple of German iron pennies on the floor; an American from the table behind picked them up and returned them to her. "These things are just a weight and a trouble," he said. "I think I shall throw mine away?"

"You've come down from Germany, then?"

"Been up at Trêves. They do you well up there."

"Not better than here!"

"No, this is an exception. It's a good place."

"Madame is a great manager."

"Hev' you got more German pennies than you know what to do with?" said the American sergeant who had advised her to drink the wine. "Because, if you hev' so hev' I and I'll play you at dominoes for them."

As Julien did not return at once, Fanny moved to his table and piled her German pennies beside her, and they picked out their dominoes from the pile.

"I want to go home," said the American, and lifted up his big face and looked at her.

"You all do."

"That's right. We all do," assented another and another. They would make this statement to her at every village where she met them, in every *estaminet*, at any puncture on the road over which they helped her — simply, and because it was the only thing in their minds.

"Do you hev' to come out here?" he enquired.

"Oh, no. We come because we like to."

Thinking this a trumpery remark he made no answer, but put out another domino—then as though something about her still intrigued his heavy curiosity: "You with the French, ain't you?"

"Yes."

"Like that too?"

He sat a little back into his chair as though he felt he had put her in a corner now, and when she said she even liked that too, twitched his cheek a little in contempt for such a lie and went on playing.

But the remark worked something in him, for five minutes later he pursued:

"I don't see anything in the French. They ain't clean. They ain't generous. They ain't up-to-date nor comfortable."

Fanny played out her domino.

"They don't know how to *live*," he said more violently than he had spoken yet.

"What's living?" she said quickly. "What is it to live, if *you* know?"

"You want to put yourself at something, an' build up. Build up your fortune and spread it out and about, and have your house so's people know you've got it. I want to get home and be doing it."

"Mademoiselle actually knows it!" said Julien in the doorway to the red-haired woman in the back room, and Fanny jumped up.

The American passed four iron coins across the table. "'Tisn't going to hinder that fortune I'm going to make," he said, smiling at last.

"What do I know?" she asked, approaching the doorway, and moving with him into the back room.

"Madame owns a house in Verdun," said Julien, "and I tell her you know it."

"*I* know it?"

"Come and drink this little glass of my wine, mademoiselle," said the red-haired woman good-humouredly, "and tell me about my poor little house. I had a house on the crown of the hill ... with a good view ... and a good situation (she laughed) by the Cathedral."

"Had you? Well, there are a great many by the Cathedral," Fanny answered cautiously, for she thought she knew the house that was meant.

"But my house looked out on the *citadelle*, and stood very high on a rock. Below it there was a drop and steep steps went down to a street below."

"Had you pink curtains in the upper windows?"

"Is it not then so damaged?" demanded the woman eagerly, dropping her smile. "The curtains are left? You can see the curtains?"

"No, no, it is terribly damaged. If it is the house you mean I found a piece of pink satin and a curtain ring under a brick, and there is a sad piece which still waves on a high window. But wait a minute, excuse me, I'll be back." She passed through the café and ran out to the car, returning in a moment with something in her hand.

"I fear I looted your house, madame," she said, offering her a small cylindrical pot made of coarse clouded glass, and half filled with a yellowish paste. "I found that inside on the ground floor; I don't know why I took it."

The woman held it in her hand. "Oh!" she wailed, and sliding down upon the sofa, found her handkerchief.

"*Mais non!*" said Julien, "you who have so much courage!"

"But it was my own *face!*" she cried incoherently, holding out the little pot. "My poor little cream pot!"

"What!"

"It was my face cream!"

"How strange!"

"I had not used it for a week because they had recommended me a new   one. Ah! miraculous! that so small a thing should follow me!"

She touched her eyes carefully with her handkerchief, but a live tear had fallen on the waistcoat.

"Tell me, mademoiselle ... sit down beside me, my dear ... the poor little house is no more good to me? I couldn't live there? Is there a roof?"

"You couldn't live in it."

"But the roof?"

"It was on the point of sliding off; it was worn like a hat over one ear. The front of the house is gone. Only on the frame of one window which sticks to the wall could I see your piece of pink curtain which waves."

"My poor, pretty house!" she mused. "My first, you know," she said in an undertone to Julien. "Ah, well, courage, as you say!"

"But you are very well here."

"True, but this isn't my vocation. I shall start again elsewhere. And Verdun itself, Mademoiselle, can one live in it?"

"No, not yet. Perhaps never."

"Well, well...."

"Madame, we must move on again," interrupted Julien. "We have a long way to go before night."

The woman rose, and turning to a drawer, pulled out a heap of soiled papers, bills and letters. "Wait," she said, "wait an instant!"

Turning them over she sought and found a couple of old sheets pinned together, and unpinning them she handed one to Fanny.

"It is the receipt for the cream," she said, "that I want to give you. It is a good cream though I left the pot behind."

* * * * *

The sun sank and the forests around Chantilly grew vague and deep. White statues stood by the roadside, and among the trees chateaux with closed eyes slept through the winter. Every tree hung down beneath its load of snow; the telephone wires drooped like worsted threads across the road.

Fanny, who had left Julien at his new billets in Chantilly, drove on alone to the little village on the Oise which was to be her home. It was not long before she could make out the posts and signals of the railway on her left, and the river appeared in a broad band below her. The moon rose, and in the river the reeds hung head downwards, staring up at the living reeds upon the bank.

"PRECY."

It gleamed upon a signpost, and turning down a lane on the left she came on a handful of unlighted cottages, and beyond them a single village street, soundless and asleep. A chemist's shop full of coloured glasses was lit from within by a single candle; upon the step the chemist stood, a skull cap above his large, pitted face.

Somewhere in the shuttered village a roof already sheltered her companions, but before looking for them she drew up and gazed out beyond the river and the railway line to where the moon was slowly lighting hill after hill. But the spectral summer town which she sought was veiled in the night.

PART III.
THE FORESTS OF
CHANTILLY

XII. PRECY-SUR-OISE

The light of dawn touched Paris, the wastes of snow surrounding her, forests, villages scattered in the forest and plains around Senlis, Chantilly, Boran, Précy. The dark receded in the west; in the east a green light spread upwards from the horizon, touched the banks of the black Oise, the roofs of the houses of Précy, the dark window panes, and the flanks of the granite piers that stood beheaded in the water—all that was left of the great bridge that had crossed from bank to bank.

Above the river stood the station hut and the wooden gates of the level crossing, upon which the night lantern still hung; above again a strip of snow divided the railway line from the road, at the other side of whose stone wall the village itself began, and stretched backwards up a hill.

Upon a patch of snow above the river and below the road stood a flourishing little house covered with gables and turrets; and odd shapes like the newel-posts of staircases climbed unexpectedly about the roof. In summer, fresh with paint, the outside of the house must wave its vulgar little hands into the sky, but now, everything that bristled upon it served only as a fresh support for the snow which hung in deep drifts on its roof, and around its balconied windows. It stood in its own symmetrical walled garden, like a cup in a deep saucer, and within the wall a variety of humps and hillocks showed where the bushes crouched beneath their unusual blanket. One window, facing towards the railway and the river, had no balcony clinging to its stonework, and in the dark room behind it the light of the dawn pressed faintly between the undrawn curtains. A figure stirred upon the bed within, and Fanny, not clearly aware whether she had slept or not, longed to search the room for some heavier covering which, warming her, would let her sink into unconsciousness. Her slowly gathering wits, together with the nagging cold, forced her at last from the high bed on to the floor, and she crossed the room towards the light. In the walled garden below strange lights of dawn played, red, green and amber, like a crop of flowers. The railway lines beyond the garden wall disappeared in fiery bands north and south, lights flashed down from the sky above and winked in the black and polished river; at the limit of the white plain beyond, a window caught the sun and turned its burning-glass upon the snow.

"Chantilly...." A word like the dawn, filled with light and the promise of light! Turning back into the dim room, she flung her coat upon the bed, climbed in and fell asleep. Three hours later something pressed against her bed and she opened her eyes again. The room was fresh with daylight, and Stewart standing beside her carried a rug on her arm and wore a coat over her nightgown. "I'm coming down to have chocolate in your room...."

Fanny watched her. Stewart climbed up beside her wrapped in the rug. A knock at the door heralded the entry of a woman carrying a tray. Fanny watched her too, and saw that she was fresh, smiling, clean and big, and that steam flew up in puffs from the tray she carried. The woman pulled a little table towards the bed and set the tray on it.

"This is Madame Boujan!" said Stewart's voice.

Fanny tried to smile and say "Good morning," and succeeded. She was not awake but knew she was in clover. The cups holding the steaming chocolate were as large as bowls, and painted cherries and leaves glistened beneath their lustre surface. Beside the cups was a plate with rolls, four rolls; and there were knives and two big pots which must be butter and jam.

"Wake up!"

Fanny rolled nearer to the chocolate, sniffed it and pulled herself up in bed. The woman, still smiling beside them, turned and hunted among the clothes upon the chair; then held a jersey towards her shoulders and guided her arms into its sleeves. Ecstasy stole over Fanny; other similar wakings strung themselves like beads upon her memory; nursery wakings when her spirit had been guided into daylight by the crackle of a fire new-lit, by the movements of just such an aproned figure as this, by a smile on just such a pink face; or wakings after illness when her freshening life had leapt in her at the sound of a blind drawn up, at the sight of the white-cuffed hand that pulled the cord.

Oh, heavenly woman, who stood beside the tray, who fed her and warmed her while she was yet weak and babyish from sleep! Beyond her the white plains of beauty shone outside the window.... She sat up and smiled: "I'm awake," she said.

And Madame Boujan, having seen that her feet were set upon the threshold of day, went out of the door and closed it softly.

They held the lustre bowls cupped in their hands and sipped.

* * * * *

During lunch in the little villa, while they were all recounting their experiences, Madame Boujan came softly to Fanny's side and whispered:

"A soldier has brought you a note from Chantilly."

"Keep it for me in the kitchen," Fanny answered, under her breath, helping herself to potatoes.

"Will you come and cut wood for the bedroom fire?" said Stewart, when lunch was over. "I bought a hatchet in the village this morning."

"Come down by the river first," insisted Fanny, who had her note in her hand.

"Why? And it gets dark so soon!"

"I want to find a boat."

"What for?"

"To cross the river."

"To cross the river! Do you want to see what's on the other side?"

"Julien will be on the other side.... I have had a letter from him. I am to dine in Chantilly. He will send a car at seven to wait for me in the fields at the other side of the broken bridge, and trusts to me to find a boat. Come over the level crossing to the river."

They passed the station hut and came to a little landing stage near which a boat was tied.

"There's a boat," said Stewart. "Shall we ask at that hut?"

The wooden hut stood above their heads on a pedestal of stone; from its side the haunch of the stone bridge sprang away into the air, but stopped abruptly where it had been broken off. The hut, once perhaps a toll-house, was on a level with what had been the height of the bridge, and now it could be reached by stone steps which wound up to a small platform in front of the door. From within came men's voices singing.

"Look in here!"

A flickering light issued from a small window, and having climbed the steps they could see inside. Two boys, about sixteen, a soldier and an old man, sat round a table beneath a hanging lamp, and sang from scraps of paper which they held in their hands. Behind the old man a girl stood cleaning a cup with a cloth.

"They are practising something. Knock!"

But there was no need, for a dog chained in a barrel close to them set up a wild barking.

"Is he chained? Keep this side. The old man is coming."

The door opened. The voices ceased; the girl stood by the old man's side.

"Yes, it could be arranged. People still crossed that way; their boat was a sort of ferry and there was a charge.

"There might be a little fog to-night, but it didn't matter. Margot knows the way across blindfold—Margot would row the lady. She would be waiting with a lantern at five minutes to seven; and again at half-past nine. Not too late at all! But Margot would not wait on the other side, it was too cold. They would lend the lady a whistle, and she must blow on it from the far bank."

"There's romance!" said Fanny, as they came away.

"Not if you are caught."

"There's my magic luck!"

"How dare you ask like that? Even if you are not superstitious, even if you don't believe a word of it, why be so defiant—why not set the signs right!"

"Oh, my dear Stewart, I hardly care! And to the creature who doesn't care no suspicion clings. Haven't I an honest face? Would you think it was me, me, of all the Section, to cross the river to-night, in a little boat with a lantern, to creep out of the house, out of the village, to dine forbidden in Chantilly, with some one who enchants me! You wouldn't. Why, do you know, if I lived up in their house, under their eyes, I would go out just the same, to cross the river. I wouldn't climb by windows or invent a wild tale to soothe them, but open the door and shut the door, and be gone. And would anybody say: 'Where's Fanny?'"

"They might."

"They might. But they would answer their own question: 'Innocently sleeping. Innocently working. Innocently darning, reading, writing.' I don't suspect myself so why should any one else suspect me!"

Fanny broke off and laughed.

"Come along and cut wood!"

They moved off into the woods as people with not a care in the world, and coming upon a snow-covered stack of great logs which had been piled by some one else, began to steal one or two and drag them away into a deep woodland drive where they could cut them up without fear of being noticed.

They worked on for an hour, and then Stewart drew a packet of cake from her coat pocket, and sitting upon the logs they had their tea.

Soon Fanny, wringing her hands, cried:

"I'm blue again, stiff again, letting the cold in, letting the snow gnaw. Where's the hatchet?"

For a time she chopped and hacked, and Stewart, shepherding the splinters which flew into the snow, piled them—splinters, most precious of all—*petit bois* to set a fire alight; and the afternoon grew bluer, deeper. Stewart worked in a reverie—Fanny in a heat of expectation. One mused reposedly on life—the other warmly of the immediate hours before her.

"Now I'm going to fetch the car," said Stewart at last. "Will you stay here and go on cutting till I come? There are two more logs."

She walked away up the drive, and Fanny picked the hatchet out of the snow and started on the leathery, damp end of a fresh log. It would not split, the tapping marred the white silence, and yet again she let the hatchet fall and sat down on the log instead. It was nearly six—they had spent the whole afternoon splitting up the logs, and making a fine pile of short pieces for firewood; the forest was darkening rapidly, blue deepened above the trees to indigo, and black settled among the trunks. Only the snow sent up its everlasting shine. Her thoughts fell and rose. Now they were upon the ground busy with a multitude of small gleams and sparkles—now they were up and away through the forest tunnels to Chantilly. What would he say first? How look when he met her?

"Ah, I am a silly woman in a fever! Yet happy—for I see beauty in everything, in the world, upon strange faces, in nights and days. Upon what passes behind the glassy eyes" (she pressed her own) "depends sight, or no sight. There is a life within life, and only I" (she thought arrogantly, her peopled world bounded by her companions) "am living in it. We are afraid, we are ashamed, but when one dares talk of this strange ecstasy, other people nod their heads and say: 'Ah, yes, we know about that! They are in love.' And they smile. But what a convention—tradition—that smile!"

There was no sound in the forest at all—not the cry of a bird, not the rustle of snow falling from a branch—but there was something deeper and remoter than sound, the approach of night. There was a change on the face of the forest—an effective silence which was not blankness—a voiceless expression of attention as the Newcomer settled into his place. Fanny looked up and saw the labyrinth of trees in the very act of receiving a guest.

"Oh, what wretched earnest I am in," she thought, suddenly chilled. "And it can only have one end—parting." But she had a power to evade these moods. She could slip round them and say to herself: "I am old enough—I have learnt again and again—that there is only one joy—the Present; only one Perfection—the Present. If I look into the future it is lost."

She heard the returning car far up the forest drive, and in a moment saw the gleam of its two lamps as they rocked and swayed. It drew up, and Stewart put out the lamps, ever remembering that their logs were stolen. There was still light enough by which they could pack the car with wood. As they finished Stewart caught her arm: "Look, a fire!" she said, pointing into the forest. Through a gap in the trees they could see a red glow which burst up over the horizon.

"And look behind the trees—the whole sky is illumined—What a fire!" As they watched, the glare grew stronger and brighter, and seemed about to lift the very tongue of its flame over the horizon.

"It's the moon!" they cried together.

The cold moon it was who had come up red and angry from some Olympic quarrel and hung like a copper fire behind the forest branches. Up and up she sailed, but paling as she rose from red to orange, from orange to the yellow of hay; and at yellow she remained, when the last branch had dropped past her face of light, and she was drifting in the height of the sky.

XIII. THE INN

They drove back to the village and down to their isolated villa, and here on the road they passed ones and twos of the Section walking into supper

"How little we have thought out your evasion!" whispered Stewart at the wheel, as they drew up at the door: "Get out, and go and dress. I will take the car up to the garage and come back."

Fanny slipped in through the garden. What they called "dressing" was a clean skirt and silk stockings—but silk stockings she dared not put on before her brief appearance at supper. Stuffing the little roll into her pocket she determined to change her stockings on the boat.

Soon, before supper was ended, she had risen from the table, unquestioned by the others, had paused a moment to meet Stewart's eye full of mystery and blessing, had closed the door and was gone.

She slipped down the road and across the field to the railway. There was a train standing, glowing and breathing upon the lines, and the driver called to her as she ran round the buffers of the engine. Soon she was down by the riverside and looking for Margot. Though there was moonlight far above her the river banks were wrapped in fog that smelt of water, and Margot's face at the hut window was white, and her wool dress white, too. She came down and they rowed out into the fog, in an upward circle because of the stream. Fanny could just see her companion's little blunt boots, the stretched laces across her instep, and above, her pretty face and slant eyes. Hurriedly, in the boat she pulled off the thick stockings, rolled them up, and drew on the silk. A chill struck her feet. She wrapped the ends of her coat lightly round her knees and as she did so the roll of thick stockings sprang out of her lap and fell overboard into the fog and the river.

"Mademoiselle goes to a party?" said Margot, who had not noticed. The soft sympathetic voice was as full of blessing as Stewart's eyes had been.

"Yes, to a party. And you will fetch me back to-night when I whistle?"

"Yes. Blow three times, for sometimes in the singing at home I lose the sound."

The opposite bank seemed to drift in under the motionless boat, and she sprang out.

"A tout à l'heure, mademoiselle."

At the top of the bank the road ran out into the fog, which was thicker on this side. She walked along it and was lost to Margot's incurious eyes. Here it was utterly deserted: since the bridge had been blown up the road had become disused and only the few who passed over by Margot's boat ever found their way across these fields. She strayed along by the road's edge and could distinguish the blanched form of a tree.

Strange that the fog should reach so much further inland on this side of the river. Perhaps the ground was lower. Standing still her ear caught a rich, high, throaty sound, a choking complaint which travelled in the air.

"It is the car," she thought. Far away a patch of light floated in the sky, like an uprooted searchlight.

"That is the fog, bending the headlights upward."

She stood in the centre of the road and listened to the sound as it drew nearer and nearer, till suddenly the headlights came down out of the sky and pierced her—she stood washed in light, and the car stopped.

Beside the driver of the car was, not Julien, but a man with a red, wooden face like a Hindoo god made out of mahogany. Saluting, he said: "We are sent to fetch you, mademoiselle." He held the door of the closed car open for her, she smiled, nodded, climbed in and sank upon the seat.

"When you get to the lights of the houses, mademoiselle, will you stoop a little and cover yourself with this rug? It is not foggy in Chantilly and the street is very full."

"I will," she said, "I'll kneel down."

Something about his face distressed her. How came it that Julien trusted this new man? Perhaps he was some old and private friend of his who felt antagonistic to her, who disbelieved in her, who would hurt them both with his cynical impassivity.

"I'm fanciful!" she thought. "This is only some friend of his from Paris." Paris sending forth obstacles already!

In Chantilly she crouched beneath the rug—her expectations closing, unwandering, against her breast. Beams might pierce the glass of the car and light nothing unusual; what burnt beneath was not a fire that man could see. Generals in the street walked indifferently to the Hotel of the Grand Condé. It was their dinner hour, and who cared that an empty car should move towards a little inn beyond? Now, she held armfuls of the rug about her, buried from the light, now held her breath, too, as the car stopped.

"Now mademoiselle!"

And there stood Julien, at the end of the passage, he whom she had left, sombre and distracted, a long twenty-four hours ago in Chantilly. She saw the change even while she flew to him. He was gay, he was excited, he was exciting. He was beautiful, admirable, he admired her.

"Fanny, is it true? You have come?" and "Que vous êtes en beauté!"

Within, a table was laid for three—three chairs, three plates, three covers. He saw her looking at this.

"We dine three to-night. You must condescend to dine with a sergeant.
My old friend—Where is Alfred?"

"I am here."

"My old friend—four years before the war. The oldest friend I have. He has heard—"

("——Of Violette. He has heard of Violette! He is Violette's friend; he is against me!")

"I am so glad," she said aloud, in a small voice, and put out her hand. She did not like him, she had an instant dread of him, and thought he beheld it too.

"I did not even know he was here," said Julien, more gay than ever. "But he is the sergeant of the garage, and I find him again.

"What a help you'll be, to say the least of it! You will drive her to the river, you will fetch her from the river! I myself cannot drive, I am not allowed."

The impassive man thus addressed looked neither gay nor sad. His little eyes wandered to Fanny with a faint critical indifference. ("Julien has made a mistake, a mistake! He is an enemy!") She could not clearly decide how much she should allow her evening to be shadowed by this man, how deeply she distrusted him. But Julien was far from distrusting him. Through the dinner he seemed silently to brag to Alfred. His look said, and his smile said: "Is she not this and that, Alfred? Is she not perfect?" His blue eyes were bright, and once he said, "Go on, talk, Fanny, talk, Fanny, you have an audience. To-night you have two to dazzle!" Impossible to dazzle Alfred. Could he not see that? One might as easily dazzle a mahogany god, a little god alive beneath its casing with a cold and angry life. Yet though at first she was silent, inclined to listen to Alfred, to hope that something in his tones would soothe her enemy fears, soon she could not help following Julien's mood. Should she want to be praised, she had it from his eye—or be assured of love, it was there, too, in the eye, the smile, the soft tone. Because of Alfred, he could put nothing into words—because he must be dumb she could read a more satisfying conversation in his face.

She began to think the occasional presence of a third person was an addition, an exciting disturbance, a medium through which she could talk with ease two languages at once, French to Alfred, and love to Julien.

When they had finished dining Alfred left them, promising to come back with the car in half an hour, to take Fanny to the river.

"You must like him!" said Julien confidently, when the door had closed.
Fanny said she would. "And *do* you like him?" Fanny said she did.

"I met him so many years ago. He was suffering very much at the time through a woman. Now he will tell you he has become a cynic."

"Did she treat him badly?"

"She ran away from him, taking his carriage and his two horses—"

"A beautiful woman?" interrupted Fanny, who liked details.

"She might equally well have been magnificent or monstrous. She was over life-size, and Alfred, who is small, adored her. Everything about her was emphatic. Her hair was heavy-black, her skin too red. And never still, never in one place. Alfred had a house outside Paris, and carriage and horses to take him to the station. One night she took the horses, put them into the carriage and was seen by a villager seated upon the coachman's box driving along the road. When she had passed him this man saw her stop and take up a dark figure who climbed to the seat beside her. They—the woman and her probable lover, who never once had been suspected, and never since been heard of—drove as far as Persan- Beaumont, near here, where they had an accident, and turned the carriage into the ditch, killing one of the horses. The other they took out and coolly tied to the station railings. They took the train and disappeared, and though she had lived with Alfred two years, she never left a note for him to tell him that she had gone, she never wired to him about the roses, she never has written one since."

"Enough to turn him into a cynic!"

"Not at first. He came to me, spent the night in my flat; he was distracted. We must have walked together a mile across my little floor. He couldn't believe she was gone, which was natural. And though next morning the horses were missing and the coach-house empty, he couldn't be got to connect the two disappearances. He rang me up from the country where he went next day, saying earnestly as though to convince himself, 'You know

I've got on to the Paris police about those horses.' And later in the day, again: 'I hear there has been a good deal of horse-stealing all over the country.' Then, when the horses were found, one dead, and the other tied to the station railings, he believed at once that she had taken them and wouldn't talk one word more upon the subject. He sold the remaining horse."

"It was then he grew cool about women!"

"Not yet. It was then that he met, almost at once, a young girl who insisted in the most amazing fashion, that she loved him. He could not understand it. He came to me and said: 'Why does she love me?'

"I thought she was merely intriguing to marry him, but no, he said: 'There's something sincere and impressive in her tone; she loves me. What shall I do?'

'Why *shouldn't* you marry her?' I said.

And then he was all at once taken with the idea to such a degree that he became terrified when he was with her. 'Suppose she refuses me,' he said twenty times a day. 'Ask her. It's simple.' 'It's staking too much. You say, "Ask her," when all in a minute she may say no.'

"He got quite ill over it. The girl's mother asked him to the house, the girl herself, though she saw him less and less alone, smiled at him as tenderly as ever. And then there came a day when he left me full of courage, and going to her house he asked her to marry him. He met her alone by chance, and before asking her mother he spoke to the girl herself. She said no, point-blank. She said 'Nothing would induce her to.' He was so astonished that he didn't stay a second longer in the house. He didn't even come to me, but went back into the country, and then to England."

"But why did the girl—?"

"There is nothing to ask. Or, at any rate, there is no answer to anything. I suppose he asked himself every question about her conduct, but it was inexplicable."

"He should have asked her twice."

"It never occurred to him. And he has told me lately that she refused him with such considered firmness that it seemed unlikely that it was a whim."

"Well—poor Alfred! And yet it was only the merest chance, the merest run of bad luck—but it leaves him, you say, with the impression that we are flawed?"

"A terrible flaw. His opinion is that there is a deep coldness in women. In the brain, too, he feels them mortally unsound. Mad and cold he says

184

now of all women, and therefore as unlike a normal man as a creature half-lunatic, half-snake."

"He thinks that of all women, young or old?"

"Yes, I think so. He tells me that whereas most men make the mistake of putting down womanly unreason to the score of their having too much heart, he puts it down to their having no heart at all, which he says is so mad a state that they are unrecognisable as human creatures."

"But—(alas, poor Alfred)—you have made a charming confidante for us!"

"Confidante? He will make the best. He is devoted to me."

"To me?"

"To anything, to any one I care for."

"Not to me. What you have told me is the key to his expression when he looks at me. If he is devoted to you it is not an unreasoning devotion, and he is judging me poisonous to you. As he has himself been hurt, he will not have you hurt. I wish he had never come. I wish he might never be my driver to the river, and your friend, and our enemy."

"Fanny!"

"I wish it. I am unhappy about him, and unhappiness is always punished. While we were in Metz every one smiled at us; here every one will spy us out, scold, frown, punish—"

"And your magic luck?"

"Alfred threatens my luck," she said. Then, with another look, "Are you angry with me? Can you love such a character?"

"I love it now."

"You have never heard me when I scold, or cry or am sulky?..."

"Never."

"But if I make the experiment?"

"I could make a hundred experiments, but I make none of them. We cannot know what to-morrow may bring."

This she remembered suddenly with all her heart.

"Come nearer to me, Fanny. Why are you sitting so far away?"

She sat down nearer to him; she put all her fingers tightly round his wrist.

"I am not always sure that you are there, Julien; that you exist."

"Yet I am substantial enough."

"No, you are most phantom-like. It is the thought of parting that checks my earnestness; as though I had an impulse to save myself. It is the thought of parting that turns you into a ghost, already parted with; that sheds a light of unreality over you when I am distant. Something in me makes ready for that parting, flees from you, and I cannot stay it, steals itself, and I cannot break through it. I have known you so short a time. I have had nothing but pleasure from you; isn't it possible that I can escape without pain?"

"Is it?"

"No, no, no!" She laid her cheek upon his hand. "Do something to make it easier. Must it be that when you go you go completely? Promise me at least that it will be gradual, that you will try to see me when you have taken up your other life."

"But if I can't? If you are ordered back to Metz?"

"Why should I be? But, if I am, promise me that you will try. If it is only an artifice, beguile me with it; I will believe in any promise."

"You don't need to ask me to promise; you know you don't need to make me promise. Wherever you are sent I will try to come. *Wherever*—do you hear? Do you think that that 'other' life is a dragon to eat me up? That it will be such bliss to me that I shall forget you completely? It isn't to be bliss, but work, hard work, and competition. It is the work that will keep me to Paris, not my happiness, my gaiety, my content with other faces. That would comfort me if I were listener, and you the speaker. But, Fanny, Fanny, I never met any one with such joy as you—it is you who change the forest and the inns we meet in, make the journeys a miracle. Don't show me another face. We have been in love without a cloud, without scenes, without tears. You have laughed at everything. Don't change, don't show me someone whom I don't know; *not that sad face!*"

"This then!" She held up a face in whose eyes and smile was the hasty radiance his fervour had brought her—and at sight of it the words broke from him—"Are you happy so quickly?"

"Yes, yes, already happy."

"Because I speak aloud of what I feel? What a doubting heart you have within you! And I believe you only pretend to distress yourself, that you may test whether I am sensitive enough to show the reflection of it. Come! Well—am I right?"

"Partly. But I need not think. Oh, I am glad your feeling is so like mine, and mine like yours! I will let the parting take care of itself —yet there is one thing about which I cannot tell. What does your heart do in absence, what kind of man are you when there is no one but Alfred, who will say: 'Forget her'?"

"What kind do you think?"

"While I am here beside you, you cannot even imagine how dim I might become. Can I tell? Can you assure me?"

Dim she might become to him, but dim she was not now as she besought him with eyes that showed a quick and eager heart, eyes fixed on his face full of enquiry, sure of its answer, feigning doubt that did not distress her.

"And I to you, and I to you?" he said, speaking in her ear when he had made her an answer. "Dim, too? Why do we never talk of your inconstancy? We must discuss it."

"Inconstancy! That word had not occurred to me. It was *your* forgetfulness that I dreaded."

"I shall not be unforgetful until I am inconstant."

"Julien!"

"My love!"

"You can afford to tease me now you have me in such a mood!"

"In such a mood! Have I, indeed? Yet you will forget me before I forget you."

"You tell me to my face that I shall change?" she asked.

"Yes. And since you are bound to forget me, I insist at least that there shall be a reason for doing so. I would rather be a king dethroned than allowed to lapse like a poor idiot."

"You would? You can say that?" Her voice rose.

"One instant, Fanny. Even when my teasing is out of taste, learn to distinguish it from what I say in earnest. My dear, my dear, why should you have to listen to the matter of *my* philosophy and *my* experience which tells me all creatures forget and are forgotten! No! I wipe out! You will not vanish—"

The door opened and Alfred entered the room.

"The car is ready," he said. "I have had trouble in getting here."

Fanny turned to him. "I am ready," she said. "It is dreadful to have to trouble you to take me so late at night to the river."

"No, no—" Alfred, glowing from the exercise in the snowy night outside, was inclined to be more friendly, or at least less sparing of his

187

words. "Here are some letters that were at your lodging." He handed three to Julien.

"When do you dine with me again?" Julien, holding the letters, placed his hand upon her shoulder.

"I cannot tell what the work will be. Perhaps little, as the snow is deep."

"It is snowing again outside," said Alfred.

"Then the snow will lie even deeper, and there will be no work."

"Get her back quickly, Alfred, or the snow will lie too deep for you. I will send you a note, Fanny."

"That is quite easy, is it?"

"Easy. But compromising."

"Oh, surely—not very?"

"In France everything is compromising, mademoiselle," said Alfred. "But he will find a way to send it."

Julien had urged her to hurry, fearing the snow; now he said, "You are going?" as though it distressed him.

"I must."

"Yes, you must, you must. Where is your leather coat? Here—"

He found it.

"Stay! I must read this before you go. It is my demobilisation paper with the final date. I will look—"

"Are you coming?" called Alfred, from the end of the passage. "It is snowing wildly."

"There is some mistake," muttered Julien, his eye searching the large unfolded document.

"When, when—?" Fanny, hanging on his words, watched him.

"One moment. It is a mistake. Alfred! Alfred, here, a minute!"

"Look," he said, when Alfred had re-entered the room. He handed the paper to him, and drew him under the light. "See, they say—ah, wait, did I register at Charleville or Paris?"

"At Charleville. As an agriculturist. I remember well."

"Then there is no mistake." He folded up the paper, pinching the edges of the folds slowly with his thumb and finger nail.

"Fanny, it has come sooner than I expected."

She could say nothing, but fastened her gaze upon his lips.

"Much, much sooner, and there is no evading it. Alfred, I will bring her in a minute."

"The snow is coming down," muttered the mahogany god, grown wooden again under the light, and retreated.

"It is worse for me; it has been done by my own stupidity. But in those days I didn't know you—"

"Oh, if you are thinking of breaking it to me—only tell me *which* day! To-morrow?" She moved up close to him.

"Not to-morrow! No, no," he said, almost relieved that it was better than she feared. "In five days, in five days. Oh, this brings it before me! I have no wish now for that release for which I have longed. Fanny, it is only a change, not a parting!"

Alfred's voice called sharply from without. "You must come, mademoiselle!
Julien, bring her!"

"One instant. She is coming. Fanny, I must think it out. Until I go—I shall have time—we will get you sent to Charleville, and Charleville I must come often to see my land and my factory."

"How often?"

"Often, I must—"

"How often?"

"Once a week at last. Perhaps more often. If we can only manage that!"

"Julien!" Alfred returned and stood again in the doorway. "This is absurd. I can never get to the river if you keep her."

"Go, go. I will arrange! You will have a note from me to-morrow. Hurry, good-night, good-night!"

She was in the car; now the door was shutting on her; yet once more he pulled it open, "Ah! Oh, good-night!"

At the side of the car, the snow whirling round his head, Julien kissed her face in the darkness; Alfred, relentless, drove the car onward, and the door shutting with a slam, left him standing by the inn.

XIV. THE RIVER

The indifferent Alfred drove his unhappy burden towards the river. Walled in by the rush of snowflakes about him he made what way he could, but it was well-nigh impossible to see. The lamps gave no light, for the flakes had built a shutter across the glass like a policeman's dark lantern. The flying multitudes in the air turned him dizzy; he could not tell upon which side of the road he drove, and he could not tell what he would do when the wall beyond the outskirts of Chantilly forsook him. As to what was happening below him, what ruts, ditches, pits or hillocks he was navigating, he had no idea; his ship was afloat upon the snow, sluggishly rolling and heaving as it met with soft, mysterious obstacles

Heaviness and gloom sat upon the velvet seat behind him. The white, wild night outside was playful and waggish compared with the black dejection behind the opaque glass windows.

Fanny, who could not see her hand move in the darkness, saw clearly with other miserable and roving eyes the road that lay before her.

"Julien, good-bye. Don't forget me!" That she would say to him in a few days; that was the gate, the black portal which would lead her into the road. That she would say, with entreaty, yet no painful tones of hers would represent enough the entreaty of her heart that *neither would forget the other*. She thought of this.

Not in wilful unreason, or in disbelief of his promise, she looked at this parting as though it might be final. Without him she could see no charm ahead. And yet.... Tough, leathery heart—indestructible spinner she knew herself to be—no sooner should the dew fall from this enchanting fabric, the web itself be torn, than she would set to work upon the flimsiest of materials to weave another. And with such weaving comes forgetfulness. She thought of this.

Not four feet away, another mind, inscrutable to hers, was violently employed upon its own problem. In this wild darkness the wall of Chantilly had bid him go on alone; it left him first without guide, second without shelter. He drove into the path of a rough and bitter storm which was attacking everything in the short plain between the forest and the town. It leapt upon him in an outbreak of hisses; cut him with hailstones, swept up false banks of snow before him till the illusion of a road led him astray. He turned too much to the right, hung on the lip of a buried ditch, turned back again and saved himself. He turned too much to the left, tilted, hung, was in danger— yet found the centre of the road again. Here, on this wild plain, the exposed night was whiter—blanched enough, foreign enough, fitful enough to puzzle the most resolved and native traveller.

He arrived at a cross-roads. Yet was it a cross-roads? When roads are filled in level with the plain around them, the plain itself wind-churned like a ploughed field, when banks are rompishly erected, or melt unstably before the blows of the storm, it is hard to choose the true road from the false. He chose a road which instantly he saw to be no road. Too late. He pitched, this time not to recover. "A river—a river-bed!" was his horrified thought. Down went the nose of the car before him, the steering-wheel hitting him in the chest. Down came Fanny and all her black thoughts against the glass at his back. The car had not fallen very far; it had slid forward into a snow-lined dyke, and remained, resting on its radiator, its front wheels thrust into the steep walls of the bank, its back wheels in the air. Alfred climbed down from a seat which had lost its seating power; Fanny opened the door and stepped from the black interior into the deep snow. The front lamps were extinguished and buried in the opposite bank, the little red light at the back shone upwards to heaven.

"Well—"

"Well!"

"Are you hurt?"

"Not at all. And you?"

"Not a bit."

Their cold relations did not seem one whit changed from what they had been in the inn. Nothing had intervened but a little reflection, a little effort, and a vigorous jerk. Why should they change? They stood side by side in the noisy violence of the storm, and one shouted to the other: "Can you get her out!" and the other answered, "No."

"I will walk on to the river."

"You would never find it."

The truth of this she saw as she looked round.

Alfred left her and descending into the dyke, went on his knees by the radiator and fumbled deep in the snow with his hand. A hissing arose as the heated water ran from the tap he had turned. He emptied the water from the generator; the tail light sank and went out.

"No one will run into her," he remarked. "No one will pass."

Aie—screamed the wind and created a pillar of white powder. Fanny, losing her balance, one foot sank on the edge of a rut, and she went down on her hands; to the knees her silk-clad legs met the cold bite of the snow.

"You must come back with me," shouted Alfred in her ear.

That seemed true and necessary; she could not reach the river; she could not stay where she was. She followed him. At the next ditch he put out his hand and helped her across. They had no lamp. By the light of the snow she watched his blue-clad legs as they sank and rose; her own sinking and rising in the holes he left for her, the buffets of wind un-steadying her at every step. She followed him. And because she was as green as a green bough which bursts into leaf around a wound, the disturbing, the exciting menace of her discovery brightened her heart, set her mind whirling, and overgrew her dejection.

They gained the Chantilly wall, and experienced at once its protection. The howling wind passed overhead and left them in a lew; the dancing snowflakes steadied and dropped more like rain upon them; she moved up abreast of Alfred.

"I will take you back to the inn," he said. "They will have a room there."

"Julien will have left and gone to his lodging."

"Yes, at the other end of the town," answered Alfred, she fancied with grim satisfaction. ("Though it is as well," she thought; "there will be less scandal in the eyes of the innkeeper.")

"To-morrow morning, mademoiselle, I will fetch you at six with another car and its driver, Foss, a man whom I can trust. We will take you to the river, and on the return journey drag the car from the ditch. It should be easy; she has not heeled over on her side."

"That will be marvellous. I cannot tell you how I apologise."

This, she began to see, was serious; her debt to the enemy Alfred was growing hourly.

"No, no," he said, as though he saw the thing in the light of common justice. "You have come over to dine with Julien; we must get you back to the river."

"Nevertheless it's monstrous," she thought, "what he has to do for me."

But Alfred regarded it less as a friendly office towards Julien than as a duty, an order given by an officer. He was a sergeant, and four years of war had changed him from an irritable and independent friend to a dogged and careful subordinate. He did not like Fanny any the more for the trouble she was giving him; but he did not hold her responsible for his discomforts. She must be got to the river and to the river he would get her.

Pray heaven she never crossed it again.

When they arrived on the pavement outside the inn, he said: "Knock, mademoiselle, and ask if there is a room. It would be better that I should not be seen. Explain that the snow prevented you from returning. If there is a room do not come back to tell me, I shall watch you enter, and fetch you at six in the morning."

She thanked him again, and following his instructions, found herself presently in a small room under the eaves—pitied by the innkeeper's wife, given a hot brick wrapped in flannel by the innkeeper's daughter, warmed and cheered and, in a very short time, asleep. At half-past five she was called, dressed herself, and drank a cup of coffee; paying a fabulous bill which included two francs for the hot brick.

At six came Alfred, in another car, seated beside Foss, the new driver, a pale man with a grave face. They moved off in the grey dawn which brightened as they drove. Beyond the Chantilly wall the plain stretched, and on it the labouring wheel-marks of the night before were plainly marked. Alfred, beside the driver, let down a pane of glass to tell her that he had already been out with Foss and towed in the other car. She saw the ditch into which they had sunk, the scrambled marks upon the bank where she had been towed out. In ten minutes they were in the midst of the forest.

Now, Fate the bully, punishing the unlucky, tripping up the hurried, stepped in again. This car, which had been seized in a hurry by cold and yawning men, was not as she should be.

"Is she oiled?" Foss had called to the real driver of the car.

"She is ... everything!" answered the man, in a hurry, going off to his coffee. She was not.

Just as the approaching sun began to clear the air, just as with a spring at her heart Fanny felt that to be present at the opening of a fine day was worth all the trouble in the world, the engine began to knock. She saw Foss's head tilt a little sideways, like a keen dog who is listening. The knock increased. The engine laboured, a grinding set in; Foss pulled up at the side of the road and muttered to Alfred. He opened the bonnet, stared a second, then tried the starting handle. It would not move. Fanny let down the pane of glass and watched them in silence. "Not a drop," said Foss's low voice. And later, "Oil, yes, but—find me the tin!"

"Do you mean there is no oil, no spare oil—" Alfred hunted vainly round the car, under the seats, in the tool box. There was no tin of oil.

"If I had some oil," said Foss, "and if I let her cool a little, I could manage—with a syringe."

They consulted together. Alfred nodded, and approached the window.

"Mademoiselle," he said, "I am going on to the next village to get a tin of oil. There is a garage. Cars will be passing soon; I must ask you to lie covered with the rug in the bottom of the car; your uniform is very visible. Foss will remain with you."

Fanny lay down in the bottom of the car, fitting her legs among a couple of empty petrol tins; Foss covered her with the rug. A quarter of an hour went by, and above her she began to hear the voices of birds; below her the cold crept up. She had no idea how far the village might be, and it is possible that Alfred had had no idea either. A bicycle bell rang at her side; later she heard the noise of a car, which passed her with a rush. Lying with her ear so close to the poor body of the motor she felt it to be but cold bones in a cemetery, dead, dead.

Outside in the road, Foss shaded his eyes and looked up the now sparkling road a hundred times. The motors increased; the morning traffic between Précy and Chantilly awoke; the cars were going in to the offices of the G.Q.G. Now and then Foss would come to the window of the car. "Don't move," he would say. The floor-boards were rattled by an icy wind that blew over the face of the snow and up under the car; the brown, silk legs lay prone and stiff between the petrol cans, lifeless now to the knee. She was seized with fits of violent shivering. At one moment she had planned in her despair to call to Foss and tell him she would walk—but she had let the moment pass and now she put away the thought of walking on those lifeless feet. Besides, she would be seen—that well-known cap, bobbing back between the trees from Chantilly so early in the morning!

"Oh, Honour of the Section, I am guarding you like my life!" She tried to raise her head a little to ease her neck.

"Don't move," said Foss.

Feet pattered past her; motors swept by; bicycle bells rang.

"Foss," she said.

The soldier leant towards her and listened.

"Choose your own time, but you must let me sit up a moment. I am in pain."

"Then, now, mademoiselle!"

She sat up, flinging the rug back, dazzled by the splendour of the forest, the climbing sun, the heavy-burdened trees. Behind her was a cart coming up slowly; far ahead a cyclist swayed in the ruts of the road. As they approached her she pleaded: "They can't know me! Let me sit up—"

But Foss knew only one master, his sergeant.

"Better go down, mademoiselle."

She went down again under the black rug, close against the wind that lifted the floor-boards, wrapping her coat more tightly round her, folding her arms about her knees.

"It must be nearly eight. I have an hour more before they come in to breakfast. Ah, and when they do, will one of them go into my bedroom with my letters?"

She tried to pick out in her mind that one most friendly to her, that one who was to destroy her. She heard in spirit her cry: "Fanny *isn't there!*"

She thought of Stewart who would have woken early, planning anxiously to save her. The faces of the Guardians of the Honour of the Section began to visit her one by one, and horror spread in her. Then, pushing them from her, attempting to escape: "They are not all the world—" But they *were* all the world—if in a strange land they were all to frown together. The thought was horrible. Time to get there yet! Alas, that the car was not facing *towards* Chantilly—so early in the morning!

"Foss, Foss, don't you see him coming?"

"The road is full of people."

A car rushed by them, yet never seemed to pass. The engine slowed down and a voice called: "What's up? Anything you want?"

It was the voice of Roland Vauclin. Ah, she knew him—that fat, childish man, who loved gossip as he loved his food. To Fanny it seemed but a question of seconds before he would lift the rug, say gravely, "Good morning, mademoiselle," before he would rush back to his village spreading the news like a fall of fresh snow over the roofs. She lay still from sheer inertia. Had Foss answered? She could not hear.

Then she heard him clear his throat and speak.

"The Captain asked me to get a bit of wood for his fire, sir. I have a man in there gathering branches, while I do a bit of 'business' with the car."

195

"Oh, right!... Go on!" said Vauclin to his own chauffeur. Again they were left alone. Talk between them was almost impossible; Fanny was so muffled, Foss so anxiously watched for Alfred. The reedy singing between the boards where the wind attacked her occupied all her attention. The very core of warmth seemed extinguished in her body, never to be lit again. She remembered their last *fourier*, or special body-servant, who had gone on leave upon an open truck, and who had grown colder and colder—"and he never got warm again and he died, madame," the letter from his wife had told them.

"I think he is coming! There is no one else on the road, mademoiselle.
Will you look? I don't see very well—"

She tried to throw off the rug and sit up, but her frozen elbow slipped and she fell again on the floor of the car. Pulling herself up she stared with him through the glass. Far up the white road a little figure toiled towards them, carrying something, wavering as though the ice-ruts were deep, picking its way from side to side. Neither of them was sure whether it was Alfred; they watched in silence. Before she knew it was upon her a car went by; she dived beneath the rug, striking her forehead on the corner of the folding seat.

"Did they see? Was any one inside?"

"It was an empty car. Please be careful."

Foss was cold with rebuke. After that she lay still, isolated even from Foss. Ten minutes went by and suddenly Foss spoke—"Did you have to go far?"

And Alfred's hard voice answered "Yes."

Then she heard the two men working, tools clattering, murmured voices, and in ten minutes Foss said: "Try the starting handle."

She heard the efforts, the labour of Alfred at the handle.

"He will kill himself—he will break a blood-vessel," she thought as she listened to him. Every few minutes someone seized the handle and wound and wound—as she had never wound in her life—on and on, past the very limit of endurance. And under her ear, in the cold bones of the car, not a sign of life! Not a sign of life, and, as though she could hear them, all the clocks in the world struck nine.

The Guardians of the Honour would be in at breakfast now! they would be sitting, sitting—discussing her absence. Stewart, upstairs, would be looking out of the window, watching the river, perhaps answering questions indifferently with her cool look. "Oh, in the garage—or walking in the forest. I don't know." Cough! She jumped as the bones in the bottom of the car moved under her, and the engine breathed. The noise died out, Foss leapt to the handle and wound and wound, fiercely, like a man who meant to make her breathe again or die. Again she struggled to life, lived for a few minutes, choked and was silent.

"How is the handle?"

"Pretty stiff," said Foss, "but getting better. Give me the oil squirt."

Alfred took his place at the handle. Suddenly the car sprang to life again on a full deep note. Fanny lifted her head a little. Foss was leaning over the carburettor with his thin anxious look: Alfred stood in the snow, dark red in the face, and covered with oil. Soon they were moving along the road, slowly at first, and with difficulty: then faster and more freely. A little thin warmth began to creep up through the boards and play about her legs.

She was carried along under her dark rug for another twenty minutes, then fell against the seat as the car turned sharply into the forsaken road that led to the broken bridge. In five minutes more the car had stopped and Alfred was at the door saying: "At last, mademoiselle!" She stammered her thanks as she tried to step from the car to the ground —but fell on her knees on the dashboard.

"Have you hurt your foot?" said Alfred, who was hot.

"I am only cold," she said humbly, unwilling to intrude her puny endurances on their gigantic labours.

She sat on the step of the car rubbing her ankles, and stared at the meadows of thawing snow, at the open porches of stone which led the road straight into the river, at the church and the sunlit houses on the other side.

Bidding them good-bye she reached the bank, and climbed down it, stumbling in the frozen mud and pits of ice till she reached the stiff reeds at the bank.

The river had floes of ice upon it, green ice which swung and caught among the reeds at the edge. "It is thin," she thought, pushing her shoe through it, "it can't prevent the boat from crossing the river." Yet she was anxious.

There on the other side was the little hut, the steps, the boat tied to the stone and held rigid in the ice. A shaggy dog ran by her feet to the river's edge and barked. Feet came clambering down the bank and a workman followed the dog, with a bag of tools and a basket. He walked up to the river, and putting his hands in a trumpet to his mouth called in a huge voice: "Un passant, Margot! Margot!" Fanny remembered her whistle and blew that too.

There was no sign of life, and the little hut looked as before, like a brown dog asleep in the sun. Fanny turned to the man, ready to share her anxiety with him, but he had sat down on the bank and was retying a boot-lace that had come undone.

Margot never showed herself at the hut window, at the hut door. When Fanny turned back to whistle again she saw her standing up in the boat, which, freed, was drifting out towards them—saw her scatter the ice with her oar—and the boat, pushed upstream, came drifting down towards them in a curve to hit the bank at their feet. The girl stepped out, smiling, happy, pretty, undimmed by the habit of trade. The man got in and sat down, the dog beside him.

"I would stand," said Margot to Fanny, "it's so wet."

She made no allusion to the broken appointment for the night before.

Fanny, noticing the dripping boards of the boat, stood up, her hand upon Margot's shoulder to steady herself. The thin, illusory ice shivered and broke and sank as the oar dipped in sideways.

Cocks were crowing on the other side—the sun drew faint colours from the ice, the river clattered at the side of the boat, wind twisted and shook her skirt, and stirred her hair. All was forgotten in the glory of the passage of the river.

Margot, smiling up under her damp, brown hair, took her five sous, pressed her town boots against the wooden bar, and shot the boat up against the bank.

Fanny went up the bank, over the railway lines, and out into the road. Two hundred yards of road lay before her, leading straight up to the house. On the left was a high wall, on the right the common covered with snow—should some one come out of the house there was no chance of hiding. She glanced down at her tell-tale silk stockings; yet she could not hurry on those stiff and painful feet. She was near the door in the wall.

She passed in—the dog did not bark; came to the foot of the steps—nobody looked out of the window; walked into the hall among their hanging coats and macintoshes, touched them, moved them with her shoulder; heard voices behind the door of the breakfast room, was on the stairs, up out of sight past the first bend, up, up, into Stewart's room.

"*Do you know...?*"

"*No one knows!*"

"Oh ... oh...." All her high nerves came scudding and shuddering down into the meadows of content. Eternal luck.... She crept under Stewart's eiderdown and shivered.

"Here's the chocolate. I will boil it again on my cooker. Oh, you have a sort of ague...."

Good friend ... kind friend! She had pictured her like that, anxious, unquestioning and warm!

Later she went downstairs and opened the door of the breakfast room upon the Guardians of the Honour.

As she stood looking at them she felt that her clothes were the clothes of some one who had spent hours in the forest—that her eyes gave out a gay picture of all that was behind them—her adventures must shout aloud from her hands, her feet.

"Had your breakfast?" said some one.

"Upstairs," said Fanny, contentedly, and marvelled.

She had only to open and close her lips a dozen times, bid them form the words: "I have been out all night," to turn those browsing herds of benevolence into an ambush of threatening horns, lowered at her. Almost ... she would *like* to have said the sentence.

But basking in their want of knowledge she sat down and ate her third breakfast.

XV. ALLIES

A thaw set in.

All night the snow hurried from the branches, slid down the tree trunks, sank into the ground. Sank into the moss, which suddenly uncovered, breathed water as a sponge breathes beneath the sea; sank into the Oise, which set up a roaring as the rising water sapped and tunnelled under its banks.

With a noise of thunder the winter roof of the villa slipped down and fell into the garden—leaving the handiwork of man exposed to the dawn—streaming tiles, ornamental chimneys, unburied gargoyles, parapet, and towers of wood.

In a still earlier hour, while darkness yet concealed the change of aspect, Fanny left the garden with a lantern in her hand. She had a paper in her pocket, and on the paper was written the order of her mission; the order ran clearly: "To take one officer to the demobolisation centre at Amiens and proceed to Charleville"; but the familiar words "and return" were not upon it.

She cast no glance back, yet in her mind sent no glance forward. She could not think of what she left; she left nothing, since these romantic forests would be as empty as tunnels when Julien was not there; but closing the door of the garden gate softly behind her, she blew out the lantern and hung it to the topmost spike, that Stewart, who was leaving for England in the morning, might bequeath it to their landlady.

All night long the Renault had stood ready packed in the road by the villa—and now, starting the engine, which ran soundlessly beneath the bonnet—she drove from a village whose strangeness was hidden from her, followed the Oise, which rumbled on a new note, heard the bubbling of wild brooks through the trees, and was lost in the steamy moisture of a thawing forest.

There was a sad, a deadly charm still about the journey. There was a bitter and a sweet comfort yet before her. There were two hours of farewell to be said at dawn. There was the sight of his face once more for her. That the man who slipped into the seat beside her at Chantilly was Julien dissolved her courage and set her heart beating. She glanced at him in that early light, and he at her. Two hours before them still.

She was to carry him with her only to lose him surely; he was to accompany her on her journey only to turn back.

All the way to Amiens he reassured himself and her: "In a week I will come to Charleville."

And she replied: "Yes, this is nothing. I lose you here, but in a week you will come."

(Why then this dread?)

"In a week—in a week," ran the refrain.

"How will you find me at Charleville? Will you come to the garage?"

"No, I shall write to the 'Silver Lion.' You will find in the middle of the main street an old inn with mouldering black wood upon the window sashes. How well I know it! I will write there."

"We are so near the end," she said suddenly, "that to have said 'Good-bye' to you, to leave you at Amiens, is no worse than this."

And faster she hurried towards Amiens to find relief. He did not contradict her, or bid her go slower, but as they neared Amiens, offered once more his promise that they would meet again in a week.

"It isn't that," she said. "I know we shall meet again. It isn't that I fear never to see you again. It is the closing of a chapter."

"I, too, know that."

They drove into Amiens in the streaming daylight.

The rain poured.

"I am sending you to my home," he said. "Every inch of the country is mine. You go to a town that I know, villages that I know, roads that I have walked and ridden and driven upon. You go to my country. I like to think of that."

"I shall go at once to see your house in Revins."

"Yes—oh, you will see it easily—on the banks of the Meuse. I was born there. In a week, in a few days, in a short time—I will come, too."

She stopped the car in a side street of the town.

Lifting her hands she said: "They want to hold you back." Then placed them back on the wheel. "They can't," she said, and shook her head.

He took his bag in his hand, and stood by the car, looking at her.

"You take the three o'clock train back to Paris when the papers are through," she said hurriedly with sudden nervousness. And then: "Oh, we've said everything! Oh, let's get it over—"

He held the side of the car with his hand, then stepped back sharply. She drove down the street without looking back.

There was a sort of relief in turning the next corner, in knowing that if she looked back she would see nothing. A heavy shadow lifted from her; it was a deliverance. "Good-bye" was said—was over; that pain was done—now for the next, now for the first of the days without him. She had slipped over the portal of one sorrow to arrive at another; but she felt the change, and her misery lightened. This half-happiness lasted her all the morning.

She moved out of Amiens upon the St. Quentin road, and was almost beyond the town before she thought of buying food for the day. Unjustly, violently, she reflected: "What a hurry to leave me! He did not ask if I had food, or petrol, or a map—"

But she knew in her heart that it was because he was young and in trouble, and had left her quickly, blindly, as eager as she to loosen that violent pain.

She bought a loaf of bread, a tin of potted meat, an orange and a small cheese, and drove on upon the road until she came to Warfusée. Wherever her thoughts fell, wherever her eye lay, his personality gnawed within her—and nowhere upon her horizon could she find anything that would do instead. Julien, who had moved off down the street in Amiens, went moving off down the street of her endless thought.

"I have only just left him! Can't I go back?" And this cry, carried out in the nerves of her foot, slowed the car up at the side of the road. She looked back—no smoke darkened the landscape. Amiens was gone behind her.

Again, on. In ten minutes the battlefields closed in beside the road.

Julien was gone. Stewart was gone. Comfort and ease and plenty were gone. "But *We* are here again!" groaned the great moors ahead, and on each hand. The dun grass waved to the very edge of the road cut through it. Deep and wild stretched the battlefields, and there, a few yards ahead, were those poor strangers, the scavenging Chinamen.

Upon a large rough signpost the word "Foucaucourt" was painted in white letters. A village of spars and beams and broken bricks—yet here, as everywhere, returning civilians hunted like crows among the ruins, carrying beams and rusty stoves, and large umbrellas for the rain.

At the next corner a Scotch officer hailed her.

"Will you give me a lift?"

He sat down beside her.

"What do you do?" she asked.

"I look after Chinamen."

"Ah, how lonely!"

"It is terrible," he replied. "Look at it! Dead for miles; the army gone, and I here with these little yellow fellows, grubbing up the crumbs."

She put him down at what he called "my corner"—a piece of ground indistinguishable from the rest.

"Is that where you live?"

"Yes."

There was a black-boarded hut from whose chimney smoke exuded, and to this ran a track across the grass. She watched him walk along it, a friendless, sandy man, left over from the armies which had peopled the rabbit warren in the ground. The Renault loped on with its wolf-like action, and she felt a spring of relief that she lived upon moving ground; passing on down the rickety road she forgot the little man.

Ahead lay the terrible miles. She seemed to make no gain upon them, and could not alter the face of the horizon, however fast she drove. Iron, brown grass—brown grass and iron, spars of wood, girders, torn railway lines and stones. Even the lorries travelling the road were few and far between. A deep loneliness was settled upon the desert where nothing grew. Yet, suddenly, from a ditch at the side of the road, a child of five stared at her. It had its foot close by a stacked heap of hand grenades; a shawl was wrapped round it and the thin hands held the ends together. What child? Whose? How did it get here, when not a house stood erect for miles and miles—when not a coil of smoke touched the horizon! Yes, something oozed from the ground! Smoke, blue smoke! Was life stirring like a bulb under this whiter ruin, this cemetery of village bones?

She stopped the car. The child turned and ran quickly across a heap of dust and iron and down into the ground behind a pillar. "It must have a father or mother below—" The breath of the invisible hearth coiled up into the air; the child was gone.

A man appeared behind the pillar and came towards the car. Fanny held out her cigarette-case and offered it to him.

"Have you been here long?" she asked.

"A month, mademoiselle."

"Are there many of you in this—village?" (Not a spar, not a pile of bricks stood higher than two feet above the ground.)

"There are ten persons now. A family came in yesterday."

"But how are you fed?"

"A lorry passes once a week for all the people in this district—within fifty miles. There are ten souls in one village, twenty in another, two in another. They have promised to send us huts, but the huts don't come. We have sunk a well now and it is drinkable, but before that we got water by lorry once a week, and we often begged a little from the radiators of other lorries."

"What have you got down there?"

"It is the cellar of my house, mademoiselle. There are two rooms still, and one is watertight. The trouble is the lack of tools. I can't build anything. We have a spade, and a pick and a hammer, which we keep between the ten of us."

"Take my hammer," said Fanny. "I can get another in the garage."

He took it, pleased and grateful, and she left this pioneer of recolonisation, this obstinate Crusoe and his family, standing by his banner of blue smoke.

Another hour and a large signpost arrested her attention.

"This *was* Villers Carbonel," it told her, and beneath it three roads ran in different directions. There was no sign at all of the village—not a brick lay where the signpost stood.

Stopping the car she drew out her map and considered—and suddenly, out of nowhere, with a rattle and a bang, and a high blast on a mad little horn, a Ford arrived at her side upon the cross-roads.

"Got no gas?" enquired an American. She looked up into his pink face. His hood was broken and hung down over one side of the car. One of his springs was broken and he appeared to be holding the car upright by the tilt of his body. His tyres were in rags, great pieces of rubber hung out beyond the mudguards.

"Dandy car you've got!" he said with envy. "French?"

Soon he was gone upon the road to Chaulnes. His retreating back, with the spindly axle, the wild hood, the torn fragments of tyre flying round in streamers, and the painful list of the body set her laughing, as she stood by the signpost in the desert.

Then she took the road to Peronne.

"I won't have my lunch yet——" looking at the pale sun. Her only watch had stopped long since, resenting the vibrations of the wheel. She passed Peronne—uprooted railways and houses falling head foremost into the river, and beyond it, side roads led her to a small deserted village, oddly untouched by shell or fire. Here the doors swung and banged, unlatched by any human fingers, the windows, still draped with curtains, were shut, and no face looked out. Here she ate her lunch.

The rain had ceased and a little pale sunshine cheered the cottages, the henless, dogless, empty road. A valiant bird sang on a hedge beside her.

With her wire-cutters she opened the tin of potted meat, and with their handle spread it on the bread.

"Lord, how lonely it is—surely some door might open, some face look out——" At that a little gust of wind got up, and she jumped in her seat, for a front door slammed and blew back again.

"I couldn't stay here the night——" with a shiver—and the bird on the branch sang louder than ever. "It's all very well," she addressed him. "You're with your own civilisation. I'm right *out* of mine!"

The day wore on. The white sun, having finished climbing one side of the sky, came down upon the other.

Here and there a man hailed her, and she gave him a lift to his village, talked a little to him, and set him down.

A young Belgian, who had learned his English at Eton, was her companion for half an hour.

"And you are with the French?" he asked. "How do you like the fellows?"

"I like them very much. I like them enormously." (Strange question, when all France meant Julien!)

"Don't you find they think there is no one else in the world?" he grumbled. "It is a delicious theory for them, and it must be amusing to be French!"

"Little Belgium—jealous young sister, resentful of the charm of the elder woman of the world!"

A French lieutenant climbed to the seat beside her.

"You are English, mademoiselle?" he said, she thought with a touch of severity. He was silent for a while. Then: "Ah, none but the English could do this——"

"What?"

"Drive as you do, alone, mademoiselle, amid such perils."

She did not ask to what perils he alluded, and she knew that his words were a condemnation, not a compliment. Ah, she knew that story, that theory, that implication of coldness! She did not trouble to reply, nor would she have known how had she wished it.

They passed an inhabited village. From a door flew a man in a green bonnet and staggered in the street. After him a huge peasant woman came, and standing in the doorway shook her fist at him. "I'll teach you to meddle with my daughter—"

"Those are the cursed Italians!" said the French lieutenant, leaning from the car to watch.

A mile further on they came to a quarry, in which men prowled in rags.

"Those are the Russians!" he said. And these were kept behind barbed wire, fenced round with armed sentries.

She remembered an incident in Paris, when she had hailed a taxi.

"Are you an American?" asked the driver. "For you know I don't much like driving Americans."

"But I am English."

"Well, that's better. I was on the English Front once, driving for the French Mission."

"Why don't you like Americans?"

"Among other things they give me two francs when three is marked!"

"But once they gave you ten where three was marked!"

"That's all changed!" laughed the taxi-man. "And it's a long story. I don't like them."

* * * * *

"Go away!" said France restlessly, pushing at the new nations in her bosom. "It's all done. Go back again!"

"Are you an Ally?" said the Allies to each other balefully, their eyes no longer lit by battle, but irritable with disillusion—and each told his women tales of the other's shortcomings.

Along the sides of the roads, in the gutters, picking the dust-heap of the battlefields, there were representatives of other nations who did not join in the inter-criticism of the lords of the earth. Chinese, Arabs and Annamites made signs and gibbered, but none cared whether they were in amity or enmity.

Only up in Germany was there any peace from acrimony. *There* the Allies walked contentedly about, fed well, looked kindly at each other. *There* were no epithets to fling—they had all been flung long ago.

And the German people, looking curiously back, begged buttons as souvenirs from the uniforms of the men who spoke so many different languages.

XVI. THE ARDENNES

The day wore on—

The sun came lower and nearer, till the half-light ran with her half-thought, dropping, sinking, dying. "Guise," said the signpost, and a battlement stared down and threw its shadow across her face. "Is that where the dukes lived?" She was a speck in the landscape, moving on wheels that were none of her invention, covering distances of hundreds of miles without amazement, upon a magic mount unknown to her forefathers. Dark and light moved across the face of the falling day. Sometimes when she lifted her eyes great clouds full of rain were crossing the sky; and now, when she looked again the wind had torn them to shreds and hunted them away. The shadows lengthened—those of the few trees falling in bars across the road. A turn of the road brought the setting sun in her face, and blinded with light, she drove into it. When it had gone it left rays enough behind to colour everything, gilding the road itself, the air, the mists that hung in the ditches.

Before the light was gone she saw the Ardennes forests begin upon her left.

When it was gone, wood and road, air and earth, were alike stone-coloured. Then the definite night, creeping forward on all sides, painted out all but the road and the margin of the road—and with the side lights on all vision narrowed down to the grey snout of the bonnet, the two hooped mudguards stretched like divers' arms, and the blanched dead leaves which floated above from the unseen branches of the trees.

Four crazy Fords were drawn up in one village street, and as her lights flashed on the door she caught sight of the word "Café" written on it. Placing the Renault beside the Fords she opened the door. Within five Frenchmen were drinking at one table, and four Americans at another. The Americans sprang up and claimed her, first as their own kin, and then at least as a blood sister. They gave her coffee, and would not let her pay; but she sat uneasily with them.

"For which nation do you work? There are no English here," they said.

"I am in the French Army."

"Gee, what a rotten job!" they murmured sympathetically.

"Where have you come from?"

"We've just come back from Germany, and you bet it's good up there!"

"Good?"

"Every darn thing you want. Good beds, good food, and, thank God, one can speak the lingo."

"You don't speak French then?"

"You bet not."

"Why don't you learn? Mightn't it be useful to you?"

"Useful?"

"Oh, when you get back home. In business perhaps—"

"Ma'am," said the biggest American, leaning earnestly towards her, "let me tell you one thing. If any man comes up to me back in the States and starts on me with that darn language—I'll drop him one."

"And German is easier?"

"Oh, well, German we learn in the schools, you see. How far do you make it to St. Quentin?"

"Are you going there on those Fords?"

"We hope to, ma'am. But we started a convoy of twenty this morning, and these here four cars are all we've seen since lunch."

"I hardly think you'll get as far as St. Quentin to-night. And there's little enough to sleep in on the way. I should stay here." She rose. "I wish you luck. Good-bye."

She thanked them for their coffee, nodded to the quiet French table and went out.

One American followed her.

"Can you buzz her round?" he asked kindly, and taking the handle, buzzed her round.

"I bet you don't get any one to do that for you in your army, do you?" he asked, as he straightened himself from the starting handle. She put her gear in with a little bang of anger.

"You're kind," she said, "and they are kind. That you can't see it is all a question of language. Every village is full of bored Americans with nothing to do, and never one of them buys a dictionary!"

"If it's villages you speak of, ma'am, it isn't dictionaries is needed," he answered, "'tis plumbing!"

She had not left him ten minutes before one of her tyres punctured.

"Alas! I could have found a better use for them than arguing," she thought ruefully, regretting the friendly Americans, as she changed the tyre by the roadside under the beam from her own lamps.

When it was done she sat for a few minutes in the silent car. The moon came up and showed her the battlements of the Ardennes forest standing upon the crest of the mountains to her left. "That is to be my home—"

Julien was in Paris by now, divested of his uniform, sitting by a great fire, eating civilised food. A strange young man in dark clothes—she wondered what he would wear.

He seemed a great many difficult miles away. That he should be in a heated room with lights, and flowers, and a spread table—and she under the shadow of the forest watching the moon rise, lengthened the miles between them; yet though she would have given much to have him with her, she would have given nothing to change places with him.

The road left the forest for a time and passed over bare grass hills beneath a windy sky. Then back into the forest again, hidden from the moon. And here her half-stayed hunger made her fanciful, and she started at the noise of a moving bough, blew her horn at nothing, and seemed to hear the overtaking hum of a car that never drew near her.

Suddenly, on the left, in a ditch, a dark form appeared, then another and another. Down there in a patch of grass below the road she caught sight of the upturned wheels of a lorry, and stopping, got down, walked to the ditch and looked over. There, in wild disorder, lay thirty or forty lorries and cars, burnt, twisted, wheelless, broken, ravaged, while on the wooden sides the German eagle, black on white, was marked.

"What—what—can have happened here!"

She climbed back into the car, but just beyond the limit of her lights came on a huge mine crater, and the road seemed to hang on its lip and die for ever. Again she got down, and found a road of planks, shored up by branches of trees, leading round on the left edge of the crater to firm land on the other side. Some of the planks were missing, and moving carefully around the crater she heard others tip and groan beneath her.

"Could that have been a convoy caught by the mine? Or was it a dumping ground for the cars unable to follow in the retreat?"

The mine crater, which was big enough to hold a small villa, was overgrown now at the bottom with a little grass and moss.

On and on and on—till she fancied the moon, too, had turned as the sun had done, and started a downward course. It grew no colder, she grew no hungrier—but losing count of time, slipped on between the flying tree trunks, full of unwearied content. At last a light shone through the trees, and by a wooden bridge which led over another crater she came on a lonely house. "Café" was written on the door, but the shutters were tight shut, and only a line of light shone from a crack.

From within came sounds of laughter and men's voices. She knocked, and there was an instant silence, but no one came to answer. At length the bolts were withdrawn and the head of an old woman appeared through the door, which was cautiously opened a little.

"An omelette? Coffee?"

"You don't know what you speak of! We have no eggs."

"Then coffee?"

"No, no, nothing at all. Go on to Charleville. We have nothing."

"How far is Charleville?"

But the door shut again, the bolts were shot, and a man's voice growled in the hidden room behind.

"Dubious hole. Yet it looks as though a big town were near——" And down the next slope she ran into Charleville. The town had been long abed, the street lamps were out, the cobbles wet and shining.

On the main boulevard one dark figure hurried along.

"Which is the 'Silver Lion'?" she called, her voice echoing in the empty street.

Soon, between rugs on a bed in the "Silver Lion," between a single sheet doubled in two, she slept—propping the lockless door with her suitcase.

The Renault slept or watched below in the courtyard, the moon sank, the small hours passed, the day broke, the first day in Charleville.

PART IV.
SPRING IN CHARLEVILLE

XVII. THE STUFFED OWL

A stuffed bird stood upon a windless branch and through a window of blue and orange squares of glass a broken moon stared in.

A bedroom, formed from a sitting-room, a basin to wash in upon a red plush table—no glass, no jug, no lock upon the door. Instead, gilt mirrors, three bell ropes and a barometer. A bed with a mattress upon it and nothing more.

This was her kingdom.

Beyond, a town without lights, without a station, without a milkshop, without a meat shop, without sheets, without blankets, crockery, cooking pans, or locks upon the doors. A population half-fed and poor. A sky black as ink and liquid as a river.

Prisoners in the streets, moving in green-coated gangs; prisoners in the gutters, pushing long scoops to stay the everlasting tide of mud; thin, hungry, fierce and sad, green-coated prisoners like bedraggled parrots, outnumbered the population.

The candle of the world was snuffed out—and the wick smoked.

The light was gone—the blinding light of the Chantilly snows, the lights on the Précy river—moonlight, sunlight—the little boat crossing at moonrise, sunrise.

"Ah, that long journey! How I pressed on, how I fled from Amiens!"

"What, not Charleville yet?" I said. "Isn't it Charleville soon? What hurry was there then to get there?"

The stuffed bird eyed her from his unstirring branch, and that yellow eye seemed to answer: "None, none..."

"This is his home; his country. He told me it was beautiful. But I cannot see beauty. I am empty of happiness. Where is the beauty?"

And the vile bird, winking in the candle's light, replied: "Nowhere."

But he lied.

Perhaps she had been sent, stuffed as he was, from Paris. Perhaps he had never flown behind the town, and seen the wild mountains that began at the last house on the other bank of the river. Or the river itself, greener than any other which flowed over black rocks, in cold gulleys —the jade-green Meuse flowing to Dinant, to Namur. Perhaps from his interminable boulevard he had never seen the lovely Spanish Square of red and yellow, its steep-roofed houses standing upon arches—or the proud Duc Charles de Gonzague who strutted for ever upon his pedestal, his stone cape slipping from one shoulder, his gay Spaniard's hat upon his head—holding back a smile from his handsome lips, lest the town which he had come over the mountains to found should see him tolerant and sin beneath his gaze.

That bird knew the rain would stop—knew it in his dusty feathers, but he would not kindle hope. He knew there was a yellow spring at hand— but he left her to mourn for the white lustre of Chantilly. Vile bird!... She blew out the candle that he might wink no more.

"To-morrow I will buy a padlock and a key. If among these gilt mirrors I can have no other charm, I will have solitude!" And having hung a thought, a plan, a hope before her in the future, she slept till day broke—the second day in Charleville.

* * * *

She woke, a mixture of courage and philosophy.

"I can stand anything, and beyond a certain limit misfortune makes me laugh. But there's no reason why I should stand this!" The key and padlock idea was rejected as a compromise with happiness.

"No, no, let us see if we can get something better to lock up than that bird." He looked uncommonly dead by daylight.

"I would rather lock up an empty room, and leave it pure when I must leave it!"

Dressing, she went quickly down the street to the Bureau de la Place. The clerks and secretaries nodded and smiled at each other, and bent their heads over their typewriters when she looked at them.

"Can I see the billeting lieutenant?"

"He is not here."

"I saw him enter."

"We will go and see...."

She drummed upon the table with her fingers and the clerks and secretaries winked and nodded more meaningly than ever.

"*Entrez*, mademoiselle. He will see you."

The red-haired lieutenant with pince-nez was upon his feet looking at her curiously as she entered the adjoining room.

"Good morning, mademoiselle. There is something wrong with the billet that I found you yesterday?"

She looked at him. In his pale-blue eyes there was a beam; in his creased mouth there was an upward curve. The story of legitimate complaint that she had prepared drooped in her mind; she looked at him a little longer, hesitated, then, risking everything:

"Monsieur, there is a stuffed owl in the room."

He did not wince. "Take it out, mademoiselle."

"H'm, yes. I cannot see heaven except through orange glass."

"Open the window."

"It is fixed."

Then he failed her; he was a busy, sensible man.

"Mademoiselle, I find you a billet, I instal you, and you come to me in the middle of the morning with this ridiculous story of an owl. It isn't reasonable...."

The door opened and his superior officer walked in, a stern captain with no crease about his mouth, no beam in his olive eye.

Ah, now ... Now the lieutenant had but to turn to his superior officer and she would indeed be rent, and reasonably so.

"What is the matter?" said the newcomer. "Is something fresh needed?"

The billeting lieutenant never hesitated a second.

"*Mon capitaine*, unfortunately the billet found yesterday for this lady is unsuitable. The owner of the house returns this week, and needs the room."

"Have you some other lodging for her?"

"Yes, *mon capitaine*, in the Rue de Clèves."

"Good. Then there is no difficulty?"

"None. Follow me, mademoiselle, the street is near. I will take you to the *concierge*."

She followed him down the stairs, and caught him up upon the pavement.

"You may think, mademoiselle, that it is because I am young and susceptible."

"Oh, no, no...."

"Indeed, I *am* young; But I slept in that room myself the first night I came to Charleville...."

"My room with the owl? Do you mean that?"

"Yes, I put him upon the landing. But even then I dared not break the window. Here is the street."

"How you frightened me when your captain came in! How grateful I am, and how delighted. Is the house here?"

"Mademoiselle, I do not truly know what to do. *It is an empty house.*"

"So much the better."

"But you are not afraid?"

"Oh, no, no, not at all. Has it any furniture?"

"Very little. We will see."

He pulled the bell at an iron railing, and the gate opened. A beautiful face looked out of the window, and a young woman called: "*Eh bien! More* officers? I told you, *mon lieutenant*, we have not room for one more."

"Now, come, come, Elsie! Not so sharp. It is for the house opposite this time. Have you the key?"

"But the house opposite is empty."

"It will not be when I have put mademoiselle into it."

"Alone?"

"Of course."

The young *concierge*, under the impression that he was certainly installing his mistress, left the window, and came through the gate with a look of impish reproof in her eyes.

Together they crossed the road and she fitted the key into a green iron door let into the face of a yellow wall. Within was a courtyard, leading to a garden, and from the courtyard, steps in an inner wall led up into the house.

"All this ... all this mine?"

"All yours, mademoiselle."

215

The garden, a deserted tangle of fruit trees and bushes, fallen statues, arbours and grass lawn brown with fallen leaves, was walled in by a high wall which kept it from every eye but heaven's. The house was large, the staircase wide and low, the rooms square and high, filled with windows and painted in dusty shades of cream. In every room as they passed through them lay a drift of broken and soiled furniture as brown and mouldering as the leaves upon the lawn.

"Who lived here?"

"Who lived here?" echoed the *concierge*, and a strange look passed over her face. "Many men. Austrians, Turks, Bulgarians, Germans...."

"Were you, then, in Charleville all the time?"

"All the time. I knew them all."

In her eyes there flitted the image of enemies who had cried gaily to her from the street as she leant out of the open window of the house opposite. "Take anything," she said, with a shrug, to Fanny. "See what you can make from it. If you can make one room habitable from this dust-heap, you are welcome. See, there is at least a saucepan. Take that. So much has gone from the house in these last years it seems hardly worth while to retain a saucepan for the owner."

"Who is the owner?"

"A rich lady who can afford it. The richest family in Charleville. She has turned *méchante*. She will abuse me when she comes here to see this—as though *I* could have saved it. Her husband and her son were killed. Georges et Phillippe. Georges was killed the first day of the war, and Phillippe ... I don't know when, but somewhere near here."

"You think she will come back?"

"Sometimes I think it. She has such a sense of property. But her daughter writes that it would kill her to come. Phillippe was the sun ... was the good God to her."

"I must go back to my work," said the lieutenant. "Can you be happy here in this empty house? There will be rats...."

"I can be very happy—and so grateful. I will move my things across to-day. My companions ... that is to say six more of us arrive in convoy from Chantilly to-morrow."

"Six more! Had you told me that before ... But what more simple! I can put them all in here. There is room for twenty."

"Oh...." Her face fell, and she stood aghast. "And you gave me this house for myself. And I was so happy!"

"You are terrible. If my business was to lodge soldiers of your sex every day I should be grey-haired. You cannot lodge with an owl, you cannot lodge with your compatriots!..."

"Yet you were joking when you said you would put us all here?"

"I was joking. Take the house—the rats and the rubbish included with it! No one will disturb you till the owner comes. I have another, a better, a cleaner house in my mind for your companions. Now, good-bye, I must go back to my work. Will you ask me to tea one day?"

"I promise. The moment I have one sitting-room ready."

He left her, and she explored the upper storey with the *concierge*.

"I should have this for your bedroom and this adjoining for your sitting-room. The windows look in the street and you can see life." Fanny agreed. It pleased her better to look in the street than into the garden. The two rooms were large and square. Old blue curtains of brocade still hung from the windows; in the inner room was a vast oak bed and a turkey carpet of soft red and blue. The fireplaces were of open brick and suitable for logs. Both rooms were bare of any other furniture.

"I will find you the mattress to match that bed. I hid it; it is in the house opposite."

She went away to dust it and find a man to help her carry it across the road. Fanny fetched her luggage from her previous billet, borrowed six logs and some twigs from the *concierge*, promising to fetch her an ample store from the hills around.

All day she rummaged in the empty house—finding now a three-legged armchair which she propped up with a stone, now a single Venetian glass scrolled in gold for her tooth glass.

In a small room on the ground floor a beautiful piece of tapestry lay rolled in a dusty corner. Pale birds of tarnished silver flew across its blue ground and on the border were willows and rivers.

It covered her oak bed exactly—and by removing the pillows it looked like a comfortable and venerable divan. The logs in the fire were soon burnt through, and she did not like to ask for more, but leaving her room and wandering up and down the empty house in the long, pale afternoon, she searched for fragments of wood that might serve her.

A narrow door, built on a curve of the staircase, led to an upper storey of large attics and her first dazzled thought was of potential loot for her bedroom. A faint afternoon sun drained through the lattice over floors that were heaped with household goods. A feathered brush for cobwebs hung on a nail, she took it joyfully. Below it stood an iron lattice for holding a kettle on an open fire. That, too, she put aside.

But soon the attics opened too much treasure. The boy's things were everywhere, the father's and the son's. Her eyes took in the host of relics till her spirit was living in the lost playgrounds of their youth, pressing among phantoms.

"Irons ... For ironing! For my collars!"

But they were so small, too small. His again—the son's. "Yet why shouldn't I use them," she thought, and slung the little pair upon one finger.

Crossing to the second attic she came upon all the toys. It seemed as though nothing had ever been packed up—dolls' houses, rocking-horses, slates, weighing machines, marbles, picture books, little swords and guns, and strange boxes full of broken things.

Returning to the floor below with empty hands she brooded by the embers and shivered in her happy loneliness. Julien was no longer someone whom she had left behind, but someone whom she expected. He would be here ... how soon? In four days, in five, in six. There would be a letter to-morrow at the "Silver Lion." Since she had found this house, this perfect house in which to live alone and happy, the town outside had changed, was expectant with her, and full of his presence. But, ah ... inhuman... was Julien alone responsible for this happiness? Was she not weaving already, from her blue curtains, from her soft embers, from the branches of mimosa which she had bought in the market-place and placed in a thin glass upon the mantelpiece, from the gracious silence of the house, from her solitude?

XVIII. PHILIPPE'S HOUSE

What a struggle to get wood for that fire? Coal wouldn't burn in the open hearth. She had begged a little wood from the cook in the gar-age, but it was wet and hissed, and all her fire died down. Wood hadn't proved so abundant on the hills as she had hoped. Either it was cut and had been taken by the Germans, or grew in solid and forbidding branches. All the small broken branches and twigs of winter had been collected by the shivering population of the town and drawn down from the mountains on trays slung on ropes.

Stooping over her two wet logs she drenched them with paraffin, then, when she had used the last drop in her tin, got down her petrol bottle. "I shall lose all my hair one day doing this...."

The white flame licked hungrily out towards her, but it too, died down, leaving the wet wood as angrily cold as ever.

Going downstairs she searched the courtyard and the hayloft, but the Bulgarians and Turks of the past had burnt every bit, and any twigs in the garden were as wet as those which spluttered in the hearth. Then—up to the attics again.

"I *must* have wood," she exclaimed angrily, and picked up a piece of broken white wood from the floor.

It had "Philippe Seret" scrawled across it in pencil. "Why, it's your name!" she said wonderingly, and held the piece of wood in her hand. The place was all wood. There was wood here to last her weeks. Mouse cages— white mouse cages and dormouse cages, a wooden ruler with idle scratches all over it and "P.S." in the corner—boxes and boxes of things he wouldn't want; he'd say if he saw them now: "Throw it away"—boxes of glass tubes he had blown when he was fifteen, boxes of dried modelling clay....

"I must have wood," she said aloud, and picked up another useless fragment. It mocked her, it wouldn't listen to her need of wood; it had "P.S." in clumsy, inserted wires at the back. His home-made stamp.

Under it was a grey book called "Grammaire Allemande." "It wasn't any use your learning German, was it, Philippe?" she said, then stood still in a frozen conjecture as to the use and goal of all that bright treasure in his mind—his glass-blowing, his modelling, the cast head of a man she had found stamped with his initial, the things he had written and read, on slates, in books. "It was as much use his learning German as anything else," she said slowly, and her mind reeled at the edge of difficult questions.

Coming down from the attics again she held one piece of polished chair-back in her hand.

"How can I live in their family like this," she mused by the fire. "I am doing more. I am living in the dreadful background to which they can't or won't come back. I am counting the toys which they can't look at. Your mother will never come back to pack them up, Philippe!"

She made herself chocolate and drank it from a fine white cup with his mother's initials on it in gold.

* * * * *

Work was over for the day and she walked down the main street by the "Silver Lion," from whose windows she daily expected that Julien's voice would call to her.

"Mademoiselle has no correspondence to-day," said the girl, looking down at her from her high seat behind the mugs and glasses.

"He ought to be here to-day or to-morrow, as he hasn't written," and even at that moment thought she heard hurrying feet behind her and turned quickly, searching with her eyes. An old civilian ran past her and climbed into the back of a waiting lorry.

"I am in no hurry," she said, sure that he would come, and walked on into the Spanish Square, to stare in the shops behind the arcaded pillars. Merchandise trickled back into the empty town in odd ways. By lorry, train, and touring car, merchants penetrated and filled the shops with provisions, amongst which there were distressing lacks.

The trains, which had now been extended from Rheims over many laborious wooden bridges, stopped short of Charleville by four miles, as the bridges over the Meuse had not yet been made strong enough to support a railroad. To the passenger train, which left Paris twice a week, one goods truck full of merchandise was attached—and it seemed as though the partic- ular truck to arrive was singled out casually, without any regard to the needs of the town. As yet no dusters, sheets or kitchen pans could be bought, but to-day in the Spanish Square every shop was filled to overflowing with rolls of ladies' stays; even the chemist had put a pair in the corner of his window. Fanny inquired the cause. A truck had arrived filled with nothing but stays. It was very unfortunate as they had expected condensed milk, but they had accepted the truck, as, no doubt, they would find means of selling them—

for there were women in the country round who had not seen a pair for years.

A man appeared in the Square selling boots from Paris—the first to come to the town with leather soles instead of wooden ones. Instantly there was a crowd round him.

It was dark now and the electric street lamps were lit round the pedestal of the Spanish Duke. The organisation of the town was jerky, and often the lights would come on when it was daylight and often disappear when it was dark. Where Germans had been there were always electric light and telephones. No matter how sparse the furniture in the houses, how ragged the roof, how patched the windows—what tin cans, paper and rubbish lay heaped upon the floors, the electric light unfailingly illumined all, the telephone hung upon the wall among the peeling paper.

A little rain began to fall lightly and she hurried to her rooms. There, once within, the padlock slipped through the rings and locked, the fire lighted, the lamps lit, the room glowed before her. The turkey carpet showed all its blues and reds—the mimosa drooped above the mantelpiece, the willow palm in the jar was turning yellow and shedding a faint down.

"You must last till he comes to tea!" she rebuked it, but down it fluttered past the mirror on to the carpet.

"He will be here before they all fall," she thought, and propped open her window that she might hear his voice if he called her from the street below.

She boiled her kettle to make chocolate, hanging it upon a croquet hoop which she had found in the garden—Philippe's hoop. But Philippe was so powerless, he couldn't even stop his croquet hoop from being heated red-hot in the flames as a kettle-holder ... One must be sensible. He would allow it. That was the sort of device he would have thought well of.

"He rushed about the town on a motor-bicycle," the *concierge* had said, when asked about him. But that was later. There had been other times when he had rocked a rocking-horse, broken a doll's head, sold meat from a wooden shop, fed a dormouse.

"Did Philippe," she wondered, "have adventures, too, in this street?" She felt him in the curtains, under the carpet like a little wind.

* * * * *

The days passed.

Each day her car was ordered and ran to Rheims and Chalons through the battlefields, or through the mountains to Givet, Dinant or Namur. Changes passed over the mountains as quickly as the shades of flying

221

clouds. The spring growth, at every stage and age from valley to crest, shook like light before the eyes. There were signs of spring, too, in the battlefields. Cowslips grew in the ditches, and grass itself, as rare and bright as a flower, broke out upon the plains.

A furtive and elementary civilisation began to creep back upon the borders of the national roads. Pioneers, with hand, dog, and donkey carts, with too little money, with too many children, with obstinate and tenacious courage, began to establish themselves in cellars and pill-boxes, in wooden shelters scraped together from the *débris* of their former villages. In those communities of six or seven families the re-birth and early struggles of civilisation set in. One tilled a patch of soil the size of a sheet between two trenches—one made a fowl-yard, fenced it in and placed a miserable hen within. Little notices would appear, nailed to poles emerging from the bowels of the earth. "Vin-Café" or "Small motor repairs done here."

All this was noticeable along the great national roads. But in the side roads, roads deep in yellow mud, uncleared, empty of lorries and cars, no one set up his habitation.

A certain lawlessness was abroad in the lonelier areas of the battlefields. Odds and ends of all the armies, deserters, well hidden during many months, lived under the earth in holes and cellars and used strange means to gain a living.

There had been rumours of lonely cars which had been stopped and robbed—and among the settlers a couple of murders had taken place in a single district. The mail from Charleville to Montmédy was held up at last by men in masks armed with revolvers. "We will go out armed!" exclaimed the drivers in the garage, and polished up their rifles.

After that, when the Americans hi the camps around, hungry upon the French ration, or drunk upon the mixture of methylated spirits and whisky sold in subterranean *estaminets* of ruined villages, picked a quarrel, there were deaths instead of broken heads and black eyes. "They must ... they MUST go home!" said the French, turning their easy wrath upon the homesick Americans.

Somewhere beyond Rheims the wreck of a cindery village sprawled along a side road. Not a chimney, not a pile of bricks, not a finger of wood or stone reached three feet high, but in the middle, a little wooden stake rose above the rubbish, a cross-bar pointing into the ground, and the words "Vin-Café" written in chalk upon it. Fanny, who was thirsty, drew up her car and climbed across the village to a hole down which the board pointed. Steps of pressed earth led down, and from the hole rose the quarrelling, fierce voices of three men. She fled back to the car, determined to find a more genial *café* upon a national road.

The same day, upon another side road, she came on the remains of a village, where the road, instead of leading through it, paused at the brink of the river, over which hung the end spars of a broken bridge.

"I will make a meal here," she thought, profiting by the check—and pulled out a packet of sandwiches, driving her car round the corner of a wall out of the wind. Here, across the road, a donkey cart was standing, and a donkey was tied to a brick in the gutter.

Upon the steps of a doorway which was but an aperture leading to nothing, for the house itself lay flat behind it and the courtyard was filled with trestles of barbed wire, a figure was seated writing earnestly upon its knees. She went nearer and saw an old man, who looked up as she approached.

"Sir ..." she began, meaning to inquire about the road—and the wind through the doorway blew her skirt tight against her.

"I am identifying the houses," he said, as though he expected to be asked his business. She saw by his face that he was very old—eighty perhaps. The book upon his knee contained quavering drawings, against each of which a name was written.

"This is mine," he said, pointing through the doorway on whose step he sat. "And all these other houses belong to people whom I know. When they come back here to live they have only to come to me and I can show them which house to go to. Without me it might be difficult, but I was the oldest man here and I know all the streets, and all the houses. I carry the village in my head."

"That is your donkey cart, then?"

"It is my son's. I drive here from Rheims on Saturdays, when he doesn't want it."

He showed his book, the cheap paper filled with already-fading maps, blurred names and vague sketches. The old man was in his dotage and would soon die and the book be lost.

"I carry the village in my head," he repeated. It was the only life the village had.

So the days went on, day after day, and with each its work, and still no letter at the "Silver Lion," Though vaguely ashamed at her mood, she could not be oppressed by this. Each cold, fine, blooming day in the mountains made him less necessary to her, and only the delicate memory of him remained to gild the town. When hopes wither other hopes spring up. When the touch of charm trembles no more upon the heart it can no longer be imagined.

XIX. PHILIPPE'S MOTHER

The horn of a two days' moon was driving across the window; then stars, darkness, dawn and sunrise painted the open square; till rustling, and turning towards the light, she awoke. At the top of the window a magpie wiped his beak on a branch, bent head, and tail bent to balance him —then dropped like a mottled pebble out of sight. She sat up, drew the table prepared overnight towards her, lit the lamp for the chocolate —thinking of the dim Julien who might pay his beautiful visit in turn with the moon and the sun.

She got up and dressed, and walked in the spring morning, first to the bread shop to buy a pound of bread from the woman who wouldn't smile ... so serious and puzzling was this defect that Fanny had once asked her: "Would you rather I didn't buy my bread here?"

"No, I don't mind."

Then to the market for a bunch of violets and an egg.

And at last through the "Silver Lion"—for luck, opening one door of black wood, passing through the hot, sunny room, ignoring the thrilled glances of soldiers drinking at the tables, looking towards the girl at the bar, who shook her head, saying: "No, no letter for you!" and out again into the street by the other black door (which was gold inside).

She passed the morning in the garage working on the Renault, cleaning her, oiling her—then ate her lunch in the garage room with the Section.

Among them there ran a rumour of England—of approaching demobilisation, of military driving that must come to an end, to give place to civilian drivers who, in Paris, were thronging the steps of the Ministry of the Liberated Regions.

"Already," said one, "our khaki seems as old-fashioned as a crinoline. A man said to me yesterday: 'It is time mademoiselle bought her dress for the summer!'"

(What dream was that of Julien, and of a summer spent in Charleville! The noise of England burst upon her ears. She heard the talk at parties—faces swam so close to hers that she looked in their eyes and spoke to them.)

And how the town is filling with men in new black coats, and women in shawls! Every day more and more arrive. And the civilians come first now! Down in the Co-operative I asked for a tin of milk, and I was told: 'We are keeping the milk for the "Civils".' 'For the "Civils"?' I said, for we are all accustomed to the idea that the army feeds first."

"Oh, that's all gone! We are losing importance now. It is time to go home."

As they spoke there came a shrill whistle which sounded through Charleville.

"Ecoute!" said a man down the street, and the Section, moving to the window, heard it again, nameless, and yet familiar.

Unseen Charleville lifted its head and said, "Ecoute."

The first train had crawled over the new bridge, and stood whistling its triumph in the station.

As spring became more than a bright light over the mountains so the town in the hollow blossomed and functioned. The gate bells rang, the electric light ceased to glow in the daytime, great cranes came up on the trains and fished in the river for the wallowing bridges. Workmen arrived in the streets. In the early summer mornings tapping could be heard all about the town. Civilians in new black suits, civilians more or less damaged, limping or one-eyed, did things that made them happy with a hammer and a nail. They whistled as they tapped, nailed up shutters that had hung for four years by one hinge, climbed about the roofs and fixed a tile or two where a hundred were needed, brought little ladders on borrowed wheelbarrows and set them against the house-wall. In the house opposite, in the Rue de Clèves, a man was using his old blue puttees to nail up his fruit-trees.

All the men worked in new Sunday clothes; they had, as yet, nothing old to work in. Every day brought more of them to the town, lorries and horse carts set them down by the "Silver Lion," and they walked along the street carrying black bags and rolls of carpet, boxes of tools, and sometimes a well-oiled carbine.

"Yes, we must go home," said the Englishwomen. "It's time to leave the town."

The "Civils" seemed to drive them out. They knew they were birds of passage as they walked in the sun in their khaki coats.

The "Civils" were blind to them, never looked at them, hurried on, longing to grasp the symbolic hammer, to dust, sweep out the German rags and rubbish, nail talc over the gaping windows, set their homes going, start their factories in the surrounding mountains, people the houses so long the mere shelter for passing troops, light the civilian life of the town, and set it burning after the ashes and dust of war.

There were days when every owner, black-trousered and in his shirt-sleeves, seemed to be burning the contents of his house in a bonfire in the gutter. Poor men burned things that seemed useful to the casual eye — mattresses, bolsters, all soiled, soiled again and polluted by four years of soldiery.

Idling over the fire in the evening, Fanny's eye was caught by a stain upon her armchair. It was sticky; it might well be champagne—the champagne which stuck even now to the bottoms of the glasses downstairs.

"I wonder if they will burn the chair—when *they* come back." Some one must come back, some day, even if Philippe's mother never came. She seemed to see the figure of the Turkish officer seated in her chair, just as the *concierge* had described him, stout, fezzed, resting his legs before her fire—or of the German, stretched back in the chair in the evening reading the copy of the *Westfälisches Volksblatt* she had found stuffed down in the corner of the seat.

How, how did that splash of wax come to be so high up on the face of the mirror? Had someone, some predecessor, thrown a candle in a temper? It puzzled her in the morning as she lay in bed.

On the polished wooden foot of the bed was burnt the outline of a face with a funny nose. A child's drawing. That was Philippe's. The nurse had cried at him in a rage, perhaps, and snatched the hot poker with which he drew—and that had made the long rushing burn that flew angrily across the wood from the base of the face's chin. "Oh, you've made it worse!" Philippe must have gibed.

("B"—who wrote "B" on the wall? The Bulgarian—)

She fell asleep.

The first bird, waking early, threw the image of the world across her lonely sleep. He squeaked alone, minute after minute, from his tree outside the window, thrusting forests, swamps, meadows, mountains in among her dreams. Then a fellow joined him, and soon all the birds were shouting from their trees. Slowly the room lightened till on the mantelpiece the buds of the apple blossom shone, till upon the wall the dark patch became an oil painting, till the painting showed its features —a castle, a river and a hill.

In the night the last yellow down had fallen from the palm upon the floor.

The common voice of the tin clock struck seven. And with it came women's voices—women's voices on the landing outside the door—the voice of the *concierge* and another's.'

Some instinct, some strange warning, sent the sleeper on the bed fly-ing from it, dazed as she was. Snatching at the initialled cup of gold veining she thrust it behind the curtain on the window sill. An act of panic merely, for a second glance round the room convinced her that there was too much to be hidden, if hidden anything should be. With a leap she was back in bed, and drew the bedclothes up to her neck.

Then came the knock at the door.

"I am in bed," she called.

"Nevertheless, can I come in?" asked the *concierge*.

"You may come in."

The young woman came in and closed the door after her. She ap-proached the bed and whispered—then glancing round the room with a shrug she picked up a dressing-gown and held it that Fanny might slip her arms into it.

"But what a time to come!"

"She has travelled all night. She is unfit to move."

"Must I see her now? I am hardly awake."

"I cannot keep her any longer. She was for coming straight here when the train came in at five. I have kept her at coffee at my house. *Tant pis!* You have a right to be here!"

The *concierge* drew the curtain a little wider and the cup was exposed. She thrust it back into the shadow; the door opened and Philippe's mother walked in. She was very tall, in black, and a deep veil hung before her face.

"*Bonjour*, madame," she said, and her veiled face dipped in a faint sa-lute.

"Will you sit down?"

She took no notice of this, but leaning a little on a stick she carried, said, "I understand that it is right that I should find my house occupied. They told me it would be by an officer. Such occupation I believe ceases on the return of the owner."

"Yes, madame."

"I am the owner of this house."

"Yes."

"May I ask of what nationality you are?"

The *concierge* standing behind her, shrugged her shoulders impatiently, as if she would say, "I have explained, and explained again!"

"I am English, madame."

The lady seemed to sink into a stupor, and bending her head in silence stared at the floor. Fanny, sitting upright in bed, waited for her to speak. The >*concierge*, her face still as an image, waited too.

Philippe's mother began to sway upon her stick.

"Do please sit down," said Fanny, breaking the silence at last.

"When will you go?" demanded the old lady, suddenly.

"Go?"

"Who gave you that lamp? That is mine." She pointed to a glass lamp which stood upon the table.

"It is all yours," said Fanny, humbly.

"Mademoiselle borrowed it," said the voice of the *concierge*. "I lent it to her."

"Why are my things lent when I am absent? My armchair—dirty, soiled, torn! Paul's picture—there is a hole in the corner. Who made that hole in the corner?"

"I didn't," said Fanny feebly, wishing that she were dressed and upon her feet.

"Madame, a Turkish officer made the hole. I spoke to him about it; he said it was the German colonel who was here before him. But I am sure it was the Turk."

"A Turk!" said Philippe's mother in bewilderment. "So you have allowed   a
Turk to come in here!"

"Madame does not understand."

"Oh, I understand well enough that my house has been a den! The house where I was born—All my things, all my things—You must give that lamp back!"

"Dear madame, I will give everything back, I have hurt nothing—"

"Not ruined my carpet, my mother's carpet! Not soiled my walls, written your name upon them, cracked my windows, filled my room downstairs with rubbish, broken my furniture—But I am told this is what I must expect!" Fanny looked at her, petrified. "But I—" she began.

"You don't understand," said the young *concierge* fiercely. "Don't you know who has lived here? In this room, in this bed, Turks, Bulgars, Germans. Four years of soldiers, coming in one week and gone the next. I could not stop it! When other houses were burnt I would say to myself, 'Madame is lucky.' When all your china was broken and your chairs used for firewood, could I help it? Can *she* help it? She is your last soldier, and she has taken nothing. So much has gone from this house it is not worth while to worry about what remains. When you wrote to me last month to send you the barometer, it made me smile. Your barometer!"

"Begone, Elsie."

"No, madame, no! Not till you come back with me. They should not have let you come alone. But you were always wilful. You cannot mean to live here?"

"I wish this woman gone to-day. I wish to sleep here to-night."

"No, madame, no. Sleep in the house opposite to-night. Give her time to find a lodging—"

"A lodging! She will find a lodging soon enough. A town full of soldiers—" muttered the old woman.

"I think this is a question for the billeting lieutenant," said Fanny. "He will explain to you that I am billeted here exactly as a soldier, that I have a right to be here until your arrival. It will be kind of you to give me a day in which to find another room."

"Where are *his* things?" said the old woman unheedingly. "I must go up to the attics."

A vision of those broken toys came to Fanny, the dusty heap of horses, dolls and boxes—the poor disorder.

"You mustn't, yet!" she cried with feeling. "Rest first. Sit here longer first. Or go another day!"

"Have you touched *them*?" cried Philippe's mother, rising from the chair. "I must go at once, at once——" but even as she tried to cross the room she leant heavily upon the table and put her hand to her heart. "Get me water, Elsie," she said, and threw up her veil. Her ruined face was grey even at the lips; her eyes were caverns, worn by the dropping of water, her mouth was folded tightly that nothing kind or hopeful, or happy might come out of it again. Elsie ran to the washing-stand. Unfortunately she seized the glass with the golden scrolling, and when she held it to the lips of her mistress those lips refused it.

"*That*, too, that glass of mine! Elsie, I wish this woman gone. Why don't you get up? Where are your clothes? Why don't you dress and go—"

"Madame, hush, hush, you are ill."

"Ah!" dragging herself weakly to the door, "I must take an inventory. That is what I should have done before! If I don't make a list at once I shall lose something!"

"Take an inventory!" exclaimed the *concierge* mockingly, as she followed her. "The house won't change! After four years—it isn't now that it will change!" She paused at the door and looked back at Fanny. "Don't worry about the room, mademoiselle. She is like that—*elle a des crises*. She cannot possibly sleep here. Keep the room for a day or two till you find another."

"In a very few days I shall be going to England."

"Keep it a week if necessary. She will be persuaded when she is calmer.
Why did they let her come when they wrote me that she was a dying woman! But no—*elle est comme toujours—méchante pour tout le monde.*"

"You told me she thought only of Philippe."

"Ah, mademoiselle, she is like many of us! She has still her sense of property."

XX. THE LAST DAY

Around the Spanish Square the first sun-awnings had been put up in the night, awnings red and yellow, flapping in the mountain wind.

In the shops under the arches, in the market in the centre of the Square, they were selling anemones.

"But have you any eggs?"

"No eggs this morning."

"Any butter?"

"None. There has been none these three days."

"A pot of condensed milk?"

"Mademoiselle, the train did not bring any."

"Must I eat anemones? Give me two bunches."

And round the Spanish Square the orange awnings protecting the empty shop-fronts shuddered and flapped, like a gay hat worn unsteadily when the stomach is empty.

What was there to do on a last day but look and note, and watch, and take one's leave? The buds against the twig-laced sky were larger than ever. To-morrow—the day after to-morrow ... it would be spring in England, too!

"*Tenez*, mademoiselle," said the market woman, "there is a little ounce of butter here that you may have!"

The morning passed and on drifted the day, and all was finished, all was done, and love gone, too. And with love gone the less divine but wider world lay open.

In the "Silver Lion" the patient girl behind the counter shook her head.

"There is no letter for you."

"And to-morrow I leave for England."

"If a letter comes where shall I send it on?"

"Thank you, but there will come no letter now. Good-bye."

"Good-bye."

It was the afternoon. Now such a tea, a happy, lonely tea—the last, the best, in Charleville! Crossing the road from the "Silver Lion" Fanny bought a round, flat, sandwich cake, and carried it to the house which was her own for one more night, placed it in state upon the biggest of the green and gold porcelain plates, and the anemones in a sugar-bowl beside it. She lit the fire, made tea, and knelt upon the floor to toast her bread. There was a half-conscious hurry in her actions.

("So long as nobody comes!" she whispered. "So long as I am left alone!") she feared the good-byes of the *concierge*, the threatened inventory of Philippe's mother, a call of state farewell from the billeting lieutenant.

When the toast was done and the tea made, some whim led her to change her tunic for a white jersey newly back from the wash, to put on the old dancing shoes of Metz—and not until her hair was carefully brushed to match this gaiety did she draw up the armchair with the broken leg, and prop it steadily beside the tea-table.

But—

Who was that knocking on the door in the street?

One of the Section coming on a message? The *brigadier* to tell her that she had some last duty still?

"Shall I go to the window?" (creeping nearer to it). Then, with a glance back at the tea-table, "No, let them knock!"

But how they knocked! Persistent, gentle—could one sit peacefully at tea so called and so besought! She went up to the blue curtains, and standing half-concealed, saw the *concierge* brooding in the sunlight of her window-sill.

"Is *nobody* there?" said a light voice in the hidden street below, and at that she peered cautiously over the edge of the stonework, and saw a pale young man in grey before the door.

She watched him. She watched him gravely, for he had come too late. But tenderly, for she had been in love with him. The *concierge* raised her two black brows in her expressive face and looked upwards. Her look said: "Why don't you let him in?"

Yet Fanny stood inactive, her hands resting on the sun-warmed stone.

"Julien is here—is here! And does not know that I go to-morrow!"

But she put *to-morrow* from her, and in the stillness she felt her spirit smiling for pleasure in him. She had mourned him once; she never would again.

In her pocket lay the key of the street door, and the curtain-cord, long rotted and useless, dangled at her cheek. With a quick wrench she brought its length tumbling beside her on the sill, then knotted it to the key and let it down into the street.

The young man saw it hang before his eyes.

"Are you coming in?" said a voice above him. "Tea is ready."

"Fanny!"

"It has been ready for six weeks."

"Only wait—" He was trying the key in the door.

"What—still longer?" said the voice.

He was gone from the pavement, he had entered her house, he was on her stair—the grey ghost of the soldier!

She had a minute's grace. Slipping her hand into the cupboard she drew out another cup and saucer, and laid the table for two.

There was his face—his hands—at her door! But what a foreign grey body!

"Come in, Ghost!" she said, and held out her hands—for now she cared at least for "he who cared"—lest that, too, be lost! Does a ghost kiss? Yes, sometimes. Sometimes they are ghosts who kiss.

"Oh, Fanny!" Then, with a quick glance at the table, "You are expecting someone?"

"You. How late you come to tea with me!"

"But I—You didn't know."

"I waited tea for you," she said, and turning to a calendar upon a wooden wheel, she rolled it back a month.

She made him sit, she made him drink and eat. He filled the room with his gaiety. He had no reasons upon his tongue, and no excuses; she no reproaches, no farewell.

A glance round the room had shown her that there were no signs of her packing; her heavy kitbag was at the station, her suitcase packed and in the cupboard. She put her gravest news away till later.

"You came by the new train—that has arrived at last in Charleville?"

"Yes, and I go up to Revins to-night."

She paused at that. "But how?"

"I don't know," he answered, smiling at her.

Her eyes sparkled. "Could I?" (She had that morning delivered the car to its new driver.) "Of course. I could! I will, I will, I'll manage! You counted on me to drive you to Revins?"

"Will it be difficult to manage?"

"No—o—But I must get the car out before dark or there will be no excuse—" She pushed back her chair and went to the window. The sun was sinking over the mountains and the scenery in the western sky was reflected in the fiery pools between the cobbles in the street.

"I must go soon and get it. But how—"

She paused and thought. "How do you come down to-morrow?"

"I don't. I go on to Brussels. There is a car at Revins belonging to my agent. He will take me to Dinant for the Brussels train."

"You are bound for Brussels? Yet you could have gone straight from Paris to Brussels?"

"Yet I didn't because I wanted to see you!"

She took down her cap and coat from the nail on which they were hanging.

"Need you go yet?" he said, withdrawing the clothes from her arm, and laying them upon a chair. She sat down again.

"The sun is sinking. The town gets dark so quickly here, though it's light enough in the mountains. If I leave it later the men will be gone home, and the garage key with them."

"You're right," he said. "Put them on," and he held the coat for her. "But once you have the car there's no hurry over our drive. Yes, fetch it quickly, and then we'll go up above Revins and I'll show you the things I have in mind."

"What things?"

He drew out a fat, red note-book and held it up.

"It's full of my thoughts," he said. "Quick with the car, and we'll get up there while it's light enough to show you!"

She slipped out under the apple-red sky, through the streets where the shadows of the houses lay black as lacquer.

Before the locked gates of the garage the *brigadier* lounged smoking his little, dry cigarettes.

"We are on fire," he said, pointing up the street at the mountain. "What an evening!"

"Yes, and my last!" she said. "Oh, may I have the key of the garage?"

"But you've given up the car."

"Yes, I have, but—after to-morrow I shall never use your petrol again! And there are my bags to be taken to the station. Ah, let me have the key!"

He gave her the key.

"Don't be long then. Yet I shall be gone in a few minutes. When you come in hang the key on the nail in the office."

Once more she wound up the Renault, drove from the garage, regained the Rue de Clèves, and saw Julien leaning from her window sill.

"Come down, come down!" she called up to him, and realised that it would have been better to have made her revelation to him before they started on this journey. For now he was staring at the mountains in an absorbed excited fashion, and she would have to check his flow of spirits, spoil their companionable gaiety, and precipitate such heavy thoughts upon him as might, she guessed, spread to herself. Between his disappearance from the window and the opening of the street door she had a second in which to fight with her disinclination.

"And yet, if I've neglected to tell him in the room," she argued, "I can't tell him in the street!"

For looking up she saw, as she expected, the deep eyes of the *concierge* watching her as impersonally as the mountains watched the town.

"There'll come a moment," she said to herself as the street door opened and he joined her and climbed into the car, "when it'll come of itself, when it will be easy and natural."

By back streets they left the town, and soon upon the step road had climbed through the belt of trees and out on to bare slopes.

As they wound up the mountain, sitting so dose together, she felt how familiar his company was to her, and how familiar his silence. Their thoughts, running together, would meet presently, as they had often met, at the juncture when his hand was laid upon hers at the wheel: But when he spoke he startled her.

"How long has the railway been extended to Charleville?"

"A fortnight," she answered upon reflection.

"How about the big stone bridge on this side? The railway bridge?"

"Why that lies at the bottom of the river as usual."

"And haven't they replaced it yet by a wooden one?"

"No, not yet."

"And no one is even working there?"

"I haven't been there lately," she answered. "Maybe they are by now. Is it your railway to Revin you are thinking of?"

He was fingering his big note book.

"I can't start anything till the railway runs," he answered, tapping on the book, "but when it runs—I'll show you when we get up there."

They came to a quagmire in the red clay of the road. It was an ancient trap left over from the rains of winter, strewn with twigs and small branches so that light wheels might skim, with luck, over its shaking holes.

"You see," he said, pursuing his thought, "lorries wouldn't do here. They'd sink."

"They would," she agreed, and found that his innocence of her secret locked her words more tightly in her throat. Far above, from an iron peak, the light of the heavy sun was slipping. Beneath it they ran in shadow, through rock and moss. Before the light had gone they had reached the first crest and drew up for a moment at a movement of his hand.

Looking back to Charleville, he said, "See where the river winds. The railway crosses it three times. Can we see from here if the bridges are all down?" And he stood up and, steadying himself upon her shoulder, peered down at Charleville, to where man lived in the valleys. But though the slopes ahead of them were still alight, depths, distance, the crowding and thickening of twilight in the hollows behind them offered no detail.

"I fear they are," she said, gazing with him. "I think they are. I think I can remember that they are."

Soon they would be at the top of the long descent on Revins. Should she tell him, he who sat so close, so unsuspecting? An arrowy temptation shot through her mind.

"Is it possible—Why not write a letter when he is gone!"

She saw its beauty, its advantages, and she played with it like someone who knew where to find strength to withstand it.

"He is so happy, so gay," urged the voice, "so full of his plans! And you have left it so late. How painful now, just as he is going, to bid him think: 'I will never see her face again!'"

(How close he sat beside her! How close her secret sat within her!)

"Think how it is with you," pursued the tempting voice. "It is hard to part from a face, but not so hard to part from the writer of a letter."

Over the next crest the Belgian Ardennes showed blue and dim in the distance.

"Stop!" he said, holding up his hand again.

They were on the top of a high plateau; she drew up. A large bird with red under its wings flapped out and hung in the air over the precipice.

"See—the Meuse!" he said. "See, on its banks, do you see down there?
Come to the edge."

Hundreds of feet below lay a ribbon-loop of dark, unstirring water. They stood at the edge of the rock looking down together. She saw he was excited. His usually pale face was flushed.

"Do you see down there, do you see in this light—a village?"

She could see well enough a village.

"That's Revins. And those dark dots beyond——"

"I see them."

"My factories. Before the summer you'll see smoke down there! They are partially destroyed. One can't see well, one can't see how much—"

"Julien!"

"Yes?"

"Have you never been back? Have you never seen what's happened?"

She had not guessed this: she was not prepared for this. This was the secret, then of his absorption.

"I've not seen it yet. I've not been able to get away. And the Paris factories have held me every minute. But now I'm here, I'm—I'm wondering—You see that dot beyond, standing separate?"

"Yes."

"That's where I sleep to-night. That's the house."

"But can you sleep there?" she asked, still shocked that she had not realised what this journey was to him.

"Can I?"

"I mean is the house ruined?"

"Oh, the house is in bad order," he said. "Not ruined. 'Looted,' my old *concierge* writes. She was my nurse a hundred years ago. She has been there through the occupation. I wrote to her, and she expects me to-night. To-night it will be too dark, but to-morrow before I leave I shall see what they have done to the factories."

"Don't you know at all how bad they are?"

238

"I've had letters. The agent went on ahead five days ago and he has settled there already. But letters don't tell one enough. There are little things in the factories—things I put in myself—" He broke off and drew her to another side of the plateau. "See down there! That unfortunate railway crosses two more bridges. I can't see now, but they're blown up, since all the others are. And such a time for business! It hurts me to think of the things I can't set going till that railway works. Every one is crying out for the things that I can make here."

On and on he talked in his excitement, absorbed and planning, leading her from one point of view on the plateau to another. Her eyes followed his pointing hands from crest to crest of the mountains their neighbours, till the valleys were full of creeping shadows. Even when the shades filmed his eager hand he held it out to point here and there as though the whole landscape of the mountains was printed in immortal daylight on his mind.

"I can't see," she said. "It's so dark down there. I can't see it," as he pointed to the spot where the Brussels railway once ran.

"Well, it's there," he said, staring at the spot with eyes that knew.

The blue night deepened in the sky; from east, west, north, south, sprang the stars.

"Fanny, look! There's a light in my house!"

Fathoms of shade piled over the village and in the heart of it a light had appeared. "Marie has lit the lamp on the steps. I mustn't be too late for her—I must soon go down."

"What, you walk? Is there a footpath down?"

"I shall go down this mountain path below. It's a path I know, shooting hares. Soon I shall be back again. Brussels one week; then Paris; then here again. I'll see what builders can be spared from the Paris factories. They can walk out here from Charleville. Ten miles, that's nothing! Then we'll get the stone cut ready in the quarries. Do you know, during the war, I thought (when I thought of it), 'If the Revins factories are destroyed it won't be I who'll start them again. I won't take up that hard mountain life any more. If they're destroyed, it's too discouraging, so let them lie!' But now I don't feel discouraged at all. I've new ideas, bigger ones. I'm older, I'm going to be richer. And then, since they're partly knocked down I'll rebuild them in a better way. And it's not only that—See!" He was carried away by his resolves, shaken by excitement, and pulling out his note-book he tilted it this way and that under the starlight, but he could not read it, and all the stars in that sky were no use to him. He struck a match and held the feeble flame under that heavenly magnificence, and a puff of wind blew it out.

"But I don't need to see!" he exclaimed, and pointing into the night he continued to unfold his plans, to build in the unmeaning darkness, which, to his eyes, was mountain valleys where new factories arose, mountain slopes whose sides were to be quarried for their stony ribs, rivers to move power-stations, railways to Paris and to Brussels. As she followed his finger her eyes lit upon the stars instead, and now he said, "There, there!" pointing to Orion, and now "Here, here!" lighting upon Aldebrande.

As she followed his finger her thoughts were on their own paths, thinking, "This is Julien as he will be, not as I have known him." The soldier had been a wanderer like herself, a half-fantastic being. But here beside her in the darkness stood the civilian, the Julien-to-come, the solid man, the builder, plotting to capture the future.

For him, too, she could no longer remain as she had been. Here, below her was the face, the mountain face, of her rival. Unless she became one with his plans and lived in the same blazing light with them, she would be a separate landscape, a strain upon his focus.

Then she saw him looking at her. Her face, silver-bright in the star-light, was as unreadable as his own note-book.

"Are you sure," he was saying, "that you won't be blamed about the car?"

"Sure, quite sure. The men have all gone home."

"But to-morrow morning? When they see it has been out?"

"Not—to-morrow morning. No, they won't say anything to-morrow morning.
Oh, dear Julien—"

"Yes?"

"I think, I hope you are going to have a great success here. And don't forget—me—when you—"

"—When I come back in a week!"

"But your weeks—are so long."

"Yet you will be happy without me," he said suddenly.

"What makes you say that?"

"You've some solace, some treasure of your own." He nodded. "In a way," he said, "I've sometimes thought you half out of reach of pain."

She caught her breath, and the starry sky whirled over her head.

"You're a happy foreigner!" he finished. "Did you know? Dormans called you that after the first dance. He said to me: 'I wonder if they are all so happy in England! I must go and see.'"

"You too, you too!" she said, eagerly, and she wanted him to admit it. "See how happy, how busy, how full of the affairs of life you soon will be! Difficulties of every sort, and hard work and triumph—"

"And you'll see, you'll see, I'll do it," he said, catching fire again. "I'll grow rich on these bony mountains—it isn't only the riches, mind you, but they are the proof—I'll wring it out in triumph, not in water, but in gold—from the rock!"

He stood at the edge of the path, a little above her, blotting out the sky with his darker shape, then turning, kissed her.

"For the little time!" he said, and disappeared.

The noise of his footsteps descended in the night below. Ten minutes passed, and as each step trod innocently away from her for ever she continued motionless and silent to listen from her rock. The noises all but faded, yet, loth to put an end to the soft rustle, she listened while it grew fainter and less human to her ear, till it mingled at last with the rustle of nature, with the whine of the wind and the pit-pat of a little creature close at hand.

She stirred at last, and turned; and found herself alone with that flock of enormous companions, the hog-backed mountains, like cattle feeding about her. Above, uniting craggy horn to horn, was an architrave of stars.

"Good-bye"—to the light in the valley, and starting the car she began the descent on Charleville. There are moments when the roll of the world is perceptible to the extravagant senses. There are moments when the glamour of man thins away into oblivion before the magic of night, when his face fades and his voice is silenced before that wind of excited perception that blows out of nowhere to shake the soul.

In such a mood, in such a giddy hour, seated in person upon her car, in spirit upon her imagination, Fanny rode down the mountain into the night.

She was invincible, inattentive to the voice of absent man, a hard, hollow goddess, a flute for the piping of heaven—composing and chanting unmusical songs, her inner ear fastened upon another melody. And heaven, protecting a creature at that moment so estranged from earth, led her down the wild road, held back the threatening forest branches, brought her, all but standing up at the wheel like a lunatic, safely to the foot of the last hill.

Recalled to earth by the light of Charleville she drove slowly up the main street, replaced the car in the garage, and returned to her house in the Rue de Clèves.

"It is true," she whispered, as she entered the room, "that I am half out of reach of pain—" and long, in plans for the future, she hung over the embers.

The gradual sinking of the light before her reminded her of the present.

"The last night that the fire burns for me!" She heaped on all her logs.

"Little pannikin of chocolate, little companion!" Hunger, too, awoke, and she dropped two sticks of chocolate into the water. "The fire dies down to-night. To-morrow I shall be gone." A petal from the apple blossom on the mantelpiece fell against her hand.

"To-morrow I shall be gone. The apple blossom is spread to large wax flowers, and the flowers will fall and never breed apples. They will sweep this room, and Philippe's mother will come and sit in it and make it sad. So many things happen in the evening. So many unripe thoughts ripen before the fire. Turk, Bulgar, German—Me. Never to return. When she comes into this room the apple flowers will stare at her across the desert of *my* absence, and wonder who *she* is! I wonder if I can teach her anything. Will she keep the grid on the wood fire? And the blue birds flying on the bed? It is like going out of life—tenderly leaving one's little arrangements to the next comer—"

And drawing her chair up to the table, she lit the lamp, and sat down to write her letter.

THE END